MW00564599

CLUB OF STARS

A SAMBA OF SURVIVAL

MARIA SOUZA HOGAN

Rocket Science Press
SHIPWRECKT BOOKS PUBLISHING COMPANY

IN®
DIE

Minnesota

Cover photo by Sheli Stanford.
Cover and interior design by
Shipwreckt Books.

Copyright © 2020 Maria Souza Hogan
All rights reserved
Copyright © 2020 Rocket Science Press
ISBN-10: 1-7326274-4-4
ISBN-13 978-1-7326274-4-4

In memory of Mother

CLUB OF STARS

Contents

Part I: Castro Alves   1

Index of Family Members   3

1. The Three Marias   5

2. Paramirim Street   11

3. Tales of the Older Generation   21

4. A Very, Very Old Woman   29

5. The Club of the Stars   37

6. Scrounging   45

7. My Brother's Bravery   59

8. Mother's Nourishing Stories   69

9. The Devil's Twig   81

10. Attack of the Hookworms   89

11. Songs and Games   99

12. The Neighborhood   107

13. Leaving Town   115

Part II: Salvador—The Redeemer   125

14. Nymph of the Waters   127

15. Paralyzed Papayas   143

16. Across the Highway   155

17. The Return of the Syringe   171

18. Grace   177

19. Removal of the Invaders   191

20. College   201

21. A New Beginning   215

Epilogue   223

Acknowledgments   229

About the Author   231

Part I: Castro Alves

Vozes d'África

Deus! Ó Deus! onde estás que não respondes?
Em que mundo, em qu'estrela tu t'escondes
Embuçado nos céus?

Há dois mil anos te mandei meu grito,
Que embalde desde então corre o infinito...
Onde estás, Senhor Deus?...

Antonio Frederico de Castro Alves (1847-1871)

Voices of Africa

God! Oh God! Where are you that you don't answer?
In what world, in what star do you hide
Disguised in Heaven?

For two thousand years I have sent you my cry,
That in vain, since then, travels the infinite...
Where are you, Lord God? ...

Antonio Frederico de Castro Alves (Author's translation)

Index of Family Members

Silvina (maternal grandmother)
Joana (Silvina's sister)
Lourdes (Joana's daughter)
Belarmino (maternal grandfather)
Tutu (Belarmino's brother)
Zibina (Belarmino's sister)
Iaiá (Zibina's daughter)
Orlando Lima (Iaiá's son)
Raimunda (Silvina and Belarmino's daughter)
Heleno (Silvina and Belarmino's son)

Manuel Budin (paternal grandfather)
Maria Frebonia (paternal grandmother)
Joaquim and Romero (Manuel and Maria Fredonia's sons)
Nininha, Milu, Didi (Manuel and Maria Frebonia's daughters)

Joaquim (author's father)
Raimunda (author's mother)

Author's siblings by order of birth:
Maria Lucia (nicknamed Ua)
Celio
Maria Luiza (nicknamed Gaia)
Carlos (nicknamed Tatai)
Fernando
Miriam
Maria Leda
Eduardo
Raimundo
Wilson

1. The Three Marias

When I was born, my mother Raimunda had already given birth to ten children. Four of them died. Like the other children, I was born at home with the help of an intuitive, quick, and often unhygienic midwife from Castro Alves, the small town where we lived, and the steady help and guidance of my mother's mother, Silvina.

Castro Alves is located in the interior of northeastern Brazil, in the state of Bahia, where medical assistance at the time was seldom available. Mother had never visited a doctor, a nurse, or set foot in a hospital for any of her pregnancies. The doctors saw Mother only when her life was in danger, and then Father searched for them in a hurry, either in town or in the surrounding area. If he found a doctor, it was by pure luck.

Mother had complications after the birth of her tenth child, Miriam, the sister born before me. The midwife could not remove the placenta. It was stuck. Mother was losing lots of blood, and my siblings as well as the neighbor women who had gathered at the house to help with chores sensed danger and started to cry. When the news that Mother was near death spread around town, preparation for the Feast of the Three Kings was stopped. It was early January. When they heard the news, more women arrived at the house to help, pray, and say their final goodbye to my frail mother. My crying brothers and sisters huddled around her.

Someone then rushed into the house to announce that Dr. Jambeiro was traveling through town that day on his rounds to visit the very sick in other nearby towns. My father ran out of the house to find a friend to let him borrow his horse to find the doctor. A little while later, Dr. Jambeiro removed the placenta. My sister Ua, at nine years old, thought it looked like a chicken gizzard. Ua would repeat the stories of the birth that brought Mother close to death over and over again.

Three years after the placenta incident, I came into the world with great difficulty, breech and blue, my nose stuffed, silent. Naña, the midwife, knew she needed urgent help from a doctor or else Mother and I would die. She told my father to get Dr. Osvaldo in town. "And hurry because your wife is losing too much blood and strength." A neighbor in the room said that the doctor had left town that morning. Naña urged Father, "Go and find him wherever he is, and waste no time." Again, Father went to look for a horse and a doctor.

As always, my grandmother Silvina was present and very alert to all the details of the problems of a birth. She did not wait for Father to find the doctor. She carefully placed her mouth on my nose and mouth and sucked out the mucus that was suffocating me. She then grabbed me by my feet and hung me upside down like a dead kitten and shook my blue body, alternating splashes of hot and cold water over it. Sharp little slaps on my butt and face made me cry. Silvina laughed.

The room was littered with red rags and smelled of crushed lavender burning in the *fugareiro,* a tin container made from an empty kerosene can and filled with charcoal. It was used for cooking and for burning herbs. There were more expensive ones made from clay for those who could afford them, but ours was always of tin or of mud and set in an open area on the ground, usually by the kitchen door. The smell floated in the air. It was acrid now. The lavender had turned bitter and was mixed with the stench of blood, the placenta, and the rest of the afterbirth.

The sun in Brazil is hot on its way up, and so it was in the room at nine in the morning. My grandmother kept the doors open, swatting any flies, chickens, or gaping children that dared to enter. Mother lay quietly waiting for the doctor. The women stuck more rags under her to absorb the dripping blood. The midwife then wrapped me in a cocoon of soft cotton and set me by Mother's feet at the end of the bed while my grandmother prepared my bath. I was bathed in warm water in the small aluminum basin, my body dried, and talcum powder spread over it so that I would smell good. My grandmother dressed me in a white camisole Mother had sewn and held my body over the freshly crushed lavender the women added to the red charcoal in the *fugareiro*. I was to acquire the sweet scent of the herb. Still a little blue, I was set beside my quiet mother.

This eleventh birth was a victory, a miracle. There were no candles to light after the neighbors left. There was no birth certificate to sign and date and register with the state of Bahia. The older women mouthed prayers to themselves, but no priest blessed me as a miracle from God. I was the fourth girl born into the family, another poor person, one of many thousands born in this area of Brazil, on the seventeenth day of September 1949. On Paramirim Street there were many such births; I happened to survive this first struggle just by chance. And so, my life began.

My grandmother could not, however, apply the same practical skills and intuition she used to save my life to stop my mother's bleeding. She had to wait for Dr. Osvaldo to come. Mother was losing blood, pale and in pain, but she—more than anyone I know—knew how to wait in life. She had been accustomed to waiting patiently for changes in her fortune. She waited for a child to be born every year, for my father to quit gambling and womanizing, for the rent to be paid, for more money to buy a home of her own, and for her children to grow up and bring better days her way. She waited for many years and for many generations. I never heard Mother complaining about life's misfortunes when they came her way. And there were plenty.

The will of God and the hope for better days to come were Mother's badges of honor. In the *sertão*, the Backland of Brazil where she grew up, schooling never continued past fifth grade unless the children were sent far away to Salvador, the capital. Mother learned how to read and write, and her penmanship was very pretty. As an adult, she stayed within the confines of her own walls, backyard, daily routines, lace making, children, and survival. When times were rough, and Mother hoped for better days, I would hear her repeating one of her favorite sayings: *Nem todo tempo Sinhá Lili toca flauta*—Sinhá Lili doesn't always play the flute. She seldom left home, except to go to Mass. Ua remembers Mother not leaving the house even to buy sugar for the family if it was needed. She was more comfortable staying home.

My father was in charge and did everything for my mother. When he died in 1956, Ua, the eldest, took over the responsibilities for the family. She registered the children for school and took our big vinyl basket to the market when we had money to buy groceries.

Mother visited me in the United States when my son was born in 1985, and my husband jokingly remarked that this event for her was like the first Brazilian astronaut going to the moon. And still later, when she was operated on for cataracts, the doctor who performed the surgery commented that she was as quiet as a mouse during the whole procedure. The quietest patient he had ever had. My mother, a strong woman in her own way, did not know how to voice any of her needs or concerns.

My grandparents had raised Mother, their only daughter, with much love and dedication. She was only four feet tall, stocky and olive skinned with dark, curly hair and dark eyes. Those who knew my mother best recall her as very calm, soft spoken, compassionate, extremely generous, and kind. I remember her most as resigned to accept any condition she found herself in. She never questioned anything. Only on a few occasions do I remember Mother taking action. She had a fervent faith. She believed in the will of God and in her herbs. She burned incense in the house, spread over the red charcoal in a little tin container that she carried by its long wire handle, before she said the Rosary. She also said a liturgy, called *Ofício da Imaculada Conceição* to Mary, the mother of God, every Saturday at six in the evening. She always knelt in honor of the Virgin Mary. I knelt beside her to follow the prayer.

Mother never asked for much of anything. She was content with little and gave the little she had to those who had even less. A crippled, dirty, and hungry woman knocked on our door early one morning asking for food, just when Mother was setting the cornmeal couscous that she made on our windowsill to sell so that I could have my schoolbooks. We did not have much food in the house that day to give to the woman. Without hesitation, Mother cut a piece of the warm cornmeal couscous in the clay pot and handed it to the woman, apologizing for not having any coffee or milk to give to her to wash down the dried couscous. The woman sat on the ground by our window to quietly eat the couscous.

At the age of fifteen, my mother gave birth to her first child and thereafter endured a life of continuous pregnancy and delivery until she reached the fourteenth child. My uncle Romero, my father's brother, nicknamed my mother *Pata*, or Duck, which remained with her everywhere she went, her little ones following her. Mother became pregnant almost every eighteen months. By the time he reached the age of forty-seven, my father could no longer make babies. Six months after the birth of the last child, my brother Wilson, Father got sick.

When I was born, Mother lay waiting for death to come or for Father to find the doctor who would save her life. He came and stopped the bleeding by inserting his bare hand into my mother's womb to remove the remains from my breech birth. If she had waited much longer and if Dr. Osvaldo had not come just when he did, Mother would have died. Of that, everyone was sure. She lived and continued waiting and getting pregnant, year after year. Father left her with ten children. She delivered three more babies after her second near-death delivery and my near-death birth.

Mother named me Maria Leda. Two other girls in my family had been baptized as Marias: my elder sisters, Maria Lucia and Maria Luiza. Others called them by their middle names, Lucia and Luiza, but we called my sisters by their nicknames, Ua and Gaia. I was called Leda to differentiate me from the others. One more Maria would complete the allusion to the presence of the Holy Trinity in our family; it was my mother's conviction. She had regretted not naming the sister born just before me Maria. The family lived on Flowers Street. One day, Mother, flipping through the pages of *Vida Doméstica,* a magazine Father used to bring home for her, saw a picture of a pretty girl named Celia Miriam. The name pleased Mother, but she later realized that it did not fulfill her religious devotion.

The Maria part of my name I understand. What puzzled me for a long time, however, is where Mother found my middle name, Leda. It is not a common name where I was born, and she had only a fifth-grade education and no access to books to search for a mythical name for any child of hers. Mother's explanation was that one of the girls whom she knew on Flowers Street, the good neighborhood where she lived before I was born, had the name and she liked it. The name comes from a world completely unknown to Mother. In Greek mythology, Leda bore two mortal children with King Tyndareus of Sparta. To Zeus, who took the form of a swan to seduce her, Leda gave birth to Helen of Troy. When I was in college, years later, I was delighted one day to find my name in the title of one of W. B. Yeats' famous poems, "Leda and the Swan."

Grandmother Silvina nurtured a special connection with me. I imagine she did this because she felt that I would not have survived if she had waited for the doctor to be found. She was proud to have saved the life of her grandchild. Silvina always carried me closely on her side, and she firmly held onto me everywhere she went. I wasn't left at Mother's house in the care and mercy of my elder siblings, as was the custom with large families and busy mothers where I was born. Instead, I slept at Silvina's house, snuggled in the same bed with her. Suddenly for my grandmother, my mother, after having raised so many children before me, was not quite trusted with the care of this new child. I could not cry, crawl on the dirt floor, nor be left alone in anyone's care.

"Don't put Leda on the floor. She might put dirt in her mouth," Silvina would always say.

"But all my children before Leda crawled on the dirt floor, ate dirt, and did not die," Mother replied.

"Leda isn't going to crawl on this dirt. I'll take her to my place," replied Silvina. She then picked me up, set me snugly on her hip, my legs apart and dangling, wrapped one arm firmly around me, and walked away.

The day that I took my first steps, my grandmother carried me to her house again. She put me down on the clean floor to practice standing up and walking into her loving arms and to laugh out loud at my new skill. Silvina wanted to take pleasure in guiding my first steps by herself, away from the commotion of Mother's busy household. It seemed poetic justice that Silvina's last day on earth would be to enjoy seeing the child she had proudly rescued from the jaws of death. That was Silvina's last pleasure with her treasured child. She died suddenly later that day in Mother's backyard—some say of a heart attack; others say from tuberculosis—still with me at her side.

I have been told of my grandmother's love and attachment to me. I was also told of my physical and emotional resemblance to her: short, a bit stocky and strong, with light skin and abundant hair; quiet like my grandmother, generous, compassionate, very resilient and resourceful. Some of my older siblings call me Silvina to this day. I treasure the warmth, attention, care, and love my grandmother had for me. I only wish she had lived longer. As a child, I always thought of creating a sanctuary, far away in a hidden corner of my mother's backyard on Paramirim Street, in memory of Silvina. I wished I could visit with her when no one was around. As an adult, I have created that sanctuary in my heart. I think of Silvina when I stumble and fall in life, and in my mind's eye I can see her extended arms waiting to embrace me.

2. Paramirim Street

The house where I was born no longer stands, but its image remains vivid with me. It was on the outskirts of town where the land was muddy during the rainy season and dusty in the dry months. My family lived where worn-out houses barely sustained their own weight. On hot days, so hot that the air felt as heavy as thick clouds, our dilapidated blue house seemed to tremble from a distance. It vibrated, shifting its weight from side to side, as if dancing or seeking support from the long chain of equally worn-out homes inhabited by equally washed out souls, with their common troubles and destinies.

In front of our house was a dirt road circled by other houses directly in front of us and to the left. To the right was a small pond where my younger brothers and I sometimes played and bathed. On hot afternoons, we would come out of the water with our bodies covered with plump black leeches. One of us then would hurry home to get a piece of bar soap, kerosene, or tobacco, whichever we had in the house, to remove the leeches. The one infested would lie quietly on the ground while the others removed the many leeches one by one, carefully rubbing the pieces of soap or the other remedies over them. Back a few yards from the house, a bigger pond, covered in a green carpet of algae, with rocks of all sizes scattered all around, provided my family with water during times of little rain. The ponds also served as active playgrounds for us and the neighborhood children who gathered around them on rainy days, with plenty of fast-hopping frogs, fat leeches, and swift snakes.

Farther back from our house stood another row of rundown houses. On dark nights, the lantern light inside these homes flickered with the draft of the wind, and the light delineated the moving silhouettes of their inhabitants. I used to stand outside to watch, enchanted and intrigued by their dancing, their movements in the houses.

In our house, the smoke from the woodburning stove in the kitchen darkened the thick cobwebs that covered the mud walls that divided the two bedrooms, the small kitchen, and a center room. This middle room had a long black table on which my siblings placed the money and food they brought home. The same table served my elder brothers as a bed at night and sheltered us children during tropical rains and storms. Snuggled under the black table, my siblings and I played in the rainwater. I listened quietly to the rhythm of the heavy raindrops drumming on the roof tiles, hitting the table, dropping from its edges and cracks, then dripping on the dirt floor. My legs were covered with goosebumps. Drops forced the floor open little by little and formed puddles of warm water near my bare feet.

The bursting yellow sun would appear soon after and would quickly dry up the newly formed puddles in all corners of our house. The bigger puddles outside would accumulate fresh water and singing frogs. We would leave our temporary shelter and run outside. Life in our house would regain its usual pace. We would wade in the rainwater flowing down the alleys carrying tree branches, twigs, and whatever was left in its way, and hunt for the chanting frogs in the ponds to play with. This was our ritual on torrential rainy days.

In the house, each bedroom had one twin-size bed against a black mud wall. The three younger children shared a bed with either our older sisters or Mother. The changing of sleeping companions depended on who most often wet the bed or tossed during the night. Based on those criteria, my older sisters selected one of us since they were the ones who often carried the thin and worn-out wet straw mattresses on their shoulders into the backyard. There, they would lay them in the hot sun to dry out the urine.

Our faded mattresses endured the constant heat of the sun and numerous beatings each day, either to dry them or to dispel the bedbugs. At every flogging ritual in the backyard under the hot sun, I would watch the mattresses spit out more of thin, yellow straw through the many holes in their brown cloth coverings. They reminded me of the figure of Judas tied to a pole in the center of town on *Sábado de Aleluia* during Holy Week. Dressed in rags and stuffed with straw, Judas was packed with explosives. People would take turns beating the effigy before lighting the explosives, scattering pieces of Judas on the streets. I did not like whipping Judas even though Mother said he deserved all the pounding he got for betraying Jesus. But, unlike Judas, our mattresses would keep after the beatings, the urine drying in the sun until dusk, dissipating the accumulated urine stench, but not dispelling the resilient bedbugs. They hung on forever.

The battle against the bedbugs was constant. The insects' ferocious appetites would leave red lumps all over our bodies, day in and day out, which we constantly scratched. The war my mother and sisters fought with them was fierce, with neither an end nor a hero in sight. The parasites would not die. They kept getting fatter and multiplying, despite all the beatings, all the home remedies, such as burning dried cow manure in the house at sundown, and long hours of toasting under the hot sun. We had no choice but to deal with the biting at night and our scratching dance during the day.

"You are scratching too much. Stop it, or the wounds will get deeper and hurt you even more. Go and rub your body in warm water," Mother warned us when she saw the scratching going on for too long. We then would walk to the nearby ponds and soak ourselves in the soothing warm water. At times, I grabbed some of the herbs we had in the backyard, rubbed them on my wounds and lay down on the ground to let the sun help heal the scratches on my skin. The sun's rays felt good on my body, and I sometimes would fall asleep on the ground when my brothers did not come looking for me.

We also learned how to deal with the long red lines left on our faces from the dry straw that filled our mattresses. The lines did not cause us any pain and would disappear in just a few hours after we rubbed and soaked our faces in cold water. But soaking in water and rubbing herbs did not help us with the sticking wires from the box springs that came through the holes of the mattress and scratched our bodies and faces. These wires would find their way around the pieces of wood that Mother used to cover the many gaps on the bed frame. They stuck deep into our skin and left wounds on our bodies that we couldn't easily remedy. I dipped the small colorful remnants of my mother's and sister's sewing in warm water to cover the wounds.

Another ritual in our backyard was the battle with head lice. Everyone in our family had lice. When our heads were infested with the parasites, and we started relentlessly scratching to the point of drawing blood, we would soak our hair in gas, DDT, salt and vinegar, or alcohol. Then, we would cover it tightly with a piece of cloth for a few hours and wash it out with a strong soap we called "poisonous soap" because it could blind you if it touched your eyes. When these remedies did not work, we sat outside on our black rock and my mother or sisters would run their fingers through our hair searching for lice. They sat by a rock where they set the lice to crush it with their thumb nails. *Mata piolho* is the popular term for "thumb" in Portuguese, due to its crucial role as a lice killer. Women probing for lice in someone's hair in their front yards and their backyards was a common sight.

My parents moved to this house on the periphery of town, with their six children, long before my birth. My family had moved from a more comfortable house on Flowers Street, in the heart of town, where my brothers and sisters attended better schools, had enough to eat, and made friends with other children. But Father's trading business was not doing well, and the family had to leave Flowers Street; he was deep in debt, late with the rent and with his children's school payments. Father sent my elder siblings to private school because public schools were underfunded and teachers were poorly trained.

Father had a fourth-grade education and grew up helping his parents, Manuel and Maria Frebonia, tend the family farm and sell livestock at the open market. That's how he learned to become an entrepreneur. My paternal grandparents raised a family of three girls: my aunts, Nininha, Milú, and Didi, and two boys, my father Joaquim and my uncle Romero. They maintained a small farm where they raised cows, chickens, and goats. Manuel sold his goats at the Saturday market. He was known by the nickname of Manuel Budin, derived from *bode*, or goat. My grandfather had some money and many mistresses. He was known for taking his five children to visit his lovers on Sundays.

My grandmother died young. Many say from a broken heart. For years, Frebonia harbored a deep pain. At her husband's request, she repeatedly dressed her children with the very clothes she had spent hours sewing by hand, sitting in a corner by the window. Frebonia later ironed her children's clothes with a heavy iron filled with red-hot charcoal only to see her loved ones marching through the streets on their way to visit Manuel's mistresses.

"There goes Manuel Budin showing off his children and killing Frebonia softly," the women neighbors who watched the parading group would say.

Frebonia hardly left home. She knew the town gossiped about her, and the humiliation and suffering were too much to bear.

The house on Paramirim Street was Silvina's house. My maternal grandmother gave this house to Mother and found another small place to live. Silvina was able to purchase her home a few years earlier with the money that she had won playing a lottery game called *jogo do bicho*—the animal game in which each animal corresponds to a number. Players would choose their favorite animal to bet on. Silvina played the lottery every day. The night before she won, she had gone to bed hungry and in complete darkness because she did not want to use any of her savings for groceries or kerosene for her lamp. She was keeping the money for the lottery. That day, as soon as she got up in the morning, Silvina threw a bucket of water on her whitewashed wall to see what animal formation the splash would make. The figure of a monkey appeared in her imagination. She bet all her money on it and won.

In the late 1940s, my father Joaquim, to deal with his gambling and debt, sold the best pieces of furniture in the old house on Flowers Street, including Mother's sewing machine, so crucial to her and to my sisters for the family's clothes. Even a simple picture on the wall that Ua loved couldn't be saved. Everything of any value was sold. Father had done things like this in the past. A few years earlier, he had bought furniture for the house and then sold all of it in just one month because he was short on cash. To evade the landlord, Father hurriedly put the clothes and family in a mule-driven wagon and moved them to the poor outskirts of town in pouring rain. Life took a wrong turn for the family.

Previously, my father had done well as an entrepreneur: running his own business selling, trading, and bartering with tobacco, a local cheese called *requeijão*, butter, leather, sugar cane, manioc farina, which was made from yuca, softened in cold water and roasted under a hot fire, and other regional products. But he spent what he earned playing poker and lending money that was never repaid to his brother Romero, the owner of the Farmácia Bahia, the town's prosperous pharmacy. My uncle had a large family and a proud wife. His house was one of the nicest in town, with a garden, maids, a well-stocked refrigerator, and cooks to prepare the best dishes. But he always claimed to be on the brink of bankruptcy.

The first time Ua saw ice coming from a refrigerator was at

Romero's family dining room. She had taken the dresses she had sewn for my uncle's daughters to their house. The ice really amazed Ua. She could not believe her eyes. Ua also ate the beans that Romero's maids cooked, and they were the best she had ever tasted. She came home telling us kids this story. But my uncle and his family seldom visited our shabby house in the outskirts. We were too poor. When he came with his whole family, I would run and hide in the bushes in the backyard. I did not like seeing my well-off relatives in our shabby house. Besides, there was nothing for them to do at our house. They just stared at us for the most part of their visits. Romero, though, would come running when he was in trouble with his debtors and struggling to maintain the undisturbed appearance of the good life his family led. When times were bad for my uncle, he always looked to my father for help.

"Lend me some more money, Joaquim. I'm ruined. But no one should know anything, especially my wife and children," my uncle told Father at a warehouse where he ran his trading business in good times.

"Come back at the end of the month, Romero. I'll lend you money," Joaquim always replied.

Before my birth, Father took Mother and the six children they had at the time and traveled on horseback with their belongings to small towns in the area. There, Father would set up a new store and buy the local tobacco crops, which he would sell for a profit in nearby areas. Once established, the family would prosper again, and the relatives left behind in the old town, Castro Alves, would come to visit my parents in their new home.

It was during this flourishing time for Father's business that my family moved to a small town in the interior of Bahia, called Santo Antonio do Arguim. Mother was soon pregnant again, with her seventh child and decided she needed help with the chores around the house. The six children, the herd of goats, and the chickens and pigs my Mother raised in her spacious, new backyard left her exhausted. She needed help.

So, her mother, Silvina, thought of Lourdes, Mother's twelve-year-old cousin, who lived in a poor rural region with her mother, Joana, Silvina's sister. Joana had the habit of walking around town wearing shoes on the wrong feet. People called her names like *Joana do Sapato Errado*— Wrong Foot Shoe Joana, and *a tabaroa do Jebe*

Jebe— hillbilly. Joana grew up without ever owning a pair of shoes, and she never learned which shoe went with which foot. My great aunt lost her dignity, humanity, and identity to ignorance and poverty. Her daughter Lourdes came to live with my family and help Mother with the children and the chores. She matured, got well acquainted with the family, and became comfortable in her surroundings. At sixteen, she was very pretty and soon started dating the boys in town. Mother's voice would tremble, and her eyes would be fixed, as if the past scenes rolled in front of her, when she began telling us children the story of Lourdes and Joaquim.

My father would complain about every boyfriend Lourdes would find. When she did not pay attention to his advice, warnings, and name calling of her friends, Joaquim would lose his temper and start slapping Lourdes in public and spanking her in all corners of the house when she hid from his rage.

"I already told you to stay away from these boys," Father reminded Lourdes.

"Why?" Lourdes asked, puzzled. "This is a new boyfriend and a nice one. The old one you told me was bad. So, I sent him away. This one is completely different," she explained.

"You won't be happy with these irresponsible young men or with any other man in this town," Father said.

Father would go after the girl with his heavy belt every time she was in a relationship with any of the "irresponsible" young men around town. And Lourdes had to end every relationship and accept Joaquim's simple explanation that he was only interested in her happiness and well-being. Mother became very suspicious of Father's extreme zeal for her cousin and approached him one day.

"Joaquim," she asked, "why is it that every boyfriend Lourdes finds is a bad young man in your eyes? Why can't she bring her friends here to the house for you to supervise them more closely?"

Another of Mother's sayings, *Debaixo desse pirão tem carne, Joaquim, e o pedaço não é pequeno.*—"There is meat hidden in this dough, Joaquim, and the piece isn't small," expressed her belief that Joaquim was not showing all his cards; he was hiding something.

"Are you out of your mind? I don't want any bum around Lourdes, my house, or my family," was his reply.

"Joaquim, you're showing a lot of jealousy and extra care toward this girl," Mother continued. "Do you have any hidden interest in Lourdes? If so, it's time you tell me."

"These are unfair accusations you're making against me," replied my enraged father.

Joaquim's passion did not divert Lourdes' eyes from the young men in town. And he kept his grip on his belt, beating her and condemning the boys. My apprehensive mother kept her eyes and ears open for both of them. She delivered her seventh child, Raimundo Luis, and stayed in bed with her newborn one morning past her usual early hour. She had not heard any human voices but heard her clucking chickens and noisy animals invading the kitchen through the back door. She pulled herself out of bed to shoo them away, wondering who had left the door open. She found Lourdes lying on top of the unlit mud stove, Father on top of her, the two of them brewing love in the early hours of the morning.

Mother went back to bed in shock but later confronted Joaquim. She demanded an explanation.

"You're making up stories and false accusations again," Father told Mother.

"I saw it with the eyes that God gave me, Joaquim," she said. "I don't want Lourdes here in the house anymore. I'm writing mother, asking her to take Lourdes back to Joana," she said with a broken heart and teary eyes.

Mother then wrote Silvina a letter explaining what had happened. My grandmother wrote Father immediately, demanding that he bring Lourdes back to Castro Alves so that she could return the girl to Joana. Father completely ignored my grandmother's request and Lourdes remained with the family. My elder siblings were aware of what was going on because of Mother's constant crying. The young woman Lourdes had Father's head spinning—*ficou de cabeça virada*. Even when Mother asked him to bring home butter and other grocery items, he would forget completely.

Again, Mother's settled life came apart. The shock, the stony silence, the rage, the lack of motivation, the long hours of crying, the nights of star gazing, the long days facing the bedroom walls, and the lack of nourishment led Mother to exhaustion. She neglected her newborn, who soon died of dehydration. Mother's condition got worse. The child's death was even harder on her than

Father's betrayal. She had always been deeply loving and protective of her children. But with the severe depression she was experiencing, her abundant patience with them had worn thin.

"Stop asking me for things and get away from me," Mother yelled when her youngsters approached her throughout the day with their many small demands.

Mother's disenchantment with life and the loss of a child did not discourage Father from pursuing his affair. He had always been resolute in these matters, and his business in this new town was booming. When he finally returned to Castro Alves, he did so to establish a new life of indulgence, not to give Lourdes back to Silvina. He rented a house on Church Street, furnished it, and took in his young, pregnant mistress, away from Mother's teary eyes, then traveled by horse from one town to the other to maintain mistress and wife.

Mother's watery eyes dried out, and soon she was pregnant again. That is the way it was with my mother: one pregnancy after another. Father continued traveling to see his mistress, but Mother did not find out about it until later. When she did, the crying, star gazing, and hunger strike restarted and led her to another period of exhaustion and to the premature delivery of her baby. When the time came to deliver the baby, she hadn't the strength to concentrate on the hard task that she had earlier mastered so well. The child was born dead.

A family friend, Filadelfo, seeing Mother's unhappiness, approached her one afternoon and told her to dry her tears and not to worry too much. The people in Castro Alves, he had heard, were saying that Father's young mistress was *dando corno*—cuckolding him. People had seen another man entering Lourdes' house in the dead hours of the night. This news was spreading like wildfire in town. It soon reached Father's ears. Upset, he set out to learn the facts.

Joaquim first hired a man to stand guard by Lourdes' house at night. He confirmed the news. Still in disbelief, Father disguised himself as a traveler on horseback and arrived at night to "see it with his own eyes," as he later told his friends. He tied his horse far from his mistress's house and hid under the church's arched entry to better see the lover approaching and to avoid questions and speculation from any possible passerby. Father waited. The lover, an old friend of his, appeared at Lourdes' doorstep in the quiet of the night. As his hand rested on the doorknob, my Father's flashlight startled the figure before him.

"It's true. It's you, Florencio," said Father in a quiet voice.

The shock of Joaquim's appearance at the doorstep of the disputed young mistress caused the aspiring lover to run away and disappear in the dark of night.

Father did not confront Lourdes that night or ever again, the story goes. His new dream life of over one year had been shattered. He took the long road home on his horse that same night, under the shroud of darkness.

Father soon had all the new furniture he had bought for Lourdes' house removed. Her new lover brought her new items but soon had to remove them. The townspeople were talking again about seeing other men entering Lourdes' house in the middle of the night. The new lover had to leave. The young mistress became a famous prostitute in town.

Lourdes raised my father's son until the boy was seven years old, then she gave him away to be adopted in Rio de Janeiro. I never had any contact with my half-brother, although my siblings did. We all knew that his nickname was *Bode*, or Goat. We knew he was a very troubled young man. We knew that townspeople talked about the story of his conception amidst the noise of Mother's livestock in the kitchen. It was only years later that I clearly understood Mother's pain, sadness, and the quivering of her voice every time she told us the story of her young cousin. At other times, she was cheerful when she told us children stories of the *sertão*—the Backland where she grew up and other accounts of her family and experiences.

3. Tales of the Older Generation

I n the barren *sertão* of northeastern Brazil, rain is inconsistent. The temperature often stays above 90 degrees for days on end, turning green foliage into thin brown stalks. The shallow rivers dry up. Evergreens wither and die. The ground becomes red and splits, leaving pockmarks in the once vital beds of ponds and rivers, littering them with lifeless bushes and the white carcasses of dead animals. But with just a little rain, the vegetation comes back to life again, as if by a miracle, and then the cycle of rejuvenation repeats itself.

For centuries, there have been horrendous famines, droughts, and numerous exoduses from the area. People who live in the torrid *sertão* cannot survive droughts that last for more than three years. Many abandon the region. They flee the scorching sun and desolate land. They are forced to leave everything behind to seek relief from the persistent dryness and inconsistent rainfall that devastated their crops, livestock, and lives.

While fleeing the severe droughts in this poor and backward place, people sometimes carried just a change of clothes bundled on their heads or packed in small wooden trunks. They had to leave behind or give away their few possessions—a cow, a goat, a horse, a chicken, a bed or a table—and walk for days and miles across the wasteland, thirsty, tired, dirty, and covered by dust in a shadow of despair. Some traveled on flatbed trucks, *Pau de Arara* or Macaw's Perch, an allusion to the cultural habit of tying live birds to a pole upside down for transport and sale at the market. These trucks were equipped with wooden benches, a brown canvas canopy, and metal rails for the migrants to hold onto. They were common and are still in use. Some of the migrants ate a cactus called *mandacaru* in order to survive the journey; others died along the way. Others gave up on the long journey, deciding instead to settle in any small village that showed signs of life. Out of desperation, others fled the town in large groups packed in trucks.

My maternal grandparents, Belarmino and Silvina, were among these people. They fled Mairí, a small town in the *sertão*, during the severe drought of 1928. They traveled to Castro Alves with my mother, who was twelve. Their only son, Heleno, and Mother's only sibling, was left behind, buried in Mairí. A horse had killed him. He was just ten years old. Heleno's job in Mairí was to care for the horses that travelers rode from the rural areas when they came to see his father, the barber Belarmino. One day, Heleno carelessly ran behind a horse, scared him, and was kicked in the head. My grandparents, lacking access to medical care, used coffee grounds to stop the bleeding, as they believed it to be a miracle cure. The deep wounds to Heleno's head became infected. Tetanus set in and killed him a short time later.

Belarmino did not want to go on living after Heleno died. He let his hair and beard grow long and sat day and night on his son's bed, crying and repeating in a low voice over and over: "I lost my beloved son Heleno. I lost my son." Several months went by and Belarmino would not leave Heleno's bed. He would not eat, sleep, or talk with anyone who tried to console him, neither family nor friends.

Silvina thought that Belarmino had lost his mind. She prayed and cried while preparing the tobacco leaves to make the cigars that she sold to help support the family. My mother went completely silent and sat in a corner all day outside Heleno's bedroom, where Belarmino chanted his litany. The townspeople worried about their good barber and brought the priest to the house to say Mass for Belarmino and Heleno. They also gathered around the house at six every evening to say the rosary to the Virgin Mary. Nothing helped. The barber's hair and beard grew longer, as did the hair and beards of other men in town. His body grew thin and weak, and his soul remained buried in sorrow.

Belarmino sat on his son's bed one day chanting the same chorus he had been repeating for three months, "I lost my beloved son Heleno ... I lost my son ... ." Suddenly, he stopped chanting to listen to the whisper of a soft voice in the room, "Father, do not say that you have lost me. I am here. I am suffering to see you this way. Please get up, leave my room, cut your hair and shave your beard."

My grandfather stood up and searched under the bed, in the closet, in the laundry basket of Heleno's small room. He found no visible sign of anyone who might have whispered such words. Belarmino left Heleno's room, gave himself a close shave, cut his hair, and changed his clothes, doing what "the undeniable voice," as he later told my grandmother and my mother, had commanded him to do. He never again mentioned that he had lost Heleno. For years, Mother would cry every time she told us this story, as she did many times over; I always cried with her. Grief affects one's soul deeply. I understood grief better much later in my life, when I experienced a death in the family firsthand.

One year after Belarmino's change in behavior, another drama began. Because of the severe drought in the *sertão,* he decided to move to Castro Alves, east of Mairí, where there were a few prosperous surrounding towns. His relatives, who had fled one of the most severe droughts in the *sertão* in 1907, were living there.

Two years after my grandparents had settled in, a man in town set his eyes and heart on their young daughter, Raimunda, and would not let go. She was pretty, her hair and eyes dark as coal, her complexion cinnamon; she was calm, petite and sweet. The man was considered an older widower. Desperate to protect his daughter, Belarmino kept Raimunda indoors, letting her out only in the company of her mother. The man then sent love notes and boxes of candy to the house when he didn't see Raimunda playing outside with the cloth dolls that her mother had made for her.

"Seu Joaquim sent this package and his love to the pretty Raimunda," a delivery boy told Silvina one afternoon after a knock at her door.

"Take your damn candy and evil note back and tell the man who sent you to leave my daughter alone," Silvina replied and shut the door. This happened many times.

After around six months, my grandparents again packed up their few belongings and left town, leaving behind their steady clientele Belarmino had established as a barber. They had fled the drought in the *sertão* to preserve their lives; now they had to protect their daughter from a suitor who refused to take no for an answer and who appeared at their front door at all hours, day and night, when candy and notes did not seem to be working. There were no authorities for Belarmino and Silvina to ask for help. So, my grandparents found refuge in another town in the interior of Bahia, called Vitoria da Conquista. … or so they thought.

In Vitoria da Conquista, my grandparents kept an eye on their daughter. She was told to stay around the house, help her mother with the chores and play with her cloth dolls. They tried to keep their new whereabouts a secret, telling only relatives. But the experienced man found the refugees wherever they went. Joaquim rode his horse for days on the long dirt road from Castro Alves to Vitoria da Conquista, around 173 miles southwest of Castro Alves, and found my grandparents and their daughter.

"The whole time I rode my horse I thought of nothing but your daughter," Joaquim told Belarmino when he appeared at his door early one morning. "I came to marry her," he added firmly.

"The girl is young and innocent. We don't want her to get married to you or to anybody else for now," Belarmino answered.

"I can take very good care of your daughter and can be a good husband," insisted Joaquim.

It was difficult to flee again. There weren't many promising places in the area during the drought. It was too hard to fight both the harsh climate and the resolute man. My grandparents were tired and gave in, scourged by one and conquered by the other. Joaquim and Raimunda married in Vitoria da Conquista one week later and returned to Castro Alves. Belarmino and Silvina followed later. It was 1930. Mother was fourteen and Father twenty-four years old.

Belarmino reestablished his barbershop. Silvina supplemented their income by rolling tobacco bits into perfect cigars. She would do this day in and day out. My grandfather's relatives, his mother, two brothers and one sister, were already established in Castro Alves and welcomed his return. The townspeople were happy about having their good barber and now a perfect cigar maker back in town.

In Castro Alves, Belarmino's sister, Zibina, cared for Joaquina, their mother, who was blind, crippled and bedridden. Zibina also was raising her three children alone, supporting the family by making lace, which she sold in town. Her husband had abandoned her and the children for a young mistress. Raimunda became a good friend of Zibina's daughter, Iaiá, who was close to her in age. During her visits to the house to chat with Iaiá, Zibina taught Mother to make lace, which she learned with a passion.

Mother's Aunt Zibina lived to be ninety-six years old. I would visit her when I had not eaten for days and my siblings' resources had failed them. Zibina fed me beans cooked with squash and fresh okra. The smell and the taste of them are ingrained in my brain. Aunt Zibina often complained and sometimes ran after her granddaughter Lia, one of my playmates, when she refused to walk to Durico do Sabão's store to buy my aunt *cachaça*, the Brazilian rum she loved to drink when things were rough for her and the eight grandchildren she was raising. One day, to flee from Zibina, Lia and I ran to the backyard and climbed a leafy guava tree to gather the fruit. As I ate my guava, Lia told me about Lourdes, her mother.

Her father João had married Lourdes, his seventeen-year-old sweetheart. They were living comfortably on Flowers Street with their five children. João owned a popular pharmacy in town. One day, a friend approached him and asked if he would employ a needy fourteen-year-old girl named Francisca from a poor rural area. João gave the girl a job and soon began a love affair. Later, he decided to rent a house in town, not too far from his own family, to maintain his young mistress. His wife Lourdes, in pain and shame, became a prisoner in her home, not leaving the house much to avoid leering looks and unflattering comments. She only ventured out to the Saturday market to buy the family groceries. When Lourdes and the young mistress happened to cross paths accidentally, big fights would erupt in the middle of the busy market to the amusement of the rural vendors, who were unaware of the drama.

Seeking revenge for the bites and scratches that Lourdes had left on her daughter's face and arms, Francisca's mother decided to take action. She practiced *candomblé*, a religious ritual of African origin, very common in the area. It is a devotion to the African gods and goddesses, the *Orixás,* who grant people their wishes if they sacrifice animals in their names and offer them earthly gifts. People in town said that Francisca's mother had caught a bullfrog to sacrifice to the *Orixás* and inflict further suffering on Lourdes. She kept the frog captive in a big clay pan by her kitchen door and fed it leftovers. The bullfrog grew bigger and bigger until one day it exploded.

Meanwhile, Lourdes' life worsened. João soon started another family with his mistress, while getting his wife pregnant three more times. Lourdes cried every day, felt rejected and was an object of derision. Her children witnessed her unhappiness and rebelled. João started drinking, complaining, and beating Lourdes and the children who came to her defense. Finally, one day he told his wife to leave the house if she was going to continue being miserable. Lourdes left for the capital, where she took a job as a janitor at a hospital, sweeping and scrubbing floors. She was not used to heavy work. In the house she left, she had had servants while she watched the children and directed the household. Now, sad and weakened by the physical labor and the work conditions, Lourdes soon got sick with pneumonia.

She returned to her parents' home in the *sertão* heartland of Ipirá and begged her father to take action on her behalf, asking her husband to allow her to return home and see her children. João adamantly denied his wife's request, and Lourdes refused to eat. Her health worsened, and she died on her knees one evening, praying the rosary to the Virgin Mary. Lourdes was thirty-two years old. Lia retold the story of her mother many times, sitting on the guava tree branches with the fruits we had gathered. She and I would weep every time. Later, each time I knelt down with Mother at six in the evening on Paramirim Street to say the rosary, I would think of Lourdes and wonder how it must have felt to die while whispering prayers.

Eventually, my grandfather Belarmino became known as the best barber in town. Every day, he would grate a big bar of soap to make foam to shave men with long, unclean, and snarled up beards and straggly hair who would appear in his shop. His life was somewhat content until one day his brother Tutu woke up with hiccups that would not stop, even after following every piece of advice his friends and family gave him.

"Drink big gulps of water without stopping, Tutu," some said.

"Hold your breath as long as possible," others added. Family members even would hide around the house, behind doors and under the bed to startle Tutu. Everyone believed it would stop the hiccupping. Nothing did.

Tutu realized at one point that his hiccupping must be a sure sign that death was knocking at his door, as he put it, and he had no other choice but to let it in. He called together family members, neighbors, and friends and requested that everyone be at his home at exactly midnight. He explained that Death, an old, skinny, toothless woman in black carrying a small axe on her shoulder, would soon come to take him.

"My hour has come," Tutu announced calmly.

People from near and far rushed through their day's routine, planning their visit to Tutu's home at the appointed time. They put on their best outfits. The women carried flowers; the men had white candles in their pockets. I can still imagine them circling Tutu, their eyes moving back and forth, from the face of the hiccupping man to the hands of the ticking clock on a shelf on the wall, waiting for midnight to strike.

The hiccups did not go away. Tutu waited, lying down, dressed in his best white clothes, hands cupped together resting on his chest, holding a white candle, ready to lighten his descent into the dark tunnel of death at midnight. Surrounded by compliant faces, Belarmino's brother fulfilled his own omen. Not a second before or after the clock hands rested at midnight, Tutu had his last hiccup. His spasms gave way to stillness.

"My hour is here," he said softly.

Every eye in the room was fixed on Tutu, who quietly closed his eyes and died. Panic, despair and amazement filled the room, the house, and the town. It was 1939. Iaiá, his niece, Zibina's daughter and Mother's best friend, who was then twenty-three and who had sat beside Tutu's deathbed wearing her pink flowered dress, still remembered the story at ninety-one years old.

Forever after, Belarmino's brother lived in the minds, hearts, and wonderment of the townspeople of Castro Alves. "Were there any other such accurate predictions in his life before this hiccupping insanity?" they asked. "Who was Tutu, anyway? Where did he come from? And how had he lived his life before this?" they wondered. "How could he predict death's path?" The talk about the barber's brother's enigmatic death went on forever. The family members knew only for sure that Tutu was a very quiet man, reserved. He never prayed or went to church; he liked to work hard and have few glasses of *cachaça* once in a while. Whenever anyone walked by his house or searched for an explanation about the barber's brother, the story of the killer hiccups was remembered, told, and retold. And there were no other cases of hiccupping in Castro Alves like Tutu's.

4. A Very, Very Old Woman

When I was almost seven, Father got sick with a terrible pain that would not go away. At first, Mother believed it was not serious. It would soon be cured, using the herbal teas and concoctions from plants in our backyard, like many other maladies that she was used to diagnosing and treating. This one, however, was different. The pain got worse, not better. My sister Gaia and elder brothers Célio and Carlos, nicknamed Tatai, took turns walking the long road to the town pharmacy to ask Orlando Lima, the pharmacist and a son of Aunt Zibina's daughter, Iaiá, to please come and help.

"Orlando, Father is weeping like a child in pain, and Mother asked you for the love of God to come in a hurry and give him something to relieve his suffering," Célio begged every time.

"Let me get the syringe, and I'm on my way," Orlando replied.

I stood quietly and watched Orlando come to our house with a huge syringe to relieve my father's unbearable pain, rain or shine. But the shot he gave Father would last for only a few hours. Orlando also helped several sick and downtrodden people in town, providing relief for all their infirmities. He would never turn away anyone. He was not a medical doctor, nor had he received any kind of formal training. But Orlando would find a remedy for young and old, anyone who appeared at the counter of the pharmacy where he worked, with either a toothache, a broken arm, persistent diarrhea, a machete cut, a snake bite, a mysterious infection, or just a bellyful of hookworms. Orlando would try to cure them all. There were many people who couldn't pay him. He never demanded payment and never stopped curing and caring. Orlando must be in heaven today.

When I stepped on a broken bottle in our backyard and my toe was left bloody and dangling, my siblings carried me on their backs to Orlando for stitches. When my brother Eduardo's finger was caught in a tin can and became blue and swollen, no one could get it out. My siblings took him to see Orlando, who got the finger out. He soaked it in iodine and wrapped it in gauze. My siblings and I took turns carrying Eduardo home on our backs, his bandaged finger held high in the air.

Eduardo and I would take Mother's brief notes to Orlando, asking for more help. "Orlando, my son, we haven't eaten for days, if you could send us a little help for coffee, beans, and farina, God will protect you and deliver you from all evil in this world," Mother would write. I remember Orlando always sending us home with some money. Sometimes he would not even bother reading the notes I handed him. I didn't read them either. Mother always said the same thing. When Orlando saw us approach, he would automatically reach in his pocket. Mother also would send similar notes to an old friend of Father's in town: "Almir, I ask for charity today because the children and I are in great need. We haven't eaten anything for days. Any help is good. God blesses and protects you always, your *comadre* Raimunda."

Much later, in 1997, when Orlando Lima was sick with cancer and died, people came from near and far on mules and horses, and on flatbed trucks. They walked under the baking sun, dusty and dirty, to pay their respects to Orlando. The residents of Castro Alves had never seen so many people at anyone's funeral before, not even for the mayor, the judge, a famous doctor, or other politicians at any time. In my dreams, I follow Orlando Lima's procession. I bring him a white *sempre viva chuveirinho*—Paepalanthus polyanthus—a plant common in the area. I dig a hole on his grave and plant the *sempre viva*. I would like it to spread and create a big carpet, alive forever like the goodness and humanity Orlando carried in his heart.

Orlando had come to the house many times to help Father. Mother felt embarrassed sending my brothers to him again. We would then go instead to Uncle Romero, who would hurry to Paramirim Street with cotton wrapped in a blue paper. Each time, I would stand by the doorframe to watch Uncle Romero place the dried cotton right on the spot of Father's pain. He then lit a handful of the cotton on fire and set an empty glass on it. The cotton would heat the glass, which filled with smoke and rested on Father's painful side. My father would agonize for a while and then stop crying and quietly close his eyes in relief. The white cotton turned yellow and would glow until it died out. It soothed the pain and left a black mark on Father's lower abdomen. I repeatedly closed and opened my eyes and felt sad for Father and tormented when I saw those black marks on him. I wished that I could make the pain and the bruise disappear. They did not.

Then Father, tired of suffering, begged God for mercy. "Oh, God, have compassion for me! What have I done to deserve this? Please take this pain away or carry me away to you so that I might rest."

"Every minute, I pray for you to get better, Joaquim, be patient, and God will listen to my prayers," Mother would respond.

"I really don't want to die and leave you with the children, but I can't stand this suffering anymore," he would reply.

"I'm going to add more herbs to the teapot to make it stronger, Joaquim," Mother said, trying to console him.

Father's pain worsened. Mother took him on a slow-moving steam train to find help in Salvador, where doctors at the Santa Isabel public hospital could diagnose the malady and provide care. It turned out that he had cancer of the spleen and nothing could be done, they told Mother. Father was never told of his illness and was sent home to die with a few bottles of Atroveran, a painkiller commonly used at the time. The pain and his condition were agonizing for him and the family. He moaned, cried, yelled, and wept day and night for an entire month after that visit to the doctors in Salvador. He rolled on the ground as if performing an unusual trick. But no matter how loud the crying and moaning or how incredible his contortions, the pain did not go away, except when I saw Orlando hurrying in with the syringe or Romero coming with the cotton. Father, in his last few days, gathered his children around and gave his blessing to each of us, recognizing that it would be impossible for his body to sustain life anymore. He died at the age of forty-seven in the early hours of dawn in May 1956.

On that May morning, after hearing Mother scream that Father had died, Ua left the house crying and ran through the sleepy town to give one of his sisters, our Aunt Didi, the news. Ua's visit at that early hour, breathless and weeping, did not surprise my aunt. She was already up. Aunt Didi shook Ua out of her despair and led her to a kitchen chair where she tearfully delivered the news of Father's death. Aunt Didi looked at her husband Agilio and commented in a reassuring voice, "Didn't I tell you Joaquim died? He came here just a little while ago to give me a hug."

Back at our house, the sobbing, crying, and yelling soon awoke the neighbors, who gathered inside and out. The women comforted the family while the men cleaned the body, dressing Father in his best white outfit and setting him in the coffin that his friends had bought. It lay on a pile of empty wood crates in the middle of the front room. His feet were pointed toward the door to avert death returning to the house anytime soon, as the elders believed. The neighbors brought candles, carnations, angelicas, dahlias, and incense to perfume the body and the house. The smoke and the scent of the incense coming from the *fugareiro* by the kitchen filled the room, along with the women's soft murmured prayers. The older women wore black veils on their heads; some held a rosary in their hands and repeated a litany of prayers over and over again. My younger siblings and I mingled among the guests, entering and exiting the house throughout the day. The women, who remained in our house consoling and arranging things, lifted my younger brothers and the shorter visitors to kiss our father goodbye.

"Do you want to give your father a kiss?" a neighbor asked me.

"No," I said.

Seeing Father quiet and still in a box wearing a white shirt, his dark hair combed back, his thin face washed, and his beard shaved intrigued me. His constant moaning, groaning, and weeping had built in me a sense of helplessness. Watching him writhe in pain day after day for what seemed like an eternity had roiled my spirit.

The sounds of his voice still echo loudly in my ears. The sight of his agony still flashes in my memory from time to time, decades later. The huge syringe and the cotton on fire were constants in my mind's eye. I could not comprehend a power on earth that would suddenly end Father's suffering. I could not conceive how such long and torturous days and nights would simply stop one day. But it was Death, the old toothless woman in black carrying an axe, as I often heard Death referred to, that finally silenced him.

I stared at his face for a long time, contemplating his stillness. I had yearned for that silence for a long time. Everywhere I went, I seemed to hear Father's moaning. My mind always drifted toward the image of him. The sounds seemed stuck in my ears. I did not cry for my father that day. I never cried afterward and never understood the profuse sobbing of my mother and sisters. What I felt was a mixture of sadness and profound relief. It was as if I were in a different time and place. I knew I would never see Father again.

I was used to death all around me in Castro Alves, but I also knew I was free from his continuous moaning in pain. That gave me peace.

Burial happens fast in the tropics. Before sundown, his male friends carried my father's casket in a solemn procession through town to the cemetery on Pedrinhas Street. Two women neighbors, Benedita and Marta, swept the floor, carefully starting from the back door to the front entrance. They threw the dust mixed with fallen leaves and flower petals into the street just as the casket left the house. It was a cultural cleansing ritual to ward off further deaths. While piling up the dust the women chatted.

"This job is sad, but I'm glad we don't have to climb a ladder to reach someone's roof," said Benedita.

"Yes," replied Marta. "Last week, when Dona Almerinda died of tuberculosis, the men took off all the roof tiles to air the house for a few days and to let the hot sun kill the bacteria. They then had to paint all the walls white; that was a big job. It took days."

"I remember it," said Benedita. "And the men still had to carry the bedpans full of blood to throw in the nearby bushes."

In our living room, the aroma of flowers, mainly carnations, mixed with incense and dust floated in the air.

The funeral procession stopped for a brief rest and a change of bearers; the mourners carried small bouquets of flowers to be thrown on the casket when it was set in the grave. Townspeople appeared in their windows, while in the streets people took off their straw hats or stopped for a moment of prayer as the parade of mourners marched on, turning a corner here and there, and disappearing in the distance to Pedrinhas Street.

My elder sisters must have missed Father, but I imagine that they were also relieved that his intense agony was over. The constant gathering of medicinal herbs and tree bark, boiling of tea, and running to get Orlando Lima with his syringe and Romero with the cotton had ended. My father's suffering had ceased. My siblings were delivered from the battle they had fought with Father's cancer. But now that Father was dead, my family was left to face the ultimate dance: the one for survival.

For many years, my mother and sisters relived my father's months of suffering and the night before he died. They told the story of *uma velha bem velhinha*—a very, very old woman—to the rest of us, sitting on the warm ground during nights too dark to sing our usual songs or play games. Mother started by taking us back to that night before Father's death.

That dark night, Mother and my elder sisters, Ua and Gaia, took turns going out to our backyard carrying our tin kerosene lamp, our *fifó*, to light their way to the bushes to gather leaves from the medicinal plants that Mother grew and to get wood from the pile that we kept at the side of the house. The women watched over the teapot brewing the strong herbal concoction Mother believed would help give Father some relief from his pain.

First, it was on her turn, Mother said, that she clearly saw the figure, a very old and tall woman of cinnamon complexion, calm and preoccupied with her hair tied up in a bun, and wearing a white blouse and long skirt tied at the waist with a piece of white string, the way many older women dressed at the time. She had a white shawl wrapped around her head and neck. The figure paced the ground behind our house and peeked through the holes into the kitchen.

Mother kept her vision to herself, not wanting to scare my sisters, who had to gather the leaves and wood to maintain the mixture brewing on the stove for Father. But when Mother went outside to collect the needed items, the old woman had disappeared into the darkness. There was no one to be seen. Mother shivered in fear but controlled it well, she said, and came back quietly into the house to add the wood to the fire and the herbs to the pot.

"Where did the old woman go? Who is she? What does she want?" Mother asked herself.

On Gaia's outing, the old woman in white reappeared, pacing around the yard again, her head down. My sister saw the woman peeking into our kitchen and approached the figure. Taking the figure for a worried neighbor, she offered some news. "My father's pain is worse, and he hasn't been able to sleep all night," said Gaia. But she heard no reply. Suddenly, there was no one in sight. The apparition had dissolved into the dark and quiet of the night. Gaia ran into the house searching for the woman that she was sure she had seen and spoken to, but Father's agony diverted her fear and puzzlement. Like Mother, Gaia was quiet and went back outside to gather more medicinal herbs.

When it was Ua's time to gather the herbs and wood, the old woman reappeared, pacing the ground more restlessly and peeking through the holes. Ua saw the figure but also kept quiet, saying nothing to either Mother or Gaia. Once Ua was outside, the old woman hurried toward her, as if trying to convey a message, but Ua ran into the house in horror, dropping all her leaves. She described her vision to Mother and Gaia. The three women realized then that they had seen the same figure. It was four in the morning. Day was breaking and Father was dying. It was when my siblings and I woke up with Mother yelling to my sisters, "Call Amélia (a neighbor) to light a candle in your father's hand. He's dying."

Mother told us she was convinced that she and my two sisters had seen a spirit of her ancestors that night, trying to warn them of Father's departure from this world. She told us that she believed that the old woman in white had come to warn her and my sisters that there was no hope for Father. Death had come for him. The nights that my elder sisters sat listening to Mother's story, they nodded their heads in firm agreement. Petrified, we children remained silent during the whole story. Long after it was told, with a mixture of fear and high regard, we were convinced that the women in our family really had seen a ghost.

When it was my elder sisters' turn to tell the story of the Very, Very Old Woman the night Father died, they complemented each other's version of the account by adding some missing detail and by sharing their bravery and emotion. Father's agony that night had become secondary to the apparition of the figure peeking into the kitchen. With the passing of time, the story seemed more intriguing, and my goosebumps returned. Sitting on the warm ground, my body would stiffen in suspense. My ears were alerted to every detail of the story and to every sound around me. By night's end, the bright sun shining again through that one glass tile, the scarcity of food in our house would snap me and my siblings back to the reality of fighting for sustenance another day.

5. The Club of the Stars

L eft with ten children, no money in the bank, and virtually nothing to eat after the men carried my dead father away, Mother despaired. I remember her sobbing out of control and running after the funeral procession as it left the house. She carried our beaten-up straw mattress on her head and shoulders like the crazy man I had heard about, fleeing naked around town carrying his clothes in a bundle. Our male neighbors chased, caught and then locked up the man in a room used to store garlic. They said a rabid dog had bitten him. He ate all the garlic in the room, which was piled to the ceiling, in just a few days. When the townspeople came later to check on the man, he was sitting on the floor quiet and cured. As for Mother, the neighborhood women ran after her. They held her hands and carried the mattress back to the house. But in our house, there was no pile of garlic for a quick cure.

Shortly after the funeral, my siblings and I were sent off among friends and relatives or anyone willing to feed us for a few days and give Mother a chance to calm her nerves. I went with a female acquaintance in town, a mother with many children whose name I do not remember. Right away, I felt very comfortable in the company of my new family, although I had never seen them before. The house where I stayed was some distance from town and had a backyard filled with fruit trees. On the table, there was plenty of food; on the roof, a complete row of tiles with no holes or leaks through which heavy rain poured, black tarantulas fell, or blue sky peeked in. On the bed, a soft mattress covered a board. I could rest my body and set my face down without being poked by wires or scratched by dried straw all night. It never felt so good to eat and play.

There was more to life in places other than my own house on Paramirim Street, I discovered, and I wished that I could stay with my temporary family. When Mother and my siblings came to take me home, I felt crushed to say goodbye to a table with food and a backyard with fruit. I didn't want to go back, and I ran away as fast as I could and hid in the bushes. I cried bitterly, so disappointed when my siblings found me hiding in the greenery. Mother was sad and scolded me: "How could you forget your brothers and sisters so fast?" I said nothing and sobbed all the way home.

After having experienced a full stomach for a few days, I dreamed of building a fence around our house on Paramirim Street and planting fruit-bearing trees that would provide plenty of shade. Building a fence is still a theme in my dreams, appearing in different forms. Sometimes the fence is tall and solid, surrounded by trees; other times, a white small fence, decorated with fruits and flowers. I was happy with all of my dream fences. When I was very hungry and the food fantasy danced in my head, I dreamed of gathering mangoes, avocados, and cashews under blue skies dotted with cottony white clouds. There, I could lie down in the shade, protected from the hot afternoon sun, and eat my fruit. I dreamed of fixing the holes in the walls and roof of my family's house, of a paved floor we could sweep clean without having to sprinkle with water first to keep the dust from flying up into our nostrils. I dreamed of counting the silver stars, of playing with my younger brothers, and of coming home to food laid out on the black table, just as it was at my temporary family's house.

I dug a hole in the ground in a sunny spot in the backyard one day and planted a big mango seed that Ua had bought at the market one Saturday. I watched it grow and wished that it would grow faster so that I could harvest the fruit, but it did not grow fast enough for me. I then cleared a square piece of ground in a shady area, away from the hot sun, and planted cilantro, peppers, and okra seeds that I had collected from a neighbor's backyard. I took a bucket to the pond to water my garden when it didn't rain. To my disappointment, the cilantro seeds, peppers, and okra that I later harvested did not make much of a difference for my family. They did nothing to kill our hunger.

After Father's death, life became much harsher. I did not know the reason, nor could my siblings explain it to me. I assume now that the townspeople who had given us so much during Father's illness had grown weary of helping us or maybe we had gotten bigger and hungrier.

Mother sent us off once again. I went to Aunt Didi, whom I hardly knew and who had never come to visit my family. She lived in the center of town, facing the big church that sat on a small hill. There was a steep hill with a small chapel on top behind the church. On Church Street, there were homes with maids, furniture, and the constant aroma of food that inundated my senses. There wasn't a backyard where I could run freely like I was accustomed to. I smelled the beans cooking in the morning. It brought back the feeling of contentment knowing that I would have food on my plate while at my aunt's house, the same emotion that I had experienced while staying with my temporary family after Father's death. But now the new surroundings intimidated me. I thought Aunt Didi was very rich. She had food and furniture in the house. The furniture, I later learned, was made from a very popular wood in Brazil called *jacarandá*.

Maids were also common, even in households of very modest means. I didn't feel comfortable staying indoors all day. I had spent most of my life outdoors. I wished I could take the long walk home, carrying Aunt Didi's pots and pans filled with food to our black table, where my mother and siblings could eat, and I could come and go as I pleased.

My aunt sat at a treadle-operated sewing machine all day, clacking the pedals of her Singer to make garments to sell and help her husband, Uncle Agilio, a barber in town. Their children had gone to live in the capital to continue their education past the fifth grade, and my uncle and aunt worked to support them. I spent my days inside the dark house, smelling the beans cooking. I was told to help the maid sweep the floors, make the beds, and empty the chamber pot that my aunt kept under her bed.

One morning, I saw a balloon floating in Aunt Didi's chamber pot as I carried it to empty in the bushes or over the fence, away from the house. I kept the pot as still as I could, far from my nostrils but close to my lower body, with a firm grip so that I would not spill the urine on me. I walked slowly, one small step at a time, keeping my arms extended and stiff. I tried not to look at the contents of the white porcelain pot, and I wished that I could walk a little faster and unload the pot at the end of the long backyard by the tall wooden gate. When I reached the gateway where I was to empty the pot, I set it on the ground and looked at the yellowish balloon. I dragged it out with a twig before dumping the urine. I walked back and got water from a tall cement tank in the yard to wash the balloon. I then blew it up and entered Aunt Didi's house through the kitchen door, bouncing my newfound toy in the air and chasing after it with a big smile on my face.

When the maid saw me, she stopped what she was doing, balled her hands into fists, put them on her hips, and gave me a puzzled look.

"Where did you find that?"

"In Aunt Didi's pot," I answered in a quiet and almost inaudible voice.

She approached me, holding the broom upright in her hands to closely inspect my balloon. After a mocking laugh and with a look of disgust, the maid shared the story with my aunt. The two women told me to throw away my disgusting toy and wash my dirty hands before coming into their clean house.

I did not last long at Aunt Didi's. She was disgusted that I did not want to relieve myself in her chamber pot, preferring the bushes that I used in our backyard. I was soon sent home not knowing what I had done wrong or what was wrong with my balloon. I missed eating the food that the maid cooked and often thought of it when I was hungry.

My three sisters thought that with the death of Father the family could soon move back to Flowers Street, where they remembered life being more normal and pleasant than the harsh days that they confronted on Paramirim Street. It was on Flowers Street that the family had enjoyed electricity in the house, food on the table, nice clothes, school, and time to play with friends. My sisters dreamed of their old lives.

Ua associated the burden that had befallen on the family with my father's illness. "It's because of this miserable disease that Father can't get up and take us back to Flowers Street," Ua had repeated to herself. Now she thought that she could return to her beloved neighborhood.

Ua fancied reuniting with the group of boys and girls she had left behind on Flowers Street and their enchanting Club of the Stars. She told us about her group and the excitement of dressing up in a sky-blue outfit covered with printed stars, and the many shiny stars on the boys' caps and on the ribbons the girls wore in their hair. The Club of Stars carried small lanterns. They danced and sang on the streets accompanied by town musicians, parading all the way to the town's social club. Ua often sang for us children the song of her adored Flowers Street club.

Salve o Terno das Estrelas　　　*Hail the Club of the Stars*
Que risonho apareceu　　　　　*That cheerfully appeared,*
Mais feliz e mais brilhante　　　*Happier and more brilliant*
Que todas as Estrelas do Céu.　*Than all the Heavenly Stars.*

The Club of the Stars celebrated Christmas and the New Year. After the group sang and danced down all the streets in town, they would end the celebration at the local clubhouse on Church Street, where adults waited for the little shining stars beaming with happiness.

Father's gambling and debts, Ua often lamented, had interrupted her happy days on Flowers Street and had brought her and the family to Paramirim Street, to a house that barely stood. A house with a *fifó* that burned at night and left our noses packed with dark-caked smoke in the morning. A house with a woodburning stove and a roof that housed the big black tarantulas Ua feared and we children chased.

Ua developed a strong aversion to the black tarantulas that hid in the holes in the walls, the roof, and the black clay stove in our kitchen. Often, in the morning, she would yell and run at the sight of them. Whenever we were out of matches to start a fire to make coffee, if we had coffee to make, she would wake me and I would walk to the first neighbor whose house had smoke coming from the kitchen to ask for a *tição de fogo*—a lit piece of firewood—from their fire to start ours. I would walk back holding the lit piece in my hand, my eyes full of tears from the smoke, and give it to Ua, who would slide the ember through the slot in our stove and under a pile of dried grass to start the fire. The black tarantulas hiding in the warm stove would react to the smoke by crawling out of the hole and quickly dispersing.

Ua would scream her heart out at the sight of the giant spiders. When she did, we children rushed to get the *fifó* and chase the tarantulas with kerosene, which we poured over them. We burned the tarantulas because we believed that if the many hairs that covered their bodies got into our wounds, the scratches would become infected. So, we set the tarantulas ablaze and watched the little fireballs scatter desperately in all directions. They could run neither far nor fast and ended up burning quietly in a corner of the kitchen or in the backyard while we stood guard nearby, *fifó* in hand.

The tarantulas gave off the distinctively strange smell of burned hair as they turned into small piles of black ash, which I would gather in a tin can and bury. When the tarantulas fell from the roof on rainy days, we ran after them, beat them with wooden sticks and set them on fire.

Ua knew that the girls who lived on Flowers Street were sent to the big city to continue their studies after the fifth grade. She dreamed of studying in the capital, too. And there was also the possibility that she might somehow find a connection with those fortunate and high-spirited girls from Flowers Street, the ones who would come home from the capital on their school vacations, talking about their education and their experiences in the big city. But Ua's dreams never came true. She did leave for the capital years later, though, but with a husband who turned to drinking and became very abusive to her and their many children.

When the family left Flowers Street, my sister Gaia was forced to resign from the best-known carnival club in town and the surrounding area, the *Américo Bidulino Club*. The members rehearsed their songs and sambas for an entire year. And during the annual carnival, the group would compete and always win first place. Famous musicians and dancers from all the small towns in the region participated in the club. Members worked hard all year designing and sewing outfits for the competition. It did not matter that they spent all their money solely on the costumes while sacrificing food and other essentials. People's small savings were exhausted, but in the end, the club would always receive the highest honors.

Club members became well known. They were the envy of the town. That was what mattered most. Gaia was the star dancer of the club, with her long dark hair, curvy and flexible figure, beautiful face and contagious smile. She would lead the group through the streets. On Paramirim Street, Gaia never led the samba dancers through the streets again. Instead, she was forced into our family's samba of survival.

As for Miriam, she constantly reminisced about her time at the *Pastoral Club*. During the Three Kings celebration on the fifth of January, the girls pranced and danced around town carrying decorated lanterns in one hand and tambourines in the other. They stopped at houses with nativity scenes and performed well rehearsed plays and songs for the homeowners, guests, and townspeople. Mariam performed the group's song with enthusiasm.

A Estrela D'Alva	*The Morning Star*
No céu desponta.	*Appears in heaven.*
E a lua ainda tonta com tanto esplendor,	*And the moon still dizzy from such splendor,*
E as pastorinhas,	*And the little shepherdesses,*
Pra o consolo da lua,	*To soothe the moon,*
Vão cantando na rua	*Go singing on the street*
Lindos versos de amor.	*Pretty verses of love.*

My family never returned to Flowers Street. My sisters held on to the memories of the life that they had left behind. They kept their memories alive by repeating their stories and singing songs that captivated my imagination and entertained me on moonlit nights. As my sisters grew older and their daily fight for survival intensified, their long-awaited dream of returning to Flowers Street faded. After a while, they lost track of it, like losing sight of a shining star in the sky, after hours of gazing, when the eyes get tired from the glaring light and the neck gets stiff from turning and bending.

6. Scrounging

Soon after Father died, Mother began pacing the dirt floor on one side of our house where a white jasmine bush in constant bloom emanated a soothing aroma. She carried Wilson, our six-month-old baby brother, in her arms, and wondered where our next meal would come from. At the time, my brothers and sisters decided to help bring in some food or money any way that they could.

Ua, the eldest at nineteen, barely four feet tall with light skin, dark hair and eyes, took a job at the local movie theater after one of our cousins got pregnant. The boyfriend and the cousin had done the evil deed—*fez o mal a ela,* and she was forced to leave her job. Popular local expressions described the loss of a girl's virginity. She was lost—*se perdeu.* In most cases, after a boy deflowered a girl—*deflorou a moça,* the girl was forced to leave her parents' home—*sair de casa.* A girl's virginity was sacred; it had to be preserved until marriage. If it was lost, everyone would ostracize her, including her family. If she had a job, she would lose it, along with the respect of the community. Above all, she would lose her humanity.

Parents would usually send their daughters to stay with a distant relative or the girl had to stay indoors, not leaving the parents' home for the duration of the pregnancy. I often heard the elders say that these girls could never lead a normal life again. There were girls I saw in the neighborhood who had no distant relatives to take them in. They had no means of leaving home or raising the child. The grandparents assumed responsibility for raising the baby, and the girls stayed prisoners in their parents' home and were never again accepted in society. However, after our cousin had her child, as if by miracle, she got married to a former boyfriend and started a family. But after a few years, her husband left her for a young girl, whom she raised. The girl lived in the family's home. She helped with the children and the chores.

Ua continued working. She took all of the money she earned at her new job and a second job she had at the *Cartorio Eleitoral,* where she recorded the townspeople's voting records and registration by hand, to the market on Saturday to buy food. In addition, the sewing classes Ua had taken in better days on Flowers Street were put into practice to supplement her earnings from her two other jobs. Soon, the front window of our rundown house gained color with the display of the undergarments my sister and mother sewed on the new Singer that Father bought before his illness. They hung the clothes on a rope across the top frame. Neighbors and passersby would stop and take notice.

Surrounded by colorful panties and brassieres on the windowsill was fresh yellow cornmeal couscous, topped with white grated coconut. Mother made and sliced it into triangular portions to sell to the workers who walked by our house in the early morning on their way to Suerdieck, the town's tobacco factory. The smell of the sweet corn filled the air. We couldn't eat the couscous because we knew that Mother sold it so that we could buy beans and farina and maybe a small piece of dry meat to cook with the beans. The beans and farina would fill our stomachs more and make us less hungry. By midmorning, Mother's couscous was usually gone.

To make her couscous, Mother would soak the corn overnight, drain the water early in the morning and pound the soft kernels in a tall, thick wood mortar using a heavy black pestle. Ua, Gaia, and other female neighbors would help Mother pound the corn in the backyard. Two women would face each other over the wood mortar, each holding a heavy pestle with both hands. They stretched their arms way up and pounded the kernels in a rhythmic and naturally coordinated up-and-down movement. One pestle would reach the bottom of the mortar in full force—boom—while the other hung in the air; one woman's body bent over the mortar while the other stretched way back. They performed this ballet to the deep sound the pestle made when it thumped the mortar, boom, back and forth, … boom … boom…. The neighbors would pound coffee beans for hours this way, too, never touching each other's pestle and sometimes singing a popular jingle to the rhythm of the coordinated pounding:

Vou pilar café.	*I'm going to pound coffee.*
Vou pilar café.	*I'm going to pound coffee.*
Pila, pila meu benzinho	*Pound, pound my little sweetheart*
Que papai não quer.	*That daddy does not want you to.*

I never took my eyes away from the beloved women the whole time they ground corn or coffee in the backyard by our kitchen.

Their rhythm, grace, and agility enchanted me. I can still see their body movement and hear the deep sound of the pestle hitting the mortar.

Gaia sewed mattresses and shirts for Vinicius, the owner of a store, from Monday to Friday and took the money that she earned to the market on Saturdays. I would walk with Gaia to the store early Monday to get a big bundle of fabric for the cutting and sewing. We would stroll back late Friday with the sewn shirts and mattresses bundled up on our heads. On Saturday, I happily would march with Gaia, the money, and our dark vine basket to the market.

Gaia was seventeen when Father died. Tall, slender and agile, with cinnamon skin, very dark hair and eyes, and a luminous smile, Gaia displayed an extremely practical approach to things. She immediately thought of a new way to put food in our dark clay pan on the woodburning stove when we were hungry and there was no food in the house. In the backyard, a parade of chickens, pigs, and roosters would appear and disappear at random as they fed on earthworms, insects, and bits and pieces of whatever food that they found dispersed throughout the area. It was the neighbor's livestock. Gaia devised a plan to trap the clucking chickens in our kitchen by setting a white trail of farina or bits of earthworm. The animals would follow the trail and end up corralled in a small space in the kitchen where we waited for them.

Gaia would prepare for the event by sharpening a kitchen knife on our black stone, rubbing the knife back and forth and dropping water on the silver blade. She then set the knife by our clay bowl half filled with vinegar and put water to boil in the tall kerosene can on the stove. As soon as a chicken passed the doorframe, we carefully closed the wobbly door and chased the panicky animal into a corner. The chicken bounced back and forth against our kitchen walls and woodburning stove. The struggle did not last long, for the space was tight and the fast hands and empty stomachs were many.

Once Gaia had the chicken, she held it tightly down with her knee. She secured its head on a piece of wood, peeled off the fine feathers from its neck, tapped on it a few times, and slit the throat open with our shiny silver knife. She poured the warm blood into the clay bowl and mixed it with the vinegar so it would not coagulate. Sometimes when Gaia's knife missed the fatal vein, the stunned animal would stand up and circle the kitchen, dripping its red blood on the dirt floor and slamming its bloody head into the black walls. We would trap the disoriented animal in a hurry and give it back to our sister to finish the job with the razor-sharp knife and squeeze the remaining blood into the clay bowl. I helped Gaia immerse the chicken in a bath of cold water and then in the tall can of boiling water on the stove. We would gather to remove the feathers quickly, and Gaia would cut the chicken into small pieces, making every part count: feet and guts, which we turned inside out to clean in the nearby pond and cut into small pieces to make a stew dish called *cabidela*. The chicken tripe was sometimes full of hookworms, but they did not bother Gaia. She flushed them out. Then my sister cooked the chicken in its blood.

Eduardo and I would put the wet feathers in a bucket and carry them to be buried in a carefully dug hole in the bushes far away from our house. I carried the pail on my head and dug a hole with our old hoe while Eduardo kept a watch for animals or neighbors. The trembling fear in my stomach overcame my hunger. After burying the wet feathers, Eduardo and I stepped on the soft ground, circling around a number of times as if dancing; we covered it with leaves and twigs and ran home as fast as we could. Gaia cooked the chicken with all the windows and doors closed; even the holes in the doors and walls were stuffed with straws, so that the smell would not give us away. Thinking back, I loved roaming around in our infinite backyard, like the chickens we trapped to kill. But to eat the meal, I had to be corralled in the house, very much like the chickens. The hunter became hunted. On those days we ate. When my sister attracted more than one chicken at a time, there was good reason for celebration: we ate more. And Gaia did not have to cut the pieces too small. There was enough for everyone in our family.

Our adventure with the neighbors' chickens went on for a while until our feast along with the frequent disappearance of the animals aroused suspicions. And then, at sundown, when the women walked home from the tobacco factory and their chickens did not show up at the pen or the count of the flock was short, they would go looking for their animals. When they couldn't find them, they would stop right at our backyard by our kitchen door to ask if we had seen the chickens and describe the missing animal to us.

"Have you seen my chicken today?" they would ask.

"No. What chicken? We haven't," we would always answer.

"It was a young chicken with red stripes, and you must've seen it. We don't live too far from each other, and the chicken must've passed through your yard," they would insist.

"No. We haven't seen it," we replied.

"It was my golden hen that laid eggs like no other," some would lament.

"It was a plump white chicken," another desperate woman would explain.

"No," we persistently replied, "we haven't seen anything like it."

"Miserable bunch of liars and hungry thieves," they would yell angrily as they walked away.

We must not have been very convincing. Soon, the neighbors, one by one, started fencing their yards and keeping their flocks in. One Friday afternoon, a neighbor named Maria de Mané Vito stood firmly by our kitchen door and demanded news about her black chicken that had disappeared that day. It was the chicken that she was planning on taking to be sacrificed to the voodoo gods at sundown. I had my heart and soul in my hands that evening but stood by the story of not having seen any chicken like that one. Maria left our house calling us names at the top of her lungs, and we soon became known as the miserable chicken thieves and liars in the neighborhood.

With the disappearance of the neighbors' chickens from our backyard, my siblings had to find another way to put food on the table. On Wednesday nights, looking for relief from the midweek hunger, one of my sisters, who, decades later, still feels ashamed of this sacrifice, would take me by the hand and walk across town to pay a visit to the local priest, Padre Pedro. The two would meet in the back of the town's tall whitewashed church, standing on a small hill in the center of town. The priest would appear in a long black robe after my sister's soft knock at the church's back door. He would greet us in a soft and pious voice, take my sister by the hand, and order me to stay quiet inside the church until my sister was finished and came for me.

"All right," I answered softly.

I did not know what the priest's finishing with my sister involved. I was eight, very afraid of the priest, fascinated, and scared by the images in the church. Padre Pedro wore a long black cape that brought to mind the stories of "The Man in the Black Cape" my siblings told us in the dark, on warm and quiet nights, sitting by the side of our house. A man in black was said to wander around town on pitch-dark nights. Many people swore they had seen him in our neighborhood, taking the women and children and scaring the men away. I had heard the stories many times over, sitting stiff and snuggled against my siblings in fear. The children and women the man in the black cape was said to kidnap were never to return, and nothing was ever known of their fate.

The voices of my siblings telling this story on pitch-dark nights played over and over in my head as I entered the big white church in the shadows of candlelight. The angels with puffy round faces and lips and hands holding a torch and the human-sized statues of saints with sad faces and dressed in real clothes transported me to another world. I had never seen anything of the kind. I walked around in the dim light, and their eyes followed me everywhere I went. I could not hide from them. I sat on a pew in the back and waited.

My sister suddenly appeared, fixing her hair and straightening her red skirt with the palm of her hands. She walked to the back of the church and took me by the hand.

"Let's go home, Leda," she whispered in a very low voice.

"Are we coming back to church again?" I asked.

"I don't know," she said. "And don't say anything to anyone about this," she warned me in a firm manner.

"Yes," I said with my head down. And we walked home without saying another word.

Much later in life, when I asked my sister to elaborate on our frequent visits to the town's priest on Wednesdays, she described the occasion as being very close to my recollection. But when I asked her what exactly she did in the back of the church with Padre Pedro, she laughed a bit for a while and replied that she was in the long line with the other poor people in town, waiting for the priest's charity to buy food for the family. Then my sister became serious and sad, her head down.

On nights my sister visited church we had some money for food the following morning. We would go to the stores in town with our basket because there was no open market on Thursdays. My sister did not have to worry about my revealing her visits to the priest. No one in the family ever asked about it, though everyone knew that the priest gave my sister money on Wednesday nights. I was just happy the next day, hearing the firewood crackling, seeing the red flames under our black clay pot change from red to yellow, engulfing the round black clay pot, and smelling the beans cooking. My sister knocked on the church's back door many more Wednesdays and met with the "man in the black cape." I continued to follow her.

One of my father's sisters, Nininha, once decided to help our family and asked my sister Miriam, who was ten at the time, to help at her store on market day. Nininha lived on Church Street, across the wide street from her sister Didi. The store, which was up a hill just a short distance from her house, sold sugar, coffee, nuts, tobacco, cigars, leather and the kinds of dried goods that the vendors who came to town to sell their fresh produce took back with them. To Gaia, this was a very good opportunity to gather some money for our market day. She sewed a big pocket on the inside of Miriam's underpants and instructed my sister how to divert some of the cash from Aunt Nininha's register into her underwear pocket.

"You have to smile your natural way while doing it," Gaia said. "So, don't show any signs of being nervous."

"Fine. What do I do if people look at me?" Miriam asked.

"Just pretend nothing happened, and you're just scratching yourself," replied Gaia.

Nininha's store was popular and prosperous. Since Miriam was eager to help us back home, it worked out well. My sister quickly learned to weigh coffee, sugar, tobacco and peanuts, and to fill bottles of kerosene and palm oil to sell. She performed her new tasks efficiently. At the end of the day on Saturdays, she would arrive home walking with difficulty but thrilled, with her pocket full of my aunt's cash. Miriam would take her underwear off and empty the hidden pocket on our black table. I would watch Gaia gather the cash, count it, and then hurry to the neighborhood stores where she would buy food. It was too late in the afternoon for us to run to the open market. Miriam arrived home at dusk after the vendors had already left and the market had died down, leaving us with no time to walk across town to buy any discounted merchandise.

I was eight then, very quiet, shy, and clumsy. When I asked Gaia if I could accompany Miriam to my aunt's store to bring home money, my sister laughed and promptly sewed a similar pocket onto my underpants. I was sent to the store with Miriam. I helped my sister but could not find any way to put the money into my pocket. I could not figure out how Miriam did it so easily. I felt every eye in the store on me all the time, and at the end of the day, Miriam would walk home slowly with her pocket full. Mine was always empty.

On market day, at lunchtime, my uncle Maçu often walked the short distance from the store to home for lunch. One day, he took me by the hand and asked me to walk home with him for a warm lunch and some cash. My aunt and uncle had no children of their own, and their house on Church Street was big and had a choking stench due to the many pieces of raw leather they bought and left lying around on the floor to finish drying. I wanted to come home like Miriam, with money in my underpants pocket to dish out on our black table to see Gaia count it and take it to the store to buy food. Since I could not find a way to hide the money from my aunt's cash register, I thought I had a chance to get the needed money from my uncle. I followed him to his house.

There, my uncle led me into a bedroom with black furniture and a foul smell. He pulled his pants down, lay on the big bed, and took his penis out, telling me to play with it.

"Your aunt doesn't play with me anymore," he said. "I need some playing."

My uncle's penis looked like the huge, fat, and wrinkled earthworms I played with in the backyard on rainy days after they were flushed out of their holes and were burned by the hot sun. I liked playing with the fresh worms in my backyard, and I sometimes dug them out of the ground and gave them to Gaia to cut up into small pieces and set the trail that attracted the neighbor's chickens into our kitchen. This one worm my uncle carried between his legs did not interest me, but I still touched it, as I was told. My only thought was bringing home money to buy food for the family. I do not remember if my uncle gave me the money that he had promised, but I never went back to the store with Miriam on Saturdays and never told my family the reason. I was embarrassed for not bringing money home and confused by Uncle Maçu's actions. Miriam proudly carried out her task for a long while and Nininha never noticed the missing cash. My sister stopped bringing money home much later, only after my aunt died and her husband could not keep the store.

It was also on Saturdays, at the end of the day, that Mother went to visit Dona Ervirinha, the blonde angel of my childhood. She was a tall and very generous woman who owned a farm and lived in a big house surrounded by a tall white wall, topped with pieces of colorful broken glass, a big yard and lots of tall trees full of aromatic flowers and fruit. Outside Dona Ervirinha's house, we would get in line with many other poor mothers along with their skinny, half-naked, big bellied and barefoot children for the weekly collection of the milk, ripe avocados, bananas, and colorful vegetables that Dona Ervirinha's employees had returned unsold from the market.

My younger brothers, Eduardo and Raimundo, and I would stay in line close to our mother. When it was our turn, the blonde and blue-eyed woman, like the angels I saw in church, would fill our basket with fruits and vegetables. She would give us extra pieces of meat, a big jar of coagulated milk that had been left out in the sun, and occasional bundles of used clothes and shoes. She would always talk to Mother for a bit.

"How are you and the children doing, Dona Raimunda?" she would ask.

"We're going along as God wills it, Dona Ervirinha," Mother would always answer.

"Come back here on Wednesday, and I'll gather some more clothes and shoes for you and the children, Dona Raimunda."

"Yes, Dona Ervirinha, and God will pay and protect you," Mother replied.

My brothers and I would help Mother carry the basket on our heads across town. We would return to Dona Ervirinha's house on Wednesdays for the extras and happily carry the gifts home.

A black girl named Miuda, an orphan of ten or eleven who lived next door to me, was another angel of my childhood. Miuda was the only angel I did not see hanging from the walls and ceiling or holding candles at the altar of the town church. Brown-skinned Miuda was flesh and blood. I could touch and speak to her. She earned her nickname *Miuda*—small—because she was severely malnourished. A handicapped black woman named Dona Silvina raised Miuda.

The young and the old in Dona Silvina's house depended upon each other almost entirely. They earned a living by selling cooked cow and lamb intestines at the Saturday market. Dona Silvina's husband, João Sabino, used to push a wheelbarrow all the way to the market on Saturdays, his crippled wife holding onto the sides. Miuda followed pushing a second squeaky wheelbarrow filled with pots and pans. The rest of the week, João Sabino left the house early in the morning and returned home drunk in the evening.

Dona Silvina wanted Miuda near her all of the time. The girl could not wander in the backyard for too long or distance herself too far from the eyes of her stepmother without Dona Silvina yelling for her. "Oh, Mi-u-da, hurry up and put more wood in the fire. Check the water in the pot," she would order. "Oh, Mi-u-da, what're you doing now? Did you not hear me? Have you not done what I told you?"

Dona Silvina yelled again and again when she did not see Miuda next to her. Miuda would yell back, "I'm gathering things for the market tomorrow. I'll come right away."

In the early morning, Dona Silvina used to send Miuda to buy lamb intestines at Seu Agemiro's slaughterhouse on the outskirts of town. Miuda carried the bloody organs back home on her head in a wooden basin that we called *gamela*. When she arrived, she set the basin on the grass in the back of her house and cleaned the guts in a nearby pond. By late afternoon, the water in the pond behind Miuda's house would turn dark green with dung dancing in the water, moving from side to side according to the direction the wind blew. The muck reached the edges of the pond slowly, where it stayed, giving off a profoundly sharp smell that enveloped the backyard and unsettled my soul.

After cleaning the intestines, Miuda made up small bundles of liver, coagulated blood, tongue, heart and lung, wrapping them in pieces of stomach tied with tripe—*dobradinha*. In the afternoon, Miuda cooked the little bundles of delicacies in a black kettle that sat on top of the black clay stove in Dona Silvina's kitchen. Their kitchen wall was attached to the wall of our kitchen.

I stayed as far away as possible from Miuda's green dung pond. I held my breath when I had to come into the house, but I kept an eye on the cooking of the guts. The strong aroma invaded our kitchen and my nostrils. The distinctive smell overwhelmed my senses and tempted my hungry, weak body.

Miuda's cooking troubled my siblings, too. It disturbed us most on Friday nights when the day had come and gone and we remained with empty stomachs. Though Miuda would always find a way to hide some of the little bundles from her vigilant stepmother and pass them to Gaia's outstretched hands through the holes in our kitchen walls, there was never enough for the many dry mouths and shrunken stomachs in our house. Maybe it would have been better if Miuda had not given us anything at all, for once the little bit she gave Gaia hit our empty stomachs, our senses would wake up and transform us into ravaging hyenas.

Dona Silvina never left her woodburning stove when the bundles were cooking on Friday afternoons. She would watch us, and we would keep our eyes on her through the holes in our kitchen wall, waiting for night to fall when Gaia quietly could remove the loose adobe blocks from the wall and help herself to Miuda's bundles.

After removing the blocks, my sister would slide her thin body through the small hole and enter Dona Silvina's dark kitchen. We passed her our bucket, which she passed back to us with the warm *dobradinhas*. We were quick to carefully replace the dirt blocks, then sat on the kitchen floor in the middle of the night and in no time devoured the entrails Miuda had spent the whole day preparing.

Miuda knew we stole her bundles at night, but she continued in her role as our accomplice and friend during the day. Dona Silvina suspected the girl handed us some of her food and sometimes beat her. She knew we entered her kitchen to steal her food. She cursed the dirty starving thieves from her wheelchair in the morning if Gaia had gone too far by taking too many *dobradinhas*. But the beating, yelling, and cursing never stopped Miuda from helping us or Gaia from removing the loose blocks in the kitchen wall again and again when we had gone hungry. Gaia made some cloth dolls for Miuda to play with as a way of thanking her for alleviating our hunger.

Eduardo, a little over a year younger than me, was busy and practical, looking for ways to bring home food too. He liked the freedom that the life he lived gave him: playing in our open backyard until dark, selling Mother's couscous and my sisters' panties and brassieres at our window and at the Suerdieck tobacco factory, hunting snakes for their skins, and killing birds for food with his slingshot. His stay at school was short, like that of most of my siblings. He dropped out after second grade. Eduardo was a good conversationalist, extremely verbal, quick, cute, thin, and never shy. He loved to talk and could sell anything or make any deal. So Mother would send him on visits to the townspeople when there was nothing in our house to eat. I often followed him to the center of town to the homes that we frequently visited.

We would cross the open soccer field and pass the town's big shower house where tired donkeys waited by the curb to be loaded with heavy wooden barrels of water that would be sold around town. I remember the men whistling and singing their favorite tunes in the shower house while bathing. We would arrive at a house surrounded by tall white walls with pieces of broken colored glass cemented to the top. The shards reflected kaleidoscopic colors and shapes, as the rays of the sun hit them in the afternoon.

On more than one occasion, Eduardo knocked on the tall gate of Dona Bete's house with a rock. After a few raps, the maid came and led us to the kitchen where Dona Bete, an elegant and pretty woman, met us. She often took Eduardo by the hand and sat him on her lap to run her fingers through his tight curls and rub his skinny arms while I watched. Dona Bete never said much to me, but I knew she liked Eduardo. After a while, she would ask the maid to feed us. We ate and drank sweet pineapple juice and sat quietly at the kitchen table. Sometimes, the maid sent us home with bags of avocados, dried meat, beans, rice, old clothes and shoes. We returned to Dona Bete's house many times. My sisters said that the pretty owner of the big house had no children of her own and her husband was always traveling.

My brother Carlos, whom we called Tatai, the fourth born in our family, was short and very husky at age fourteen when Father died. Soon after, Tatai would get up with the roosters at dawn to meet with Francisco, a well-known hunter in town. They walked to the arid area and hills that surrounded town, about fifteen miles away, to catch boa constrictors and chop wood. Tatai would arrive home at dusk, sweaty and puffy, carrying a huge dead boa wrapped around his neck or a bunch of wood piled on his head. He killed boas for us to eat, and for their valuable skin, which he sold at the market. I remember watching Tatai lay the dead snake on a bed of banana leaves in the backyard, then sharpen our shiny kitchen knife on the black rock and carefully remove the snakeskin. He opened the boa's belly first and threw the guts to the neighbors' pigs and chickens. Then he pulled off the skin from one end while we held on to the other. Tatai salted the meat, briskly drying it over a big fire we built to preserve the meat since we had no refrigeration.

On Saturdays, Tatai would sell snakeskins at the market, which artisans used to make drums and tambourines. My younger brothers, Eduardo and Raimundo, naked and hungry, followed Tatai hoping to eat some of the manioc farina that the vendors spilled while filling their customers' bags. They waited for Tatai to sell his snakeskins knowing the money he made would buy groceries to bring home. When he couldn't catch a boa, Tatai carried home huge bundles of firewood tied on his head with a rope. He sold the bundles at the market, and with any money he earned, Tatai filled our black vine basket with goods. Gaia sometimes accompanied Tatai to the woods to help with chopping wood, carrying it home, and selling firewood door to door.

Our hardship was eased in other ways. Some days in December I left the house early in the morning and walked to the woods with my elder siblings to gather wild blackberries, which we called *quixaba*. I looked forward to these day trips. Upon arriving in the woods, we searched for the almost leafless prickly bushes decorated with small black and sweet fruits. We pulled down the branches, quietly satisfied our appetites, filled our buckets and carried them home on our heads late in the afternoon when the cicadas' singing echoed in the air. Another juicy and round fruit, *umbú*, from the umbra tree, very common in our area, also helped fill us up.

We used to climb tall cashew trees to pick fruits to bring home to eat. We ate the succulent, meaty part of the fruit and saved the nuts, which we later toasted on a big tin sheet made from an empty kerosene drum. We cut the drum open, flattened it out, poked holes in the center and placed the nuts on it before setting the drum on a bonfire in the backyard. To roast the nuts, we turn them constantly with a long wooden stick until they were carbon dark on the outside. Then we would sit on the ground and crack them open on a rock. I loved the warm, delicious cashews.

My siblings and I also brought home from the woods a yellowish and prickly tropical fruit called *jaca*. The sweet layer inside the *jaca* had large, hidden pits, which we also saved to cook on our kerosene tin can over the fire before eating. Sometimes we gathered the pits people had thrown on the street after eating the sweet part and brought them home to wash and cook. We also used to climb small palm trees to cut bunches of a coconut-like fruit called *licuri*, which we would cook in the backyard. I loved the excitement of gathering wood and making these big fires.

At times, when my siblings had earned some money, we would get up with the roosters at daybreak and walk with our tin cups in one hand and a little sugar mixed with manioc farina in the other to a big dairy farm in town, Seu Antonio Leone's corral. The cowboys at the corral milked the cows at dawn. When we arrived, we waited, leaning quietly on the heavy wood fence, trying not to upset the farmer, the cows or the cowboys. The scent of dried cow manure and fresh milk gave the corral a unique smell that is still deeply ingrained in my memory. It is a smell difficult to describe; there is nothing in the world like it. After a while, the cowboys would notice our presence and approach. Without much ado, they usually collected our tin cups and filled them with warm, foamy, sweet milk that we loved and looked forward to so much.

We liked to sit on the ground near the corral, add the sweetened farina to the warm milk and have a feast. The cowboys blessed us with warm milk to fill our tin cans as many times as our stomachs allowed. Then we walked home with warm milk in our tin cans for Mother.

I will always remember the rising sun greeting me on my way home, my hand holding tightly a tin cup of warm milk, contentment filling my heart. To this day, the rising sun triggers in me the warmth and satisfaction I felt those mornings holding a can of fresh milk. I wish to die on a sunny day so that the bright rays warm and guide my spirit to embrace the sun.

7. My Brother's Bravery

The happiest day in town was certainly Saturday, the big market day. The townspeople set aside their daily routines on Saturday and embraced the activity in their homes and streets. Vendors, young and old, from near and far, came to town and gathered in the open market to display their goods. They arrived on horses, donkeys, and mules. Others piled in the back of big, open trucks, sitting on improvised wood benches, snuggled together under a brown canopy.

People would carry baskets on their heads or roll their squeaking wheelbarrows along the streets. Housewives from the center of town, Church and Flowers Street, and the nicest streets, walked alongside their maids or their paid carriers, one with a purse in hand, the others carrying their wares. Vendors yelled out their merchandise and stopped in front of homes along the way for an early sale. The sound of trotting horses and mules carrying heavy baskets loaded with goods added to the excitement.

Everything was sold along the mile-long stretch of the market. In one open area, armadillos and snakes, caged or smoked, live chickens, roosters, and ducks with their feet tied up, and colorful, exotic birds were all displayed under the burning sun as well as in the pouring rain. Herbs preserved in jars claiming the power to cure maladies of the body and the soul were lined up on a bench. In another sheltered area were piles of meat: salted and fresh, fish, ham hocks, fresh pig feet and heads, half cows and pigs, all hanging from big hooks or displayed on the large cement counters.

Vibrant activity filled every corner of the market. Friends and acquaintances would stop to chat over piles of colorful women's undergarments displayed on long tables. Horses tied to trees would stamp the ground and the air, flicking away the persistent flies. Loudspeakers blasting from atop cars announced the lowest prices in town and blared popular songs to fill the intervals between sardine and soap commercials. People would come and go until sundown, when the streets were cleaned, and the cool air refreshed the ground until the following Saturday morning.

On market Saturdays, when family members had collected some money from their sewing, their begging, and the selling of wood and charcoal, Ua usually took our big vine basket to town. Miriam and I accompanied her sometimes, carrying our own small vine basket. We walked alongside Ua, who bargained with the vendors for a lower price at dusk when they wanted to quickly sell their unsold merchandise so they could go home or do their own shopping. Miriam and I trailed Ua, who stopped to buy the fruits and vegetables for the big basket she carried and to add bits and pieces to the baskets Miriam and I held. When we arrived home, Miriam and I cooked our vegetables and pieces of dried meat in our small clay pot in the backyard and then played house with our neighborhood girlfriends.

During the week, vendors and buyers in the area geared up for the market by harvesting, cooking, sewing, and preparing their goods. Seu Agemiro, the owner of the town's biggest slaughterhouse, prepared for market on Friday afternoons. He directed a group of cowboys to escort the bulls he had purchased from the local ranchers back to his corral on the periphery of town to be slaughtered at dawn on Saturday. The cowboys escorted the bulls through an area just a few miles away from the back of our house, where I saw lights glittering on dark nights.

Seu Agemiro's cowboys carried lassos in their hands. Cows with loud heavy bells wrapped around their necks accompanied the bulls, whose faces were covered with black leather blinders, leaving only the corner of their eyes exposed. This limited the bull's vision so that it focused on safely following the guiding cows and the cowboys to the corral. On many occasions, however, the fierce bulls got away from the herd and stampeded aimlessly and ferociously at full speed all over town. The bulls tricked their keepers, flashing into backyards, people's homes and stores, making everybody drop what they were doing and run for their lives. The black creatures trounced everything in their path and cornered anything that moved. Every Friday afternoon, we stayed on high alert until the animals reached Seu Agemiro's corral.

Sometimes, a bull ran out of steam and planted itself in a corner, behind a tree, a wall, or a house. With abundant white froth dripping from its mouth, the bull would dig into the ground, pounding forcefully, like thunder striking the earth. The cowboys and the cows would approach the sullen beast. After being poked many times with a long, sharp stick or pulled by its tail, the animal finally would leave the corner. The cowboys and cows then quickly led the bull to Seu Agemiro's corral, where it invariably turned into the red meat displayed at the Saturday market hanging upside down from big hooks. Even dead, the bulls frightened me. I stayed far away from Seu Agemiro's tent, the dead bulls and the mountains of meat when I followed my sisters to the market.

On Friday afternoons, we ran home to lock our doors and shut the windows, afraid that the bulls would enter our house. But these efforts meant plain terror for my siblings and for me. The bulls were huge, strong, and fearless, our doors weak and wobbly.

"Lift it just a bit with both hands," Gaia would instruct the one who arrived first at the door to close it.

"No, don't hold it so high it pulls the hinges apart," she warned.

"Oh! My God! The bulls are coming, and we won't be able to close it," my sister cried.

"The hinges are getting too loose now," the other complained.

"I need a rock to tighten the nails. Go outside and fetch one," Gaia instructed again.

No one moved. No one would dare to run into the backyard for the necessary rock. The bulls were on everyone's mind. All eyes then fixed on our brother Fernando, who quickly understood our silent plea and dashed out to get the rock to hand it to Gaia. She then pounded the loose nails back into the doorframe to secure the hinges and carefully closed the feeble door.

My siblings and I rolled our *pilão*— large and heavy black wood mortar Mother used to pound the corn for her couscous—to barricade the kitchen door. We then ran for the one chair that we had and piled it on top of the black pestle in the mortar to make the pile taller. I watched through the holes in the walls and windows, attentive to the bulls' moves and to the direction they took, and sighed in deep relief when I saw the speeding giants take a different route than the dirt path that led to our backyard.

Every Friday afternoon, no matter what else we were doing, we would run home to face the same agony of resurrecting our failing backdoor and watch the bulls. I lived in constant fear that the ferocious, foaming beasts would one day decide to take the road to our house and smash through our decrepit doors like lightning and find me hiding in a corner. I feared that a bull might pick up my body with its pointed horns and toss it around.

At night, I often had nightmares about a fuming bull throwing me in the air. In my dreams back then, I saw our house completely destroyed and the black bull flying over the debris of our table, our chair, our beds, our mortar and pestle, our stove, our windows and doors, and Mother's sewing machine; the black bull levitated in the air dressed in bright red, yellow, and green like the clowns in the circus that visited town. And like the circus clowns, the bull juggled my mother and siblings in the air, as if playing tricks with the unbreakable and colorful long pins that I had seen at the circus. In my dreams, the bull appeared with large wings and chubby face like that of the angels I had seen all over the church altar, walls, and ceiling the nights that I visited the priest with my sister.

The bull flew above my bed and looked down at me from the white clouds with big, bright and brilliant eyes. It danced to the *forró*, the music I had always heard during St. John's festivities in town and at the market over the loudspeakers on Saturdays, between commercials. And in my dreams, if I hid, the bull would find me anywhere I went, even in the quietest corner in the backyard, under the bush where I often slept off my hunger. But most often in my dreams, the raging bull would fall down from the clouds, landing its weight right on top of me and crushing my body against the wires sticking out of our mattress. Sometimes, when the masked black bull appeared with enormous wings, I, too, flew from my bed through our tile roof to confront the animal in an exuberant aerial duel. I fought the beast bravely, my small and skinny figure against the big, brave bull.

My fights with the bull must have been noisy because Gaia often shook me hard to awaken me at night. She often threatened to send me to sleep on the dirt floor, for she was getting tired of my restless nights and my frequent wetting of the straw mattress. For a long time, I had to confront Gaia's anger at night and the wet mattress in the morning. My dreams of the bull became constant.

As the years went by, the dreams of flying above my bed to confront the black bull extended to flying very high in the sky. I covered long distances above extensive land, entire cities, green forests, high mountains, and ancient ruins. These dreams have stayed with me ever since. I still dream of flying to overcome any difficult barrier or problem that I encounter. In my dreams, if I find myself in a broken-down car in a remote area, for instance, I would fly over roads, oceans, homes, and ruined villages, looking for help and directions. And when I see a person and land, I am sent to yet another unfamiliar place where destruction and confusion reign. So, I am left in a cycle of searches and unsettled results. There is never a resolution to my flying dreams. I interpret it as the result of my prolonged terror and anxiety of not being able to shut our flimsy back door and protect myself and my family from the ferocious bulls.

Saturday, however, was my brother Fernando's favorite day. At three months of age, Fernando had fallen from his bed and later developed an ear infection that left him half-deaf and unsteady for life. Ever since I can remember, my brother fiddled with the yellow pus that constantly gushed out of his ears and flowed like a river down his neck and shoulder, leaving a foul odor. No one appreciated Fernando's company: not his siblings, not the neighborhood children, and not his teachers. He was the only person in the family who had the luxury of sleeping in a corner or in a bed all alone, for no one wanted to sleep beside Fernando.

My brother had the same smell of rotten flesh that invaded the air when dead animals were left in the hot sun for vultures to devour. It was like the smell of the meat we bought at the market on Saturday and kept inside the house wrapped in a dish towel during the night, uncooked for more than a day or two. We hung our meat in the backyard to dry in the sun during the day, but it attracted maggots, puffy white worms that made the meat smell rotten. Not at all minding the worms, we removed them and cooked the meat. We then started calling Fernando "Rotten Ear."

I felt sorry for Fernando and once took him by his hand and walked all the way to school with him. The teacher was really surprised to see my brother in the classroom, for he had stopped going a long time before, but she said he could stay. Fernando sat in the back. When the teacher closed the door to the room, the stench quickly filled the room. I looked back shyly and saw Fernando calmly picking at the thick yellow string of pus running down his neck from his ear and wiping his fingers on his pants. My classmates covered their noses tightly with the tips of their fingers.

After picking his ears for a while, Fernando cleared his throat, deeply and loudly, and spit the voluminous yellow mucus on the tile floor at the side of the room. The teacher got angry.

"Get up, clean your dirtiness, and go away," she told Fernando.

He did. The teacher later complained to Ua. It was the last time Fernando went to school.

When Father died, Fernando inherited an oversized brown jacket from him. One Saturday, when all our resources had been exhausted and Mother's panties and bras were left swinging in the wind back and forth from the window frame, unsold, Fernando had an idea. He put on his loose brown jacket and wrapped a piece of bloody cow lung he had found at Seu Agemiro's slaughterhouse to his leg, so it would look like a wound. He then walked all the way to the market, limping and pretending to be crippled. With the smell that emanated from his ear, no one would doubt his disability.

Then toward midday, the busiest time at the lively Saturday market, when the jolly vendors concentrated their attention on the customers and when the market had reached a chaotic peak, Fernando saw the perfect opportunity to help himself to merchandise. He stacked pieces of salt-dried meat, fish, pork feet, and whatever other unguarded goods he could find into the loose jacket. He then ran home to Paramirim Street, as fast as the raging bulls that rampaged through town on Friday afternoons.

The enraged vendors, wearing bloody aprons and screaming bloody murder, quickly jumped on the high counters for a view of the transgressor. They ran after Fernando with their shiny machetes and axes threatening to chop off my brother's hands and head. They could never catch up or get a good look at him. He arrived home red in the face, huffing and puffing, with no signs of the bloody and injured leg he had left the house with that morning. His arms were crossed over his chest, protecting the stolen goods.

One by one, Fernando pulled the pieces of salty meat and other items from inside his coat and pockets and proudly set the pile in the center of our big black table. We ate that day. It didn't trouble me to think that the precious goods might have touched my brother's rotten ear.

On one occasion, when Fernando felt daring enough to pull down a whole cow leg hanging from a large hook in the ceiling of a meat tent, he almost got caught. After grabbing the leg, he threw it over his shoulder and quickly pushed his way through the crowd.

But the leg was too big for him and the crowd too dense. This time he could not run home as fast as the raging bull. He barely escaped the vendor's vengeance. Fernando's cow leg hung in our backyard in the sun for the rest of the week to finish drying. I kept guard over it, protecting it from the ravenous vultures outside and from the white worms it could get if kept inside the house. Everyone enjoyed Fernando's cow leg. Mother made soup, stew, and added pieces of the white bone with its yellow marrow to our cooking beans. We were happy and thankful to Fernando.

Successfully challenging the vendors at the Saturday market emboldened Fernando to defy the voodoo gods at the town's crossroads. As was the custom, both the *mães-de-santo and pais-de-santo*—voodoo priestesses and male priests arrived at midnight with large baskets of offerings on their heads, offerings they left at busy intersections for the *orixás*—the gods. The state of Bahia is rich in African culture and traditions introduced to the area by slaves originally brought to work on the sugar plantations in the sixteenth century. Many of the wonderful foods, beliefs, and practices that came from Africa remain very strong and well cultivated in this region of Brazil.

One of these is *candomblé*, a religious ritual during which the chiefs celebrate the African gods and goddesses. The ceremony starts by taking the god's offerings, known as *despacho,* to the crossroads, where the most famous god, Exu, reigns. Acting as a go-between, Exu, the most fearful god in the African pantheon, who is often compared to the devil in the Christian tradition, receives gifts at the crossroads and communicates to the other African *orixás*—gods, the human desires that he hears from the priestesses and priests.

The offerings left at the intersections usually included live or dead chickens and roosters, animal organs still warm and pulsing, a bottle of *cachaça*—rum, Exu's favorite gift; clothes tied in knots, fresh flowers, candles, dishes of fresh okra cooked in yellow palm oil, money, tobacco, cigars, huge bullfrogs, black cloth dolls stuck with lots of clothespins, and many other offerings. Fernando saw stealing these gifts as another opportunity to bring food to our black table.

On the night of the *candomblé*, the African drums resounded at sundown to announce the event. As night fell, we were on the alert. At midnight, Fernando put on his loose brown coat, carried our *fifó* in one hand and our market basket in the other, and left the house. He headed to the most popular and well-known crossroads in our neighborhood, far behind our house, a favorite spot for the *mães-de-santo* and *pais-de-santo*. No one in the family dared to follow my brother, fearing revenge from Exu. Exactly at midnight, the voodoo chiefs arrived with gifts for the gods, which they placed at the center of the cross.

When Fernando reached at the crossroads, he blew out the *fifó*, hid behind the bushes, and watched the *mãe-de-santo* when she arrived wearing a colorful puffy skirt and a white turban. The voodoo priestess set her offerings on the ground at the crossroads. One by one, she lit candles around the basket and lifted the gifts in the air, calling on the gods and goddesses to accept them. Then she called on Exu to deliver the offerings.

Holding the gifts high above her head, the *mãe-de-santo* explained to the gods in a thunderous voice what each of the gifts represented. There was a chicken's heart in a jar of warm blood that embodied the heart of a mistress who had stolen a husband's love. A headless chicken, tied up and covered in the thick yellow palm oil, represented a curse on the body and soul of a lover for betraying the beloved. A bullfrog held down with long pins, its mouth sewed up with notes inside, was a fetish intended to bring pain on the body and stop the good fortune of a disloyal friend. The eye of a goat floating in a jarful of blood was yet another curse, this upon the vision of someone once beloved for betraying another. A tied-up, tangled-up shirt or dress represented the knot of destiny belonging to a betrayer, a stagnation of their progress and prosperity. And there was always money, a gift for Exu, along with a bottle of *cachaça* for Exu to enjoy.

At the completion of the ceremony, the *mãe-de-santo* disappeared into the quiet of night. Fernando quickly jumped from the bushes, gathered the gifts in our vine basket, set it on his head and hurried home in the dark.

My siblings and I got up at once when we heard the commotion caused by my brother's arrival. We gathered around the basket of gifts Fernando had placed on our dirt floor. But before any of us could touch anything, Fernando ordered everyone to move back from the basket.

"Wait, step back, and let me first exorcise the demons," he said.

He opened his zipper and urinated over the offerings, zigzagging and dancing back and forth. Then, he pulled his pants down and rubbed the chickens and roosters on his bare ass. Fernando was cooling down Exu's ire and dispelling any possible curse he might have carried home from the crossroads.

The curse undone and the gifts set out on our black table, we took the *fifó* and rushed to the pond on the side of the house to clean the offerings. We were quiet, taking every precaution not to be heard or seen. Stealing Exu's gifts from the crossroads was a very brave action. No one we knew would dare do so. Everyone was mortally fearful of Exu. If we suspected any sound or movement, we quickly blew out the lamp so that no one in the neighborhood knew what we were doing. If our neighbors found out, they would call us voodoo thieves, just as they called us chicken thieves. Being called chicken thieves was bad, but stealing the voodoo gifts made you evil, in league with the devil.

We cleaned some of the gifts by rubbing them on the grass to remove the greasy yellow palm oil and the bloodstains. We released the pricked frog into the pond only to find it floating belly up in the morning. We brought the clean gifts back to our table.

The following morning, we cooked the beheaded chicken, cursing the wasted blood that Gaia could have added to the pot. Fernando took the cash to the market on Saturday along with our vine basket. We used the candles at night when we did not have money to buy kerosene for the *fifó*. We cooked the goat's heart, floating in blood, and added it to our beans and rice.

But the best gift of all for Fernando was the *cachaça*, which he mixed with lemon juice and sugar or honey to make the drink we called *caipirinha*. He then relaxed on the warm rocks in the back of our house drinking in honor of Exu, who had become his favorite African god and ours too. It was my brother's way of thanking the god, I suppose, for Exu never showed any signs of revenge toward anyone in our family.

For many years, Fernando ventured out to the crossroads at midnight with our *fifó* and basket and brought home all the voodoo offerings he could find. Sometimes he revisited the sites very early in the morning to make sure nothing was left behind. He once found five chickens and a red rooster. We ate the chickens, and he sold the rooster to the father of Ua's sweetheart. That made my sister very afraid and angry at Fernando because her future father-in-law found traces of the yellow and thick *dendê* oil on the rooster and suspected the bird came from the crossroads. But we were forever thankful to Fernando for his courage and to Exu for his mercy.

8. Mother's Nourishing Stories

When all of our ways of finding food had failed us and night found us hungry, we sat on the ground still warm from the day's accumulated heat, snuggling close to each other to listen to Mother's stories. She liked to sit on a black rock at the side of our house near the pond and the jasmine bush to tell us about events in her life, her parents, and growing up in the *sertão* in Mairí.

Mother's most intriguing stories were those she had heard from many different people including her parents, Silvina and Belarmino. She recounted stories about the gangsters in the Backland where she grew up and the prowess of Lampião, the most famous rebel in all of Brazil, and his wife, Maria Bonita, the first lady of banditry. In their day they had been the talk of the town. His real name was Virgulino Ferreira da Silva, Mother told us, and he was wild with a rifle, shooting so many accurate blasts that he earned the nickname of Lampião—Big Light. His career as an outlaw started at age seventeen. It was the police who actually caused the young Lampião to rebel and avenge the murder of his father and the harassment of his relatives. When he was a young man, he only wanted to restore the honor of his displaced family and retaliate for the land and the home that he had lost to the local authorities. His siblings had been forced to leave the family farm and flee from the police that had killed some of their relatives.

Lampião, Maria Bonita, and a group of their followers traveled on foot across many states in the North. They dressed in leather cowboy pants and sandals, wore colorful bandannas on their necks topped off with wide-brim, well-decorated hats, and carried their rifles on their backs. The rebels stopped at prosperous towns and farms along the way to brand their initials on the faces and bodies of the young women they caught wearing short skirts or having short hair. It was a way to punish the women for male desires and for violating the masculine realm. The bandits killed the rich and slaughtered their herds, stole their money, jewelry, horses, and donkeys, then set their houses on fire. The rebels often took hostages and demanded high ransoms for their lives.

The outlaws formed a tightknit group. They would not tolerate the slightest treason from anyone. Lampião was particularly merciless with traitors. He once was said to have captured a defector, held the man in front of his frightened wife and crying children, gouged his eyes out with a sharp knife, pointed his rifle in the defector's eye socket, and shot him dead.

The police were afraid of confronting the rebels. They were constantly on the run and could not be found easily, for they fled from town to town, and no one ever knew where they would end up given their quick-witted stunts. They walked backward to elude the police and wore sheepskin on the bottom of their shoes to disguise their tracks. They also traveled by night to reduce the chance of being caught. Not even the Brazilian army, navy, or air force could catch Lampião, people believed. The rebels often enjoyed having money and the protection of some of the rich farmers in the region, who wanted to save their own skin, property, families, and belongings by befriending the group. Lampião was the king of the rebels and reigned in Mother's *sertão* for a long time.

The rebel was also a very religious man. He prayed in the morning, at noon, and at sundown. Mother was convinced that was the reason the police had trouble catching him. He went to church and had the blessings of a popular and well-respected priest at the time, Padre Cícero, of Juazeiro do Norte, at the very heart of the *sertão*. The priest was a sympathizer of Lampião because he stole from the rich and gave to the poor. Padre Cícero became famous throughout for blessing the rebel and for bestowing upon him protection from God in heaven.

The *cangaceiros*, or outlaws, as the group was commonly known, sometimes held ferocious battles with the farmers and people in small towns that lasted for hours or sometimes the whole day. Many who resisted were killed and left unclaimed on the streets until the rebels had left town. Sometimes, Lampião and his group of forty men would fight as many as two hundred police officers and come out victorious. They fought hard and never lost a battle.

In mockery of the police, and much to the rich townsfolk's chagrin, Lampião had the audacity to organize parties in the villages and farms that he entered. He paid for drinks and food for everyone and danced with the pretty girls all night. On one occasion, he went into a town in the North with his accordion in hand, singing *Mulher Rendeira,* or Lace Woman, a famous song in the *sertão*. The song was a village favorite, and one of Mother's favorites as well. My mother would get up from the black rock, let her body loose with hands in the air, and start singing Lampião's favorite song. We circled around her, attentive to every move that she made, her voice penetrating the air and echoing in the dark night:

Olé, Mulher Rendeira,	*Olé, Lace Woman,*
Olé, Mulher Renda,	*Olé, Woman Lacy,*
Tu me ensinas fazer renda.	*You teach me to lace.*
Eu te ensino a namorar.	*I'll teach you to flirt.*
Lampião desceu a serra,	*Lampião went down the hill,*
Deu um baile em Cajazeiras,	*Had a ball in Cajazeiras,*
Pra cantar mulher bonita	*To flirt with pretty women*
Pra cantar Mulher Rendeira.	*To sing Lace Woman.*

Mother sang Lampião's beloved song with strength and passion. We laughed hard and sang along, pretending to be the outlaws in the middle of the night, with guns and accordions. Our voices and laughter on those nights will reverberate in my memory forever.

To my amazement, one Sunday afternoon, I heard this song on the Rochester, New York, public radio station. I stopped what I was doing in the kitchen, ran closer to the radio in the living room, closed my eyes, and was transported to the rock where Mother told us her stories. I could almost see my mother's figure and hear her voice floating in the warm air on the side of our house on Paramirim Street. And oh, how I felt like dancing! In my memory, the sound of Mother's voice and her theatrical moves completely replaced the growling of my empty stomach on those nights. Her passive presence in the household and in my life carries an imprint that has never left me. That afternoon, the radio announced that an American named Tex Ritter had recorded Lampião's song for Capital Records in 1954. Ritter named his version *The Bandit*.

That was one of the few times I remember Mother singing so passionately, maybe because she identified herself with the Lace Woman embodied in Lampião's favorite song. At our house, in the cool hours of the afternoon, Mother would take her lace-making tools, a kind of rough brown duffle bag the size of a large pillow filled with straw, and set it on a small bench in front of her. She would fasten a cardboard pattern with pins into the pillow. When she had enough money to buy thread, Mother would sit in a corner on the side of our house by our jasmine bush and weave lace the way her Aunt Zibina had taught her.

Each cardboard outline pinned to the pillow was a different design. Mother would patiently follow the sketches marked by the pins with wooden sticks called *bilros* attached to white thread. From a distance, I would hear the sounds, like those of a wind instrument, that the *bilros* made touching each other as Mother's dexterous hands passed them around from hand to hand, as if playing a quiet game. I always felt happy that Mother had a chance to spend time doing what she loved. This was how the women in northeastern Brazil wove the lace that made them famous and celebrated in poems, tales, and songs. Even Lampião complimented them for their skills. The art of the making lace had its roots in the sea. The tradition began among the fishermen's wives and daughters, who were eager to find a way to be occupied and still provide for their families while the men were away. Ua would sew Mother's beautiful white laces to the dresses that she made for Miriam and me when she had enough remnants from her sewing. It was much later in life that I realized the connection between Mother's passion for making lace and her enthusiasm for the rebel's favorite song.

When our singing ended, Mother sat on the rock again and continued the Lampião story. Besides singing and dancing, the *cangaceiros* sometimes amused themselves by making their victims take off their clothes and parade naked through town, regardless of the weather or time of day. On one occasion, the rebels chose to leave the town's judge and chief of police naked in their offices instead of killing them. Some members of the group then dressed up in the officials' clothes.

But the outlaw was not all bad. He cared deeply for the sick and the old. He helped people in the North during severe droughts. For that reason, Lampião won the admiration and support of many peasants, who often hid and fed the group and lied to the police when they were asked about him. Some villagers were so fond of the rebels that they left everything behind, farms, wives, and children, and took up arms to follow them in the fight for justice.

On the Saturdays I followed Ua to the market, I joined the crowd that surrounded a vendor and stared at the covers of the many booklets for sale, hanging down from a long clothesline. Many were stories, dramas, and poetry about Lampião's prowess in the *sertão*.

The vendors dressed in leather jackets. Much like the outlaw himself, they wore sandals and hats. They entertained the crowd by reading aloud and reciting the funny lines written about the rebel.

As soon as I saw the crowd, I quickly left Ua, made my way through the gathering and turned to the performer who told the stories. In *The Arrival of Lampião in Hell*, the rebel confronts the devil, sets a market on fire, and starts a brawl, leaving most everyone behind dead. In another story, *Lampião Marries the Daughter of Satan*, the devil rewards him for his outstanding bravery.

After each tale, the crowd laughed uproariously. The performer would take a short break to open his wooden box and remove more colorful booklets to replace those he had sold. As people left, laughing with their booklets in hand, new spectators gathered around to hear stories about the incredible stunts of Lampião. I remember a popular song about his wife Maria Bonita blaring on the radio for years:

Levanta Maria Bonita.	*Wake up Maria Bonita.*
Levanta vai fazer café.	*Get up and make coffee.*
O dia já vem raiando.	*Day is breaking.*
E a polícia já tá de pé.	*And the police are awakening.*

It was much later in life that I learned the true story about Lampião from books. The outlaw was born in 1898 in the state of Pernanbuco, north of where my family lived. He was, indeed, the most famous Brazilian rebel in history. His adventures in the Backland, stealing from the rich to feed the poor—a Robin Hood of Brazil—lasted for over three decades. His fame grew throughout the country and reached far beyond our warm rock on Paramirim Street and the clothesline at the market on Saturdays. As far south as Rio de Janeiro and São Paulo, people talked about the famous rebel from the North who constantly eluded and challenged the police, seeking revenge for his family and justice for all. Newspapers all over the country carried stories about the group—some were true, others fabricated. Books, pamphlets, songs, and folk poetry fed the curiosity of generations of people.

In 1938, the police ambushed Lampião, Maria Bonita, and their followers in an early morning raid, having been tipped off by a former member of the group. Eleven of the rebels were killed and decapitated. Their heads were taken to Salvador, where they remained on display in a big jar of formaldehyde for thirty years, apparently so that any skeptics could confirm the fate of their foes or heroes.

Besides Lampião, there were other rebels in Mother's narrative repertoire. In another story she told us, outlaws with long hair and beards appeared at my grandfather Belarmino's barbershop early one morning. They caught both my grandparents by surprise. As soon as my grandparents saw the men step into their living room, which was also their shop, Silvina hurried into the house to protect my mother, then ten years old, and to hide her cash in the straw mattress. And when he saw the long beards, Belarmino rushed to the backyard to sharpen his *navalha,* a folding knife, against a rock. Silvina returned to greet the rebels after hiding Mother in a big dirty clothesbasket. Belarmino walked in with his folding knife in his trembling hands, armed for the difficult task of cutting the rebels' hair.

My grandfather, shaking and scared, faced the men. He pleaded for his life in the event he accidentally cut one of them, for their beards were extra-long and his *navalha* extra-old.

"Mister, I tried to sharpen my *navalha* as much as I could. It's old, and your beards are long, so have patience with this servant of yours and please don't kill me or my wife if my hands slip and cut your face," said Belarmino in a quivering voice.

The insurgents, after long and heartfelt laughter, explained to Belarmino and Silvina that they were not murderers.

"We're not here to kill anybody. We travel through the heart of this land to help the people. These very people don't understand us. We mean no harm. You have nothing to fear," one explained.

Mother remained quiet as a mouse in the basket in her parents' bedroom, covered by soiled clothes. Silvina rushed to put more wood on the fire to heat the water and add it to the scrapings of the bar of soap Belarmino used to shave the men's snarled beards. She also sharpened his scissors against the rock.

My grandfather accommodated the travelers in his living-room shop, inviting one at a time to sit in his barber's chair and carefully soaping their beards with the warm water and foaming soap that Silvina had brought in. He gently slid his *navalha* over their faces, attentive to every move. When he needed to touch the rebels' heads to position them for shaving, Belarmino did it most gently, as if touching fragile porcelain dolls. Mother stood up to continue her story, her hands in the air pretended to guide a rebel's head. Eventually, the rebels felt comfortable getting into Belarmino's chair, putting my grandparents more at ease as the insurgents explained their cause.

"We're no Lampião," one said. "We neither steal nor kill. We work entirely for the good of the people and for justice for the peasants, but people take us for *cangaceiros* everywhere we go," said the one who appeared to be the leader of the group.

They explained that the real head of the group was Luis Carlos Prestes, who had remained with a group somewhere in the North. They had traveled a long way to help the people. My grandparents then sighed in relief, but my mother stayed in her hiding place for safety because her parents were not taking any chances with their daughter.

The room was quiet for a long while. Belarmino worked diligently, made no significant cuts on the insurgents' faces, and they left him with a generous payment as a reward. My grandparents quickly rescued Mother from the clothes basket and took the money to town, where Belarmino bought himself a new *navalha* in case other rebels made an unexpected visit to his shop. He also bought a porcelain doll for my mother, who until then had played only with the cloth dolls Silvina had made for her. My grandparents wanted to reward Mother for the hours she had spent short of breath and silent in the dirty laundry basket.

When Mother arrived home with her new porcelain doll, all the girls in the neighborhood wanted to touch and play with it. And people came from far away to meet and talk to Belarmino, the barber who had met the rebels, touched their faces and heads, shaved their beards and cut their hair. His shop became famous for having served the *Revoltosos,* the Rebels, as the group became known.

And again, it wasn't until much later that I read about the *Revoltosos* in the history books. They were national heroes and survivors of the 1924 military revolt in São Paulo and Rio Grande do Sul led by a young middle-class military officer, Luis Carlos Prestes, born in 1898, the same year as Lampião. Prestes wanted to reform the power structure of Brazil.

Known as the Cavalier of Hope and influenced by his reading and contacts with Argentine and Uruguayan communist leaders, Prestes (who foreshadowed Che Guevara, an Argentine Marxist revolutionary born 28 years after Prestes) formed the League of Revolutionary Action and urged the people, especially the peasants, to rise up against the oligarchies that controlled Brazil's Old Republic from 1889 to 1930. He put together a group of people under his command, the Prestes' Column, and led them on the legendary Long March, a 25,000-kilometer, three-year march through the Brazilian countryside.

Prestes' march never had more than 1,500 followers at one time. Peasants joined in and dropped out along the way. The group eluded the police and local authorities because its members never remained too long in any one place. The movement never gained the understanding and full support of the people whom they had hoped would benefit the most: the peasants. Like my grandparents, the people did not understand the group's ideology. The group disbanded in 1927, with its members fleeing to Bolivia and Paraguay.

This revolt contributed to the beginning of social reform in Brazil. Later, the Revolution of 1930 brought down the Old Republic and installed Getúlio Vargas as a provisional president of Brazil. Vargas, an ex-military man, like Prestes, but far from a revolutionary, became extremely conservative and oppressive of organized labor when in office.

In exile in Buenos Aires, Prestes turned to Marxism and in 1935 formed the Brazilian Aliança National Libertadora, ANL, a left-wing party of socialists, communists, and progressives. He led the ANL against Vargas, who suppressed the group using violence and terror and forced the Brazilian Congress to be tough on the communist movement in Brazil.

All the members of the opposition were seen as subversive and their party was banned. The group began an armed insurrection in November 1935, and the authoritarian regime responded by crushing the communist movement, raiding offices and jailing leaders. Prestes was imprisoned and tortured. The fascist government under Vargas embraced anti-Semitism in Brazil and, to take revenge on Prestes, deported his pregnant Jewish wife, Olga

Benário, to Nazi Germany. There, she gave birth to a girl, Anita Leocádia, who was freed and reunited with her grandmother, Leocádia Prestes. Olga was sent to a concentration camp, where she was gassed in 1942. Prestes was later released from prison but never renounced Marxism. He died in 1990 at the age of ninety-two.

Some say the rebel Lampião once traveled the same path as Prestes' fighters and that they exchanged a few shots, each thinking that the other was a member of the police. Lampião learned that Prestes' group was a different kind of rebel force, but he didn't quite understand their cause. My grandparents and Mother never knew the factual backgrounds of Lampião and Prestes, the two most famous and mythical figures of their time. They had no access to any information other than by word of mouth. The stories were told, retold, and sometimes embellished. In the entirety of Brazil at that time, only five percent of the adult population was literate enough to vote.

Mother also took us back to *The Day that Everything Went Dark*, another of the stories she told. It happened one morning that light suddenly turned to dark. The day had started out chilly and cloudy like any other winter day in May. At that time, the family lived on Flowers Street. My older siblings had walked to school and Father had left for the day. The animals wandered in the backyard and the townspeople busied themselves with their daily routine.

Around mid-morning, it started getting dark for no apparent reason. Teachers sent children home from school. The animals in the backyard became agitated and sought shelter. The stores in town slammed their doors shut, and the townspeople ran home. The wind blew harder, shaking the leaves off the trees and onto the ground. The day became very dark and very cold.

The sun disappeared completely. In its place was a shroud of darkness. A wave of shadows descended and covered the ground. Father ran home and stayed inside with Mother and the children. Everyone sought shelter and waited inside their homes.

"Oh! meu Deus. O mundo vai se acabar—Oh, my God! The world has come to an end," Mother remembered saying.

After a short while, darkness gave way, little by little, and light cracked through the doors, windows, and the glass tiles on the roofs of the houses. The sun began to shower its golden rays again and everyone rushed out to find out what had happened. But no visible signs could explain the mystery of what had happened, and life returned to normal.

I later learned that there had been a total solar eclipse on May 20, 1947, in the region where my family lived. It lasted five minutes and eight seconds, but for a long time I only knew of this event as the enigmatic morning that light turned to dark for what seemed forever. I did find an explanation for the event later in life, but, again, Mother never understood the real reason for what had taken place.

Yet another of Mother's stories was about an old man, a stranger in town, who had appeared in the hut near the house where she lived in the *sertão*. Travelers used this shelter to tie up their horses and rest while passing through town. This traveler was too sick to continue his journey, so he lay down quietly next to his horse. Mother noticed the lonely man one afternoon and went to greet him. As she approached, the traveler yelled not to get near him.

"I'm sick with leprosy. I don't want to infect you or anyone," he yelled to Mother. "Stay away from me."

But she disregarded the man's warning and approached him anyway. "I'm not afraid, and I want to help you," Mother answered. She found out that the traveler had not eaten for many days. He was dirty and smelly. Mother hurried home to gather what she could find and gave the man some water and food. She was not afraid of contracting the disease. At the time, it was common for people to believe that leprosy was a very contagious disease; people were extremely afraid of it, avoiding victims at any cost. Mother continued caring for the sick man for a few days.

Then one night, when Mother was in the backyard gathering wood for the stove, she saw the figure of an old man in rags walking with difficulty and with open arms moving toward her and trying to embrace her. But the figure disappeared into thin air as it got closer. Mother screamed, dropped the wood, and ran into the house.

The next morning when she went to the hut to bring the old man some coffee, she found him dead. She gathered clothes to dress the man and gathered money from neighbors to bury him. Mother told us that she was sure that the spirit of the sick man had come to embrace her as he left this world. After hearing Mother's story, we avoided going into the backyard at any cost on dark nights. If we had to relieve ourselves, we would go together, holding hands. Our fear lasted only for a few days but would return after Mother retold the story.

Mother also heard voices on another dark night when she was up late sewing. Everybody was asleep and all was quiet except for the clack-clack-clack of her Singer sewing machine. This was a night when the sewing needed to be finished so the garments could be displayed on our windowsill early in the morning so that we could buy food for our noon meal. If they were not sold from the windowsill, then Gaia and Fernando would carry them to the tobacco factory at five in the afternoon to sell to the women.

Night advanced. Mother continued to pedal the squeaking sewing machine under the flicker light of our *fifó*. When she heard the whistling of voices from every corner of the room, soft murmurs at first, Mother tried to ignore them. But the noises became progressively louder, as if a gush of powerful wind suddenly rushed through the holes in our windows and doors. Mother found it impossible to ignore the voices. She stopped the treadle of the Singer and sat still in her chair. The room became dead quiet. Mother put her foot on the pedal again and the whistling started again. Mother's hair stood up all over her body. Her heart pounded, and she shivered in horror. She got up, hurriedly blew out the lamp, and snuggled quietly in a corner of the bed until daybreak. Mother was certain that the spirits of her ancestors were begging her to rest.

9. The Devil's Twig

At the start of the school year in March, Ua and I walked along the dirt path at the back of our house through bushes, twigs, and mud puddles, and past singing birds and frogs to register me for school. School began at 7 a.m. and let out at noon, so that other groups of students could start the afternoon session from 1 to 5 p.m. Children usually started school at seven years of age, but I was almost eight. The search for food and basic needs was our primary objective, and school had to wait or be skipped altogether since we were destitute. We had no government law to be followed since students were not legally required to attend school. I took the path to school the following day and for the next four years. A couple of years later, when Ua married her childhood sweetheart and gave birth to her first daughter, Maisa, I returned to the same path alone this time. I carried the baby girl's dried-up umbilical cord wrapped up in my hands to bury it behind the school. My mother and sisters had told me that children who had their umbilical cord buried on school grounds would grow up liking school, and I wanted my first niece to like school the way I did.

I knew very well the trail that my sister and I walked that first day. I had taken it alone many times to visit Seu Galdino, the owner of a small store attached to his house, to ask for a banana and for one of the sugar suckers his wife Dona Helena had made. I visited Seu Galdino's house in the afternoon, when the panties and brassieres that decorated our window were left untouched from dawn to dusk, blowing in the wind and accumulating dust. I walked when my brothers came home with empty hands and pockets after taking my mother and sisters' brassieres to sell to the women at the tobacco factories, or after wandering for hours in town. I knew that there would be no food in the house for a few days.

At school, the teacher told my sister Ua that I needed to bring my first reading book. The next morning, I stayed by our front window, guarding the fresh sliced couscous that Mother had made to sell and waited for my sister to walk to town and buy my book. It was the story of a plump and energetic red hen that, on her early rounds looking for food, finds three grains of corn, hurries back to a herd of animals in the pasture and announces:

Encontrei três grãos de milho.   *I found three grains of corn.*
Quem quer plantar esse milho?   *Who wants to sow these grains?*
Eu não, disse o galo.   *Not I, said the rooster.*
Nem eu, disse o pato.   *Not I, said the duck.*
Nem eu, disse o porquinho.   *Not I, said the little pig.*

Then the vigorous red hen takes her hoe, goes into the yard, digs three holes, and carefully sows the three grains of corn. She waters and cares for them every day. After the grains have grown into healthy plants and it is time to harvest the stock, the red hen calls upon the animals again, asking who wants to harvest the corn. One by one, the animals decline the chore, and the red hen labors alone again.

But when the time comes to eat the corn, the red hen, with her beak proudly up in the air, asks the others:

Quem quer comer o milho?   *Who wants to eat the corn?*
Eu, disse o galo.   *I do, said the rooster.*
Eu também, disse o pato.   *I do, too, said the duck.*
E eu, disse o porquinho.   *And so do I, said the little pig.*

The red hen loudly replies, "No one wanted to either sow or harvest the grains of corn. Now, no one will eat them, either." That said, the red hen finds herself a shaded area under a leafy mango tree and eats the sweet corn, a product of her sweat and hard labor. When finished, she gives the animals a final look and loudly chuckles, "Those who do not work do not eat."

I read the story of the chicken, reread it, and recited it to my mother and younger brothers over and over again, pretending to be the red hen. Soon, the teacher said that I needed a second book, and Mother made more couscous to set on our windowsill. Again, I sat by it until the yellow slices were gone, and Ua had the money to walk downtown with me to buy my book.

My second reading book told the story of the ugly duckling ignored by siblings and friends because he looked different. I carried the book under my arm and soon learned the story by heart so that I could tell my younger siblings. For other books I needed for school, Mother attempted to sell her warm couscous one more time, but it could not be sold fast enough to meet both the growing demand for food in our house and the need for books and school supplies for me and Miriam. It felt good learning at school, and I wanted to continue learning, so I started borrowing books from my classmates; I wished that I could keep the books, but I had to return them the following morning, which was the condition my classmates had imposed. I continued borrowing books when Ua could not buy them, all throughout primary school, and always felt very sad when the books left my hands.

I walked the dirt path at the back of our house to the one-room schoolhouse until fourth grade. I walked on rainy and sunny days, with shoes that had big holes in the soles. My siblings tried to repair the holes by nailing pieces of rubber from old tires that we found in the neighborhood. But after a while, the nails would come loose—like the wires on our beds that stuck through the straw mattresses and poked our faces—and poke my feet and make them bleed and hurt. I walked barefoot sometimes, stepping in mud or on the hot ground. I tried to step on the green and cool areas or on the dried twigs on the side of the road when the ground was baking hot.

And I walked with food in my stomach or without any food at all. I wore clean clothes when we had money to buy soap and Gaia took them to wash, or worn-out clothes when the remnants from Ua's sewing were short. I walked without underwear when I could not find even dirty underwear to wear again. And I walked with no pens, pencils, or paper, skipping over mud piles and rocks, with my free arms and hands bouncing up in the air and the sun on my face. I did not say much, and I waited until the neighborhood children were ahead of me so that I could be alone and go at my own pace. Their noise bothered me. I liked being alone and quiet.

Each day at school, my teacher would open a long and thick leaflet with different scenery, look at it closely, and tell us to do the same. "Now you have to describe what you see," she would say. "You can create your own story based on this scene, but do not include anything that is not in the picture."

The drawings were of a father coming home from work to a happy wife and children, a blue river flowing into a green forest, or a deep blue sky full of sparkling stars and children playing beneath them. The scene I remember the most was of a girl, about my age, wearing a white bonnet and taking corn from her clean apron to feed a flock of well-behaved chickens in front of a blue house.

I would look at the views for a while before I described them on my piece of paper. Sometimes the teacher would ask me to read my descriptions to the rest of the class. She would then comment that my writing was not a representation of the scenes. I explained that my backyard was very muddy and smelly when it rained, and dusty on sunny days, that the pigs and chickens that I was used to were dirty and loud, and that Gaia killed them for food. So, it was hard for me to imagine a picture so perfect. The teacher said I had to practice seeing beyond my backyard.

One morning at school, my classmate André, a quiet and cute boy around my age of eight or nine years old, who sat next to me at an old desk, slid his body closer to mine and little by little walked his hands toward my legs and started rubbing them. André's sudden action surprised and scared me, but I did not remove his hand, afraid of calling it to the teacher's attention. The teacher did not seem to notice anything, and André kept his hand on my leg for a while after which his fingers, little by little, ended up inside my underwear. I exchanged neither looks nor words with André. I stayed as stiff as a board.

I do not quite remember how long André's sexual assault went on that day, and on several days after the first assault, but I recall that I stayed away from him during our *merenda*—midday break. I felt deeply ashamed and naked in André's presence. One time, the teacher called me up to her desk.

"Leda, what's going on with you?" she asked. "You continue describing scenes that aren't in the picture. Your writing is getting worse."

André was on my mind. I could not concentrate on the scenes in front. I could not concentrate in school. I walked home quietly, always keeping distance from my talkative classmates who took the same dirt path home. I never wanted to see André again, but he was always looking at me from the corner of his eyes. I did not know how to tell the teacher or Ua about him. After a while, I finally asked the teacher to let me sit with Nubia, a classmate whom I liked.

Another neighborhood boy came out of the bushes one afternoon while I walked home from school. He blocked my way by standing in front of me with his arms extended and moving left and right, corralling me. Then he grabbed me by the waist when I tried to run and forced me to the ground. We rolled on the ground for a while; he tried to undress me. I tried to escape. But the boy, who was taller, heavier, and older than I was, pinned my arms tightly to the ground. I smelled the smoke from his ragged clothes and hair and his nauseating breath. After rolling back and forth for a while, he lifted my skirt and rubbed his penis on my thighs. I eventually got away, ran home and snuggled quietly in my favorite place in the backyard without telling anyone what had happened.

I had seen this boy around our neighborhood before. He had a belly button the size of a golf ball, sticking out from under his shirt, which earned him the name of *Umbigudo*—Big Belly Button. The next time I saw Umbigudo, he was with a group of friends. He laughed loudly, pointed at me and announced, "E*u comi essa menina*— I have eaten that girl," meaning that he had had sex with me. The group's loud laughter brought a wave of heat to my face and a burden of humiliation to my heart.

I ran away as fast I could, but I never told anyone about my experience. Every time I saw Umbigudo and his friends, I hid from them. It took me a long time for the intense feeling of powerlessness and shame that I had experienced to heal. I can still smell the woodburning smoke that emanated from Umbigudo.

On my way home from school at midday, when we had no food for a few days, I stopped to see Seu Galdino and his wife, Dona Helena. I begged for a brown speckled banana from the bunch hanging from the ceiling. I eyed the sweet and colorful suckers that his wife made, wrapped in colorful papers, jammed onto a stick and stacked in a big clear jar.

I would arrive and wait on the sidewalk until the customers had bought their provisions and had left the store, and Dona Helena had gone inside the house. I was too shy to ask Seu Galdino for a banana and a sucker in the presence of others, and I knew that he paid attention to me when he was alone.

When the store was empty, I appeared in front of the tall wood counter and said, "Give me a banana and a sucker, Seu Galdino." He looked at me, smiled, and sang a song he had made up which he repeated every time that I appeared in front of him:

Oh, essa menina quer um pirulito,   *Oh, this girl wants a sucker,*
Enrolado no papel e socado no   *Wrapped in paper and hardened on*
   palito.   *a stick.*

Seu Galdino walked around the counter, singing his jingle over and over and dancing, while I stood still, with my eyes fixed on the colorful suckers. He stepped back, sang once more, pulled a banana from a bunch and a sucker from the jar and gave them to me. I ate the banana right on the spot and walked home licking the sucker very slowly, wishing that it lasted forever. I went back to Seu Galdino's store many times, and only much later in life did I realize the meaning of his jingle. For me, Seu Galdino was the playful man who always alleviated my hunger with a banana and a sucker. Decades later, I still smell and see his bunch of speckled bananas hanging from the ceiling; I see him dancing and hear his jingle in my head. A mixture of sadness and laughter permeates me.

Food in our house had become scarcer. At noon, when school let out, I was hungry. I did not have the usual snack, the *merenda* that some children ate at ten. I often felt dizzy and weak, my neck stiffened, my vision blurred, my stomach growled, and my ears were buzzing to turn the corner and walk to Seu Galdino's store to beg for a banana and a sucker. I walked home, instead, knowing that we had no food, not even the manioc farina, which was a food staple in the area. We mixed the farina with salt and hot pepper from the backyard or the raw brown sugar, called *rapadura,* we sometimes ate when we had some. We alternated the portions of these mixtures with gulps of water or a bite of banana that we had near us to wash them down our throats because they were awfully dry—and either very salty or very sweet—and could easily choke us to death. During these times, we sat together on our dirt floor to eat, a symphony of coughs erupting from our irritated throats.

Often, the sound from hunger that I had in my ears felt as if a bee were stuck in my head and could not find its way out. The buzzing would not go away. No other sound could muffle its persistent, frightful ringing in my ears. It usually started when a whole week had gone by without any food, and I was lethargic and dizzy with hunger. My stomach growled loudly. It squeezed my ribs tightly, leaving a hole in the center. *A barriga pegada no espinhaço* we called it. On those days, I dragged myself home under the hot noon sun, with each step feeling as if I carried a heavy weight on my back. I found a quiet corner in our backyard, under one of the many green bushes we had, called *graveto do cão*—the devil's twig. It had no leaves, just green branches attached to each other in small knots. I thought that it was a very charming bush, but it had a white and sticky residue that itched like the devil if it touched your skin and blinded you in no time if it came in contact with your eyes. I later learned that this bush is called a pencil tree.

I slept under the *graveto do cão* even when the yellow sun shone brightly at midday. I would find a shady corner and lie on the ground. One afternoon, starving, I had a nightmare that a flock of black vultures descended on my body and tore it apart with their sharp beaks, piece by piece. Those vultures were a common sight in our backyard and throughout the area.

I often saw them circling around in the sky, flapping their huge wings, and looking for prey. They would approach the ground when they smelled or saw dead animals below. The vultures would swiftly land and envelop the body of the animals as if a dark cloud had suddenly dropped from the sky. Sometimes the animals were not even yet dead, just wounded from sickness, an attack by humans or another animal, or suffering from a broken leg that prevented them from moving. The vultures could smell death nearing and tore the animals apart, fighting each other for the best spot before starting their feast by picking out the eyes and opening the stomach. Little by little, they would devour the whole animal, leaving only a pile of stripped bones behind.

In my dream, I smelled putrid. A flock of the black birds, assuming that I was dead, slowly encircled my body, picking at my eyes, ears, mouth, and stomach and carrying parts of my intestines in their beaks. That afternoon, I awoke from my dream with an overwhelming sense of relief when I felt that my body was whole. I did not feel so dizzy and hungry, as I always felt after my deep sleep; but I was distressed and petrified by the image of the vultures in my memory, devouring my body under the *graveto do cão*. I ran home and from that afternoon on, I found another corner closer to the house to sleep off the hunger, horrified of the predators. It was difficult to avoid the sight of them. Every time I saw them circling in the sky, I quickly touched my body parts to make sure that they were in place and dismissed the thought of the vultures picking at me. And when we had no food, and I went to school hungry the next morning and came home again in the afternoon with more buzzing in my ears, I slept away from the *graveto do cão,* by the jasmine bush. Although the spot was noisy, I felt safe with my family around the house and lucky to be awakened each morning with the roosters' ku ... ku ... ru ... kus in the backyard, announcing a new dawn. I knew then that the sun would soon rise and spread its glorious rays through the glass tile on the roof of our house to brighten my day. The sunlight brought me comfort and companionship.

10. Attack of the Hookworms

When my father was alive, we had more food to eat. In the evening, when our stomachs were bloated and we had little appetite or energy, he would bring home a bottle of a thick oily medicine called *acaricida*. We took the treatment for hookworms at the crack of dawn the following morning, awakened by our reliable alarm clock: the crowing of the roosters' ku... ku... ru... kus in the backyard. We swallowed the medication in a hurry, half asleep, with our eyes half closed. It tasted awful. We chewed on pieces of oranges Mother cut up for us to dispel the bitter taste that it left in our mouths and the dread it caused our souls. A few hours later, we hurried to the bushes where we released the many hookworms that had filled our bellies and caused our troubles. The noisy pigs and chickens sensed the commotion and knew enough to wait for the feast that they would have with the releasing of the brownish worms that they seemed to enjoy eating.

We accumulated hookworms in our intestines because we had to walk barefoot everywhere, ate spoiled and undercooked meat, and drank untreated water from ponds and the big clay pot Grandmother Silvina had left in the house for Mother. We kept the pot covered with a piece of wood outside the kitchen. Mostly everyone in my family and on Paramirim Street had parasites, even Mother. She had a long white and strange parasite known as *solitária* (Taenia solium). This hermaphrodite worm has a flat body and a head that bears a double crown of hooks that attaches itself to the walls of the small intestines of humans. It is the most vicious of all the tapeworms. It normally grows to be two to three meters long, but it can develop to be as long as ten meters. Its body is formed by a chain of segments that steals nutrients from its host. It is transmitted to humans through uncooked or undercooked pork. In the area where my family lived, pigs grew up wild, and I assume that this horrific parasite must have been widespread.

Unbelievably, Mother never complained about the *solitária* that lived in her intestines although she suffered from constant headaches, severe hypertension, and lack of energy. We children knew she carried the worm in her body because we would often see it crawling on the ground when Mother relieved herself. The worm would come out in small sections, lived for some time, and would stretch out on the ground, becoming very long. I do not even know if Mother ever got rid of this terrible creature in her lifetime. I had no idea how monstrous this worm is. It sickens me to even think of my mother having to feed such a horrendous parasite for what must have been her entire life when food in our house was so scarce and hunger prevailed.

Due to the dreadful poverty around us, my family and many people in the area had to live with hookworms. I saw them everywhere and sometimes stepped on them, walking barefoot. I also read and reread, while laughing out loud, a booklet that I carried around with me. It told a story, very popular at the time, of a hick from the northeast who had hookworms: Jeca Tatu. He was a character created by the famous Brazilian writer of children's books, Monteiro Lobato (1882-1948).

Once poor and miserable, the hillbilly, Jeca Tatu, did not have the gumption or energy to plant even a head of lettuce in his backyard. Suddenly one day, he planted corn and beans on his land. It was so out of character that people were amazed and wanted to know why he had done it. Jeca explained that he no longer wanted anything to do with poverty. He wanted to get rich. Jeca started working so hard that his ambitious Italian neighbor became jealous. "*Per la Madonna*," yelled the Italian when he saw Jeca's transformation. The neighbor was not alone. Jeca stunned everyone. His wife and children wore shoes. They were healthy and happy as birds. And to the shock and admiration of all, even the animals in Jeca's farm wore shoes and rode in his car to the Saturday market.

The backwoodsman now thought only of progress and material things. He decided that All-American English was the language of the rich and began calling his *porco*—a pig, his *galinha*—a hen. Jeca wanted to visit the United States to see how things were there. He smoked cigars made especially for him; he rode only purebred Arabian horses; he even grew silkworms on his farm because he wanted everything made of silk fabric, including the bags for his produce. The hillbilly and his farm soon became famous in the area and throughout Brazil. He had electricity, a telephone, and a radio transmitter to communicate with his employees. Jeca Tatu sent for a television circuit in the United States to monitor all the activities on his farm while sitting on his porch smoking his cigars.

Jeca quickly got rich and fat. But he felt sorry for the impoverished people in the northeast and installed various clinics on his land to sell drugs for hookworms, malaria, and headaches, the diseases that once afflicted him. Thus, Jeca lived to abolish the evil that harmed his people and nation. When DDT came along, Jeca further served his deprived fellow citizens by spraying their homes and everything else with the chemical. Before even greeting the poor with a simple *bom dia*—good morning, Jeca sprayed everything with DDT, Detefon, as it was known. The sound and smog coming from his fast Detefon air pump floated in the air, like the flare of a persistent car horn: fon, fon, fon. It reached everyone's ears, clouded the air, and sparked a desire to spray more De-te-fon, fon, fon, fon.

Jeca's metamorphosis had taken place one rainy day after a local doctor stopped at his meager hut seeking shelter. He noticed Jeca's pitiful appearance and extreme poverty, living with an ugly skinny wife, pale and sad children, and malnourished pigs and chickens. Back then, Jeca did nothing all day but sit around with his equally sad looking dog, Brinquinho. The hick smoked a cigarette filled with straw; he lacked the will and energy to do anything. When his neighbors asked him why, Jeca would simply reply that it was not worth planting anything because the ants would eat it. Besides his despicable lack of motivation, Jeca had the detrimental habit of drinking a lot of *cachaça*, the popular Brazilian rum.

For a long time, life had been really miserable for poor Jeca Tatu until the doctor decided to change his fate that very rainy day. He explained to Jeca that the cause of his misery was hookworms and prescribed some drugs. The doctor also took Jeca to a humid area on the side of his hut where he pointed out nearly invisible and apparently harmless parasites that caused his pessimism and disease. The doctor warned Jeca to always wear shoes to prevent the worms from entering his body through his bare feet.

It was then that Jeca understood and his life changed forever. In just three months after the doctor's visit, no one recognized Jeca. The drugs worked like a miracle. The malnourished and miserable hick became healthy and strong, so strong that he strangled a jaguar with his bare hands one day when he was out alone chopping wood. Another jaguar nearby, seeing what had happened, ran in fear for its life. The story goes that the jaguar is still on the run this very day. Everything and everyone now feared Jeca. In the forest, when he approached the trees with his axe, they trembled. Jeca was proud. He yelled out to the world that he had taken the drugs that made him strong and that no one or anything could now fight him.

Jeca Tatu lived a long life and died at the age of 89 (a very long life for that area of Brazil) with a clear conscience that he had been a fine citizen and had done good deeds. Lobato's story ends by advising the poor boys and girls of the northeast to imitate the noble Jeca. Lobato further explains that a country is not measured by its size or population but by the quality and work of its people. To be healthy, he concludes, one needs *Ankilostomina* and *Biotonico Fontoura*, the drugs that transformed the hillbilly Jeca Tatu.

Excluding my textbooks, Jeca Tatu was the first story that I read to my younger siblings. Everyone who could read reread this story. I don't remember how it was distributed to homes for free. Later in life, I learned that Lobato wrote his Jeca Tatu story in 1924 and a year later adapted it for the Drug Company Fontoura Laboratory based in São Paulo. One hundred million copies of his story were distributed by 1982.

In the area where I lived, very few people were fortunate enough to have enough money to buy a pair of shoes, let alone drugs and chemicals. Most people had worms and suffered from the diseases they inflicted without any education or resources to prevent them. Many simply lived with hookworms all of their lives or died early deaths from them, especially children. In my family, after Father died, Mother sent us to the pharmacy with yet another of her notes to Orlando Lima, asking for the oily and awful medicine that Father used to bring home to treat our parasites. Orlando always sent us back with the same blue bottle of *caricida* that we were used to swallowing when our stomachs were bloated. We survived hookworm thanks to Mother's courage and Orlando's goodness.

In the neighborhood, many children, from the ages of four to six or seven, were not as fortunate as we were. They died from hookworm attacks after accumulating too many parasites in their stunted and malnourished bodies. At one point, the vermin would take over, as if engaged in a battle, and kill the children. Some quietly dropped dead in the bushes in the backyard while relieving themselves. Their mothers later would find the small dead bodies.

Others showed early symptoms. First, they would lose what little appetite they had. Next, they would become very pale and complain of a persistent pain that no herbs in the backyard could remedy. After some time, the children might begin vomiting some worms and faint, never to get up again.

When a child was found dead in his or her waste in the backyard, others who may have witnessed the scene ran in search of the mother, who would come out wailing. Hearing the tumult, the neighborhood women and children gathered around. Ua hurried to console the mother no matter what she was doing. I often followed Ua. She threw mounds of dirt and rocks on the panicky worms to kill them. I hurried to fill a tin container with more dirt to help Ua. The worms tried to rush out of the small dead body like a swarm of insects fleeing in all directions when you disturb their nests. They exited through all the cavities they found, mouth, nose, ears and eyes. It was the most frightful sight. I closed my eyes tight and held on to my stomach. After killing the worms, the women rescued the dead child, *O Anjinho*—The Little Angel—as we now called the corpse. They carried the *Anjinho* to the house, set him on a pile of banana leaves by the kitchen or on an old straw mat on the dirt floor and soon started a fire to warm the water for the washing.

Ua hurried home to shower and change clothes so that she could walk to Flowers Street and meet with her girlfriends who were either the owners or knew the people who owned most of the stores in town. Ua and her friends would walk to the town hall to ask the mayor for a casket, then to the store to ask the owners for donations to bury the Little Angel who had died from a hookworm attack that day. My sister collected enough money to buy a piece of a thin wire, a roll of soft white crepe paper, and a piece of white cotton cloth to make the child's burial attire.

Ua hurried back home to Paramirim Street with the material for the burial. She handed some of the money to the Little Angel's mother to buy some food and told her to walk to the town hall and choose a white casket. My sister then spread the white fabric on our black table. She took her large scissors and went to work, quickly transforming the white cotton fabric into a long gown with long sleeves, like the robe angels wear. With the thin wire, Ua made a small crown and decorated it with the pretty white flowers that she had made with the soft crepe paper. When finished, she hurried back to the Little Angel's home, and, with the women's help, she washed the frail body a second time with lavender water, trying to dispel the foul odor. They dressed the *Anjinho* in the white robe, adjusted the crown of white flowers on the small head and a bouquet in his clapped hands; she set the child in the white casket, covering the body with the fresh carnations and angelicas that the female neighbors and children had brought. Ua and the women performed this ceremony for every *Anjinho* that dropped dead from worm attacks in our neighborhood.

Roque, whom I played with sometimes, died from worm attack at the age of seven or eight. I felt very sad. I sat by Ua as she sewed Roque's funeral attire, helped her decorate his crown, and followed her back to his house. When Ua and the women finished dressing Roque and set him in the casket, I ran home to change into my special white taffeta dress that Ua had made for me from the remnants of a wedding dress that she had sewn for one of her friends on Flowers Street. I then walked to the side of our house to cut some of Mother's scented white jasmine flowers, before running back to hand the little bouquet that I arranged to Ua. I asked her to set it in Roque's clasped hands. I followed the neighborhood children as the casket paraded quietly through town to the cemetery at sundown. They set Roque in the hole that had been dug for him. We threw in the flowers that we had carried on top of the white casket, and the men covered it with black dirt.

I held on to Ua's hand as we silently walked home. I told Ua that I wished that I never had to leave Roque or any other *Anjinho* in the dark holes. Ua said that Roque and all the children who had died were happy in heaven. I started looking at the bright sky sometimes, looking for any sign of Roque and wondered if God really wanted a skinny and smelly *Anjinho* in His heaven. The angels I had seen in church were white. They smelled like incense all the time, dressed in good clothes, and were very chubby.

As for our diseases, my mother and sisters treated the mumps we had with a mixture of ashes from our woodburning stove and lemon. They soaked a long white strip of cloth with this mix and set it on our lower jaws, tying it on top of our heads. We stayed in the house with that cloth wrapped on our heads, barely able to talk. The women cured asthma and measles by feeding us a broth they made by catching, killing, and cooking a small and harmless lizard we called *lagartixa*, similar to a gecko. When the measles blisters were late in appearing on our bodies, the women put a large straw strainer that we used for our corn under the bed. They believed that this helped to draw out the blisters and cure the disease faster, instead of letting it hibernate in our bodies.

Furunculosis, a highly infectious bacterial disease, afflicted us the most. Various furuncles, hard, round, red boils, appeared under the skin everywhere on our bodies, even around our eyes and private parts, sometimes two or three at once. At first, a small yellowish and itchy head appeared. The skin around it then would get very red and tender. My mother and sisters would put bar soap scrapings and mashed fresh okra or garlic that had been mixed with farina in a small round piece of cloth and set it on the boils. They also fried the yellow fat of the chicken—*inchunda de galinha*—and used it as an ointment to soothe the swelling and the pain. Some of our boils would grow to be the size of a large lemon. They were extremely painful. After itching, burning, and hurting, the boils would mature and burst, usually while we slept. Yellow pus and blood covered our bodies and clothes. My elder siblings would sit us down to squeeze the hard core from inside the boil because we believed that if we removed it completely it would prevent new furuncles from coming up again someplace else on our bodies. But the boils never ceased showing up again and again. They left big pock marks on our skin. I still have some of these scars on my legs and bottom as a legacy of these infamous furuncles.

Mother treated other common illnesses with the many herbs that she grew in our and the neighbors' backyard. She used *alumã*, a bitter plant, for ordinary stomach pain; wormwood and rosemary for colds and headaches; anise and balm mint for diarrhea; and *mastruz*, bitter watercress, for almost everything. She mashed *mastruz*, added warm milk, and gave us the dark green mixture to drink when a persistent cough would not go away. People also used *mastruz* to treat tuberculosis, which was prevalent in the area. They even mashed *mastruz* in a hurry to treat a broken chicken leg, which was often the result of the rocks and sticks thrown at them to shoo the noisy animals when they entered kitchens other than ours. They placed the mashed herb on a piece of cloth and wrapped it tightly around the broken chicken leg. It healed.

When Mother's creative remedies and the backyard herbs did

nothing to restore our lack of energy—and we looked much like Jeca Tatu—Ua would look for Dona Dulce or Dona Marcelina, the *rezadeiras*. They were older women who would come to our house before sundown, dressed in long skirts with turbans covering their heads and carrying a bundle of local herbs—*arruda, peão roxo, losna, vassourinha-de-relógio* or rue, American purging nut, wormwood, sida hemp—and others that they gathered to pray over our bodies. It was a popular belief that the forests exerted power over the bad spirits that afflicted our bodies. We would sit on a rock in the backyard and the female *rezadeira* would pray, running the small branches of the green leaves over us from head to toe and sweeping away the disease while saying a prayer:

Com dois te botaram.	*With two they gave it to you.*
Com tres eu te tiro.	*With three I take it away*
Com os poderes de Deus e da	*With the power of God and the*
Virgem Maria,	*Virgin Mary,*
Olhar morfina e quebrante	*Evil and lethargic spell*
Vai pras ondas do Mar Sagrado	*Go to the waves of the Sacred Sea*
Onde não canta nem galo nem	*Where neither the rooster nor the hen*
galinha	*sings*
E onde não chora menino pagão.	*And where pagan children don't cry.*

The *rezadeira* would recite this litany, beating our bodies with the branches until the green leaves withered and died. We believed that such women swept away the curses that occupied our bodies. Like magic, in most cases, we would feel better and the women were happy to leave the house with a small fee or a plate of food, if we had any to give them. And if we had nothing, they would wear a big smile on their faces and would return to our house to treat the diseases that Mother's herbs failed to.

A cure did not come as easy for my brother Eduardo. Born soon after I was, he came into the world with a severely low birth weight and nearly dead. Edward's brutal case of malnourishment and dehydration prompted the family to buy a small white casket and have it ready, day and night, by his side. Ua sewed Eduardo a white gown, like the many she had sewn for the neighborhood's Little Angels and rushed him to the priest to be baptized. The priest sent the boy home with a recipe that saved his life: beat the white of an egg with a fork until fluffy and foamy, let it sit, and then feed the baby the runny white liquid every few minutes. Eduardo lived, but only to confront other challenges: one nearly ended his young life, and another finished him much later.

The first episode started around the age of two when Eduardo was taken to the back of the house for his bathroom training. My brother was very active and liked running after the wild pigs and chickens that crossed through our backyard. It was Ua who first saw the toddler's bowels drop almost completely out as he squatted in position. Ua yelled, and Mother helped her bring Eduardo into the house.

"Lay him on the side, on his stomach," said Ua.

"No. Let's set him down on the table," said Mother. "It'll be easier for us to work on him."

They then warmed almond oil, dipped their hands into it, and slid the wobbly red entrails into place. Mother thought at first that Eduardo's episode was nothing to worry about, that something must have gone wrong with his bowel movement. Maybe exerting too much force or eating something rough had caused the problem.

But the women in the house soon learned that something was terribly wrong with little Eduardo. His attack became more frequent and severe. He cried terribly each time he needed to relieve himself, and my mother and sisters feared the day their patience, courage, and care would fail to guide the child's bowels back into place. Eduardo's ordeal soon became the entire family's trial.

Mother and my sisters could not carry Eduardo into the house in a hurry all the time. They had to secure a carefully chosen place in our backyard for the toddler to relieve himself. Huge, wild and noisy pigs ran freely everywhere so my older brothers were put in charge of chasing the animals away. The pigs had an insatiable appetite for human waste. Each brother kept a long stick at the side of the house ready to use against the pigs' ferocious strength when they were attracted to Eduardo's disobedient bowels. Mother decided to lay Eduardo on a carefully arranged bed of banana leaves, then guide the red pile of entrails back into his body.

"Be very careful with it," Ua would suggest.

"I can't get the whole thing to go in all at once," Gaia would reply.

"Put more almond oil on your hands," Mother would recommend.

"But they'll get too slippery," my sisters would argue.

"Use a piece of the banana leaf to help guide it," Ua suggested.

For a while, both the child and the adults got temporary relief from the battle of guts and pigs fought on a bed of banana leaves in our backyard. Eventually, Eduardo's body signaled a new fight. And so, the war in our backyard lasted for a long time. My little brother became pure skin and bones. Mother and my sisters were petrified of feeding the toddler any rough solids. In their minds, the food he ate correlated with the battle they fought daily. They went back to the recipe of egg whites that had saved Eduardo's life as an infant and to a new concoction of herbs a neighbor prescribed. Ua remembers that Eduardo, little by little, grew a bit stronger, and that the war in his bowels became less violent as time went on. Eduardo was finally victorious.

This was the most agonizing and frightful of all encounters with the diseases that my family fought. I felt sorry for Eduardo and proud of Mother and my sisters for their wisdom and resilience. They were largely responsible for our survival.

11. Songs and Games

Our town celebrated Saint John's feast every year in June. All of the residents built large bonfires in front of their houses. A week or so before the feast day, Tatai and Gaia left early in the morning for the hills to chop the wood to build our bonfire. We spent the day arranging the pieces of wood they carried home on their heads in a square formation, leaving enough room in the center. There we planted a branch of a tree or bush and decorated it with colorful paper streamers.

We lit our tall bonfire on the night of June 24th and gathered around it, singing songs and dancing to the crackling of the wood and the sparkling flames. Our neighborhood shared the traditional boiled peanuts, liquor, and corn, which was roasted on the red charcoal or cooked wrapped in its husk. The *canjica* was made with grated green corn, sugar, coconut milk and cinnamon, cooked to a firm consistency, dished onto a plate, and placed on everyone's table. The accordion players made music until dawn; square dancing went on during the fireworks, and rising colorful paper balloons filled the skies, carrying well-wishes to distant towns.

Tatai spent hours making the colorful and enchanting paper balloons that Father had taught him to make. Tatai took pride in his balloons. We lit the torches secured by wires and waited for Tatai to lift up his hands and let go of the wondrous balloons that soon would take off and brighten the night sky, meeting with the other balloons that filled the heavens. We would gather, lifting up our heads to follow them as we sang our songs.

I always hoped that the wind would suddenly change direction and send the colorful balloons into my extended hands, with their messages of love, happiness, and good fortune for others in faraway lands. But my brother's balloons flew high in the sky. I watched them with eyes fixed, so as not to lose sight of them as they mingled with others. But after a while, my eyes could not separate Tatai's balloons from the constant gathering of burning torches and spectrum of colors that filled the night sky. My heart was left wondering what direction our balloons had taken. We sang songs as they traveled though the sky:

Cai, cai, balão.	*Fall, fall, balloon.*
Cai, cai, balão,	*Fall, fall, balloon,*
Na Rua do Sabão.	*On Soap Street.*
Não cai não; não cai não; não cai	*Do not fall; do not fall; do not*
não.	*fall.*
Cai, aqui na minha mão.	*Fall here in my hand.*

But my wish to catch the balloons was in vain. Balloons fell on roofs, treetops, electrical wires, and in backyards, away from my extended hands. In the morning, I would find balloons on the ground or dangling awkwardly from the bushes in our backyard. Only then could I search for messages, for some way of knowing what was in the hearts and minds of those who had sent the wondrous balloons.

In addition to the silent wishes we sent with the balloons on St. John's Night, we also gathered to write fortune notes on colorful paper and passed them around. Some of our favorite wishes were, "St. John said that you'll be happy and will marry a rich man," or "St. John said that you'll be around for the celebration next year." We would read the wishes many times and walk around reading our good fortunes to neighbors and friends.

Tatai also liked to embellish the sky with colorful kites. He bought the paper, string, and glue with some of the money he made selling wood door to door. Tatai spent hours gluing pieces of colorful paper to thin strips of bamboo to make large, light kites. They were the prettiest kites I had ever seen but also the most feared. Tatai ground broken glass and mixed it with glue, then spread the mixture on the string used to fly his kites, making it very sharp. Sometimes Tatai attached razor blades to the tail of his kites. When they ascended as high as they would go, he attacked other kites, rubbing his lethal string and razor against their kite string and sending them swooping down to the ground or crashing into tall trees. It was a duel of colorful kites, hissing like venomous serpents, fighting in the bright blue sky. Some of the boys ran away from my brother's kites in despair. Others pulled their kites from the sky. Others still ran home crying after watching their kites dance in the air, then suddenly disappear into faraway fields, houses and treetops. Groups of boys ran after the fallen kites but in many cases they were unable to retrieve them.

At the end of the year, around carnival time, the town prepared for the *Bumba Meu Boi*—Bang my Bull, and the *Burrinha*—Young Donkey, a popular and cheerful pastime in the neighborhood, which everyone participated in and enjoyed. Tatai would help the people paint, decorate, and sew together a large piece of hard brown canvas to make a *boi*—bull—with an opening in the center to fit a man. The *burrinha* was large enough to hide a man inside. People would dance and sing around the decorated bull and donkey figures from early evening until dawn when everyone would walk home, dirty and hoarse from the dancing and singing all night but also chatty and happy.

Various circuses often visited our town. They brought excitement and aroused enthusiasm in the children. A circus would arrive in big and colorful trucks. After digging holes to set up the canvas tent, the crew would parade through the streets of town, followed by their well-decorated trucks with loudspeakers on top and banners all around. The procession would attract the neighborhood children, who were given tickets to the shows if they accompanied the parade with a rock in each hand to make noise while singing the songs blasting on the loudspeakers. Although the blast bothered me, I stood by our house to watch the parade. Tatai always secured his ticket by either remaining with the circus parade or by helping the crew dig holes to set up the tents.

Some boys, barefoot and half-naked, followed the clowns who walked on stilts and juggled. The elephants would come next, decorated with fresh flowers and colorful banners. The horses would perform tricks standing on their hind legs. The thunderous music coming through the loudspeakers would stop periodically, and a strident voice would announce the night's show:

Hoje tem espetáculo?	*"Is there a spectacle tonight?" The voice asked.*
Tem, sim, senhor.	*"Yes, there is, sir." The children replied in unison.*
Oito horas da noite?	*"At eight o'clock, tonight?"*
Tem, sim, senhor.	*"There is, sir."*
Oh, arrasta, negrada.	*"Let me hear your voices, crowd."*
Ah, ah, ah!	*"Yap! Yap! Yap!" they shouted back.*

Mais um bocadinho,	*"A little louder!"*
Ah, ah, ah, ah!	*"Yap! Yap! Yap! Yap!"*
Mais un tiricotico...	*"A little bit louder..."*
Ah, ah, ah, ah, ah...	*"Yap! Yap! Yap! Yap! Yap..."*

Children, clowns, and animals would march on, adding more excited followers to the roaring mob at every corner.

I went with Gaia to the opening nights. She always befriended the bullfighters to secure tickets for the show. From the bleachers, I watched the spectacle in bewilderment. There were clowns in colorful outfits and funny shoes, elephants rolling on the ground, and acrobats and monkeys performing their pirouettes, walking together on ropes and jumping from place to place. But most captivating of all were the *O Globo da Morte*—The Globe of Death and the *Coração Materno*—Maternal Heart. The Globe of Death was the highlight of the show. Two riders each rode a noisy motorcycle, traveling at high speed in opposite directions around an enclosed and shiny sphere. The audience watched in complete silence, not moving during the performance, the motorcycles roaring in the lit ball echoed under the dark brown canvas. After the performance stopped, all lights came on again, and the audience would let out gasps of astonishment and relief. The triumphant riders jumped out of the globe with their motorcycles and bowed their heads to the wild roar of the spectators.

The Maternal Heart performance changed the tone, shocking and restraining the audience with the tragic story of a young lover unable, despite many tries, to convince the young woman he loved to love him in return. The young woman demanded hard proof of the suitor's love, one day requesting an ultimate sacrifice, the heart of his mother. At first, the young man could not believe what he was being asked to do, but eventually he chose to fulfill the young woman's request. He found his mother praying in front of an altar, killed her without hesitation, extracted her heart and hurried back to his lover with the bloody organ in his hands.

The young woman, never expecting her whim to be fulfilled, goes mad. The audience in the bleachers always sobbed in deep sorrow. Though I never cried, I was shocked and petrified until the clowns brought happiness back to us again. After the shows, as the noisy crowd walked home in the dark, Gaia talked with the bullfighters in the back of the big tent. She praised their performances and flirted to secure a ticket for the following night.

The circuses stopped coming to town after television arrived in 1959. The few families with electricity and a TV set lived a short distance from our neighborhood, in the better part of town. I used to go to their houses to watch shows and movies. These families would leave their front living room windows open in the evening so a group of us children gathered outside could watch the shows as well. After TV arrived, most neighborhood children walked around in groups at night and stood outside any open window that had a view of a set in a living. Eduardo and I walked with a group of our own. We liked to watch Tarzan and American westerns in black and white, dubbed in Portuguese.

Sometimes, windows were slammed shut in our faces because the young audience made too much noise, shuffling, elbowing, and fighting with each other for the best spot to watch a favorite show. Sometimes children became too excited by gunshots and men chasing after Indians. At times, the 'oohs' and 'ahs' were too loud. The window was closed, and the television was turned off right in front of our awestruck faces. Regardless, when the owner turned off the television, we would walk home and disappear like ghosts into the quiet night, only to return faithfully the following night, and many more nights.

We spent hours gathered outside on clear nights looking up at the sky, nights so bright we were able to see our shadows reflected on the ground. We played a game of deciphering the different cloud formations around the silvery moon.

"It is a little lamb I see," Miriam would say.

"Oh, yes. I see it, too. It has its little tail up in the air," Ua added.

"Oh, I found a little horse right there," I said.

"And I see an elephant right next to it," Gaia shouted enthusiastically.

"I see it, and there's a Little Angel's grave, too," Ua exclaimed.

On the streets, under the bright sky and warm air, we also sang songs and played games. The adults flirted, and the elders told stories and chatted with each other. Our hearts were filled with an inexplicable contentment no matter how hard the days had been. That contentment, in bright moonlight, like the warmth that the sun's rays brought to my heart, has remained with me. I often reminisce about the commotion and pleasure the bright moon brought to Paramirim Street. The loud voices of children and neighbors leaving their dark lives and homes to gather together and share a few hours of relief from their sorrows still echo in my ears.

Gaia sometimes sat on the side of our house where we had heard our stories on moonless nights and sang her favorite tune, her long dark hair loose and her passionate voice reverberating in the air:

Quem eu quero não me quer.	*Whom I love does not love me.*
Quem me quer mandei embora.	*Who loves me I have sent away.*
E por isso já não sei	*For this reason, I do not know*
O que será de mim agora...	*What my fortune will be...*

While Gaia sang, my younger siblings, the neighborhood children, and I played a game of the rich and the poor. We divided into two groups. To begin, one person represented the rich while the rest of us represented the poor. We then held hands tightly and walked in a row toward the rich person, back and forth, singing a song that expressed our wishes:

Eu sou pobre, pobre, pobre,	*"I'm poor, poor, poor, Demarré,*
Demarré marré, marré ...	*marré, marré ...*
Eu sou rica, rica, rica, Demarré ...	*"I'm rich, rich, rich, Demarré ..."*
"Quero uma de vossas filhas ...	*"I want one of your children ...*
Escolha qual é que quer,	*"Choose the one you want,*
Demarré...	*Demarré, marré..."*

Each time we sang these verses, we lost one of our members to the rich group. The game continued until the person representing the rich had taken all the children from the poor person's group, leaving it with just one member who, in turn, would become the rich person. The game then started again, the one rich person left, marching back and forth to the poor person's group, singing and asking for the children.

We also played a game of hide-and-seek. One of us would lean against a wall or hide behind a bush, hands covering our eyes, and sing a song. When the song ended, the singer would start searching for the rest of us. We ran as fast as we could, trying to secure a good hiding spot before the chanting ended.

The words of the song we sang sounded different from the language I spoke, but I was used to singing the song with the other children. It was one of the few games we knew and liked. Later on, when I went to the capital and studied French, I realized that we had sung a mixture of French and a twisted jumble of Portuguese. I assume it remained from the French presence in the northeast, in 1612, when they founded a second colony in Brazil. Their first settlement was in 1555, in Guanabara Bay, today's Rio de Janeiro. The Portuguese expelled the French from Rio in 1567 and from the northeast in 1614. The song that I remember singing went something like this:

Une poule sur le mur,	*A chicken on the wall,*
Depicote dependu,	*Tail hanging,*
Picoté picotá,	*Pluck, pluck,*
Quero ver quem vai ficar.	*I want to see who is on.*

In our game of *Boca de Forno*—Oven's Mouth—one of us would sing a verse challenging the rest of the group to obey an order in an allotted time. The rest of us ran at once to carry out the task. If anyone returned empty-handed or without accomplishing the given order, he or she would either stay out of the game or be struck on the palm of the hand. The tasks were sometimes very hard and cruel, such as climbing a tall tree, running long distances, or finding my brother Fernando and smelling his ears. It was easy finding my brother, but no one ever dared to smell his ears.

12. The Neighborhood

I f we had money to buy soap to wash our soiled clothes piled up in a corner of the house, Gaia gathered them in a bed sheet, tied the ends in a round bundle, and carried the bundle in our large aluminum basin to a pond or any small pool of fresh water left after it rained. Gaia spent the whole day washing. I often followed my sister. Mother stayed home. She could not walk far because of the intense pains in her legs from varicose veins.

Gaia and I left early in the morning in order to return before sundown. When she located a good place for the wash—clear water and some bushes or a fence nearby to hang the clothes to dry—Gaia removed the basin from her head and set it down. Sometimes, when we had them, we brought along *farinha* and dried beans along with our clay pot. Before doing the wash, we first gathered wood to start a fire. Gaia carefully arranged three rocks in a triangle and secured our pot for cooking.

We scrubbed our clothes on a rock and laid the soapy garments on the ground for the sun to bleach and to help with the cleaning. Our clothes formed a blanket against the green grass under the clear blue sky. To prevent the hot air from drying them too fast and the strong winds from blowing them away, we fetched water in a bucket to sprinkle over our clothes while they lay on the ground. And with each sprinkling, the scorching sun bleached the colors of the garments, leaving them discolored.

Between the bleaching and the rinsing of the clothes, we ventured into the woods with the other laundresses whom we had befriended in search of bananas and wild berries to supplement our beans and farina. In the afternoon, we gathered our clothes and rinsed them in the deep blue water that Gaia had made by diluting some indigo to infuse color in our worn-out clothes. I dipped my hands into the indigo water in the basin and searched for any small piece of clothing that I could wring out by myself. We hung our clothes to dry on the nearby barbed-wire fences or bushes and folded each piece as it quickly dried under the hot sun, bundling everything up again in our round aluminum basin and heading home when the sun set behind the evergreen hills.

On some dark nights, I followed Gaia and Miriam to Dona Maria and Dona Asteria's house to sing and hear stories. At the end of their workday at the Suerdick factory, the neighbor women carried home on their heads tall piles of tobacco leaves to be cleaned and stemmed for extra pay. Along with the neighborhood children, we gathered around the women to sing and hear the stories they told, under a flickering candlelight, while helping them stem the leaves piled up on the dirt floor in in the center of their living room. The women invented or retold most of the stories.

There was the one story of Maria Calumbi, the woman from the *caatinga,* or brushwood, whose dried and snarled hair resembled the thorny vegetation of parts of the area where we lived. Maria Calumbi appeared to the people who passed by to chop wood and pick berries, and she ran after them. It was said that many of the people who had seen Maria Calumbi and had run from her arrived in town full of fear and with scratches all over their bodies after running full force through the inhospitable vegetation. But no one ever reported being caught. Dona Astera and Seu Adriano, a couple in the neighborhood, were the two who got close but bravely escaped being engulfed by the woman's long and dirty arms.

And the mystery of Castro Alves lives in a tale these women told. It is about a noisy and powerful underground river whose source is in one of the nearby hills and that flows through the entire area. The story goes that the river would overflow and burst one day, flood the town, and carry everything with it. In anticipation of this day, the townspeople carved a big canoe and tied it to a tall, tall tree, the *gameleira,* on Pedrinhas Street, near the town's cemetery. The roots of the tree spiraled and twisted deeply into the ground. The trunk and branches are whitish, thick, and strong. The wide evergreen leaves happily danced in the wind, as if singing and waving to the blue sky up high. The brown canoe slept undisturbed in the shade of the leafy *gameleira.* On rainy days, when it filled with water, the townspeople gathered to empty it out and cleared the debris, always with the flood in mind. And when walking to Pedrinhas Street, carrying the dead to bury, the people would pause for a glimpse of the majestic tree and the canoe. And so, the sight remained in their minds and imaginations, night and day, for generations, ready to carry the survivors to safety on the day of the flood.

One day, a man with a very commanding presence came to town and bought the extensive property where the *gameleira* and the canoe stood. The town elders then rushed to warn the newcomer about the roaring river underground and the flood to come. But the man wanted his farm. Soon after, he cleared the land and cut the tree. The canoe was destroyed, and no one in town ever found a new tree equal in size and strength to the old *gameleira*. Hopes of finding one died with the passing of time.

I was mystified, and on our clear moon nights I ran with the other children. We glued our ears to the ground at various locations in the neighborhood in a contest to see who had heard the underground river rumble the loudest. The roar was louder at midnight, they said, when the land slept and all was quiet. I could never last past midnight to hear the river, and I now wish I did.

When the gypsies came to town on tired mules and horses loaded with their belongings and children, I walked to the outskirts of the neighborhood with Eduardo. We would watch them set up their tents and unload their belongings. They sometimes stayed in the huts that sheltered travelers on their way across town. I later would walk back to see them with Ua, who carefully carried the colorful clothes and wedding dresses that she had sewn for them. She would go to the tents for a fitting or two before the garments were finished. The gypsies always insisted that we let them read the lines on our hands that supposedly revealed the future, but we refused because they wanted payment.

Life in our neighborhood changed with the arrival of the gypsies. No one liked them. The women who lived in town were always attentive to the gypsy women's whereabouts. They kept close watch over their children and livestock and stood by their clothes drying in the sun, afraid the gypsies would steal them. The men in town kept watch over their horses, if they had any, because the gypsies were famous for stealing them. The merchants secured their merchandise any way they could, for all could be gone and sold someplace else in the blink of an eye, never to be retrieved.

The gypsy men took their horses and jewelry to sell or barter at the market. The women walked around the neighborhood from house to house, wearing their long, loose, and colorful clothing, selling bundles of herbs, and insisting on reading people's palms to tell their fortune. No woman in the neighborhood ever allowed a gypsy to enter her home no matter how poor the house. After about two weeks or so, the group of gypsies left. Others would soon follow.

I had befriended Creusa, a girl in the neighborhood, who lived a few houses down from mine. She lived with her grandmother, Dona Dulce, who worked at the tobacco factory during the week and at her brother's store far from the neighborhood on Saturdays. Creusa's mother lived fairly close by on another street on the periphery of town with several children, all of whom their father had abandoned. On Saturdays, Dona Dulce brought home a bag of dark brown roasted pork skin from her brother's store. When there was nothing in our house to eat, I visited Dona Dulce's house, hoping to play with Creusa. I knew Dona Dulce would feed me some of her *torresmos*.

Creusa and I started wandering around the neighborhood together, especially when some news drew us out into the street. One afternoon, we went to Dona Helena's house. She had been found dead in the morning, her two-year-old son crying on top of her body. The neighbors had heard the toddler's yelling and had broken into the house. An older daughter came to take the boy away and the neighbors brought a coffin for Dona Helena, who used to walk by our window on her way to the tobacco factory and had bought Mother's undergarments at our window.

I watched the neighbor women busy themselves at Dona Helena's house, arranging her body in the best dress they could find and placing her in the casket they had bought. The deceased lay in the center of the living room, feet facing the doorway. As always, the casket was covered with fresh dahlias, carnations and angelicas. Women and children came in and out of the house, making a quick sign of the cross and whispering a prayer. Before sundown, the men lifted the casket, and with the women, paraded it through the streets to the cemetery.

Raimunda lived across the street from our house. She was young and had many children. I had seen her walking slowly with her extra heavy and rounded pregnancy, and I looked forward to visiting her after she gave birth. The older women in the neighborhood swore Raimunda was going to deliver twins because she was extra heavy. They welcomed the twin births with extra affection, care, and commotion.

The female neighbors always gathered at the house of the mother-to-be, took care of her and her young children, and did the chores. They had a ritual of raising a chicken for the occasion. When a woman gave birth, the chicken was killed and cooked. The breast was separated. A mush of manioc farina was prepared with the broth and brought to the mother to eat in bed for the three days that she needed to rest after giving birth. The women believed this food helped restore the mother's strength. They also prepared a particular kind of infusion called *meladinha,* which was a mixture of the Brazilian sugar-cane brandy, called *cachaça,* honey, and herbs, rue, wormwood, and pennyroyal, to serve the mothers and their visitors after delivery. Virtually every house, even the poorest ones prepared a *meladinha* in advance and set the infusion aside in anticipation of the birth.

I always looked forward to visiting the women in bed, the *paridas,* as they were called. I loved to smell the chicken cooking, to taste a bit of the delicious *meladinha,* and to watch the midwives. They would pour crushed fresh lavender on the bright red charcoal burning in the *fugareiro* on the ground by the kitchen and hold the newborn's clothing near the smoking herb so that it would acquire the sweet aroma that rose in the air. After bathing and dressing the newborn, the women held the small body in their extended hands near the smoking lavender for more of the fresh herb scent. I can still smell the lavender burning and the chicken cooking.

The day Raimunda was to give birth, Creusa and I arrived at her house after the 3 p.m. soap opera and saw the women gathered outside the house talking, which was odd because they were usually very busy. They explained that in the early hours of the morning, the midwife was called to deliver the baby and had difficulty with the birth. She quickly sent for a doctor. He came and had difficulty himself. He tried different procedures but all in vain. So he tied a rope to the baby's neck to force the distressed unborn child out of the mother's womb, like Seu Agemiro's cowboy, who would sometimes pull the stubborn bulls from a corner with a lasso when the animals refused to move. The doctor detached the baby's head in the mother's womb, killing both the mother and the unborn child.

I entered Raimunda's house and saw her body lying on a long board on top of some wooden boxes in the living room. She awaited a casket, which would need to be built in a hurry because her stomach was so big. None of the available caskets in town was large enough for her and the child. I looked at Raimunda's swollen but serene face on top of the wooden boxes. Instead of the usual quiet praying in the room, the women sobbed profusely. There was no smell of chicken cooking, no sweet lavender burning in the *fugareiro*, no *meladinha* passed from hand to hand. The women's sobbing, Raimunda's mountainous stomach and calm face, and the tumultuous house and surroundings prompted me to run off and hide in my corner, where I slept away my hunger. The vision of Raimunda's body haunted me for a long time.

The excitement of a birth was comparable to the hubbub surrounding the soap operas. There were always two programs, one at nine in the morning, the other at three in the afternoon. The women would arrange their household chores around their favorite program. Edna and Mara were the two neighbors who owned small battery-operated radios, which they kept safe on a high wooden pedestal in a corner of their living rooms. When it was time for the soap opera, the women would remove the radios from their pedestals and set them on a small table in the center of their living rooms where the other neighborhood women gathered around to listen.

Most people in the neighborhood did not own a clock or a watch to tell time, so they depended on each other and on the sun's position in the sky to orient them. At nine in the morning, as the sun's heat rose, the women would begin their ritual of calling on each other across the yard, through an open back door or a front window. They often would step outside to check on each other's doings and whereabouts, reminding them of the upcoming soap opera.

"It's almost time, Antonia," one would shout.

"I know, Joana. I'm hurrying and will meet you in a few minutes," the other would reply.

When it felt like it was time for the show, the women would leave their homes and chores behind, walk to the closest house, Mara's or Edna's, and gather around the radio; the older women sat closest and the younger ones circled around them. At mid-afternoon, another wave of women would walk together. After checking the time again, and each other, the women converged once more to listen to the longest and most popular afternoon soap opera.

Creusa and I followed the women to Mara's house to stand in the crowded living room and listen to the mid-afternoon soap opera most popular at the time: *O Direito de Nascer*—The Right to be Born. It told the story of a powerful patriarch, Don Rafael, who one day finds out that his daughter, Maria Helena, is pregnant. The fiancé refuses to marry the girl and does not recognize the child, who becomes the target of the grandfather's rage. Fearing for the child, the black servant, Mother Dolores, who had also raised Maria Helena at her master's home, leaves the family to raise the child alone since the mother entered a convent after giving birth. The child, Alberto, grows up and becomes a medical doctor. One day by accident, he reconnects with the family that had rejected him. He falls in love with a cousin and ends up saving the life of Don Rafael, the grandfather who had tried to deny him the right to be born.

This soap opera brought pain, rage, and tears to the women's eyes. They would walk home passionately discussing the events of each episode only to converge again at Edna's or Mara's living room the following day and for the duration of the soap opera and for many more popular dramas to come. These soap operas were not relevant to my life. My drama revolved around having food and basic necessities.

13. Leaving Town

During better times, when Father was alive and my family lived on Flowers Street, Ua started flirting with Louri, a neighbor boy she had met in school. They were twelve years old then and became sweethearts. Father did not approve of the boy and refused to allow him near the house, but Ua kept seeing him at school and around the neighborhood. They sent each other notes and arranged secret rendezvous. After Father died, Louri appeared in front of our house at four in the morning with a friend and a guitar. The commotion woke us. As soon as we recognized Louri's voice, my sisters and I got out of bed, and peeked at him through the holes in the front door. I rushed to find a place to best hear Louri's deep voice. Under the bright sky, his serenade reminded me of the birds I had heard happily announcing the break of dawn:

Diga que já não me quer.	*Say you no longer want me.*
Neque que me pertenceu.	*Deny you belonged to me.*
Eu mostro a boca molhada,	*I'll show the wet mouth,*
Ainda marcada pelos beijos teus.	*Still marked by your kisses.*

I jumped out of bed many more early mornings, the moon still shining, to rub the sleep out of my eyes and peg my ears to the holes in the door to listen to Louri's romantic serenades. But Louri's singing annoyed Fernando, who once borrowed a rifle from a neighbor and ran after the lover when the serenade became too long, too passionate, and so loud that no one in the house was able to sleep. That did not stop Louri, however, who was soon back at the front window again, serenading even longer and more passionately. Three years after Father died, after many more serenades, Ua married Louri and he moved in with us. Just as 1960 neared, the lives of my family members would take another unexpected turn.

Ua went to the Saturday market with the money that Louri gave her for their groceries. It became difficult for my sister to continue helping the family. Money was short and her husband had to eat because he worked late into the night as a tailor. Under an imperfect kerosene lamp, the *fifó*, Louri transformed piles of fabric into perfect pants and suits that he sold in his shop. His speed at sewing earned him the nickname of *Vento*—Wind. He worked sewing a pair of pants from night till day.

It became difficult to smell the beans and rice cooking every day at our house, or to smell the salted meat Ua fried for Louri on our black stove. He had to eat, but there was never enough for us. Soon after getting pregnant with her first child, Ua had to leave her job at the local movie theater.

Ua continued a tradition she had started a few years earlier of building a little nativity scene in a corner of our living room against the black mud wall. The nativity village started small but grew bigger and more elaborate with the years, and all of us took part in it. We would get up at daybreak early in December and walk a few miles deep into the woods to gather many colorful leaves and exotic mosses to decorate the village we called *presépio*. We also searched the ponds for the smooth clay we used to mold the figurines that adorned and gave life to Ua's nativity scene.

After returning from the woods, my sisters and I would spend hours in the backyard molding the clay into little houses, churches, people, priests, lambs, donkeys, ducks and figures of Mary, Joseph, Baby Jesus, and the Three Kings. We loved making figurines and became experts at it. Miriam was such an authority on molding the figures that one day she bet she could shape perfect little lambs with her eyes completely closed. And she did, amazingly. I tried to imitate Miriam but couldn't. After sculpting the figures, we would let them dry in the sun and later would paint them with different colors. The village was arranged on top of adobe blocks and empty wooden boxes we gathered in the neighborhood. We covered the blocks and boxes with brown paper decorated with the brightly colored leaves and mosses that we had gathered in the woods. On Christmas Eve, we would leave our shoes—those with holes in the soles or with soles intact—behind our wobbly front door for *Papai Noel,* Father Christmas, who was supposed to have a key to all homes so that he could leave us a gift in our shoes. But it was Mother Christmas, Ua, who left us the gifts of cloth dolls and dresses that she sewed for Miriam and me and shorts and shirts, or sometimes a plastic toy for my three younger brothers. We proudly wore the new clothes on Christmas and on New Year's Day.

When Father was alive and doing well on Flowers Street, he noticed that my elder brother Célio was not interested in school. Instead, Célio preferred to travel far on foot to break wild horses. He liked to spend all day under the burning sun riding the animals. The family worried about him. He arrived home sunburned late in the evening. Father greeted Célio armed with a long leather whip to beat Célio's legs. Father used a heavy flat wooden piece known as *palmatória* to beat the palms of my brother's hands. Célio's legs bled and his hands swelled from the strokes. Father had dreamed of my elder brother growing up to become the man of the house. The beatings did nothing to change Célio's fate. They may have contributed to it.

Célio was eighteen when Father died in 1956. Dona Ervirinha, the blonde angel who lived in the house that Mother visited to ask for food, found a job for Célio as an elevator operator in a building in the regional capital, Salvador, and he left. The train to the big city left our town in the early hours, and we woke with the call of the roosters to walk Célio to the station. From a distance, in the cool stillness of dawn, I heard the whistle and felt the rhythm of the old coal engine the townspeople called *Maria Fumaça*—Smoky Maria— named for the gush of black smoke it blew into the air and the long trail it left behind. The engine approached the station slowly, as if running out of steam.

Mother cried as she hugged and kissed Célio goodbye. He boarded the train silently after the final goodbyes. He took a seat by the window to wave a white handkerchief at us until his hand and the white cloth became smaller and smaller in the distance, and I could no longer see it. The train's whistle and its tired engine could only be heard in the distance. The white handkerchief faded away in the wind: passing houses, poles, pastures, cows, and far beyond my waving hands. Célio was gone. I heard the faraway whistle blowing and the engine puffing, cutting through our vast land and sad souls. My family walked home detached, slowly, and silently. There was no news from Célio for a long time.

Townspeople who returned from visiting Salvador reported that Célio had become a heavy drinker. Tatai left for Salvador soon after he turned eighteen. The rest of us were growing older and hungrier. The couscous Mother sold, the panties and bras she made, the trips we took to the factories and into the woods to forage, and the donations we received from our Castro Alves neighbors were not enough to feed us. Tatai thought that he could join Célio in Salvador and earn enough money to send to Mother. After he arrived in the capital, however, he rarely sent money home. When my brothers did send money, they gave it to Seu Cafezeiro, a town resident who also worked in Salvador, to bring to Mother, who spent it quickly. When it was gone, we were again left waiting and hoping for other townspeople visiting from the capital to bring Mother some of our brothers' money.

Then the worst of all possible things happened. Gaia got pregnant. When she was in her early twenties, Gaia went to a nearby town to visit an old girlfriend who had once lived in our neighborhood. Gaia's friend asked Mother to let Gaia spend some time with her family and Mother agreed. Gaia met a young, handsome farmer there who found her too pretty to resist and promised her marriage, a house and food on the table. I imagine that it was very difficult for Gaia to resist, living under the conditions we did. A few weeks later, Gaia came home with a stomach a little too full.

And when Gaia's belly started growing and her hips protruding, despite the severe shortage of food in our house, she found a waistband and tightly wrapped it around her stomach. My sister tried to disguise her pregnancy until she could no longer hide it from Mother and Ua. It was a complete shock to them. I remember Mother and Ua crying in the backyard the day that they discovered the truth. I did not know enough to cry.

Day in and day out, Gaia stayed in the bed that I shared with her; on dark nights and on clear nights, when the rain danced on the roof tiles and when the sun shone brightly through the cracks, even when we had soap to wash the clothes that had piled up in the corner, Gaia stayed in bed. The circus came and went. Gaia never again secured our tickets to the shows.

My sister wore her black skirt in bed, day and night, and never left the house again. Her voice was silent on nights that the moon shone brightly in the clear sky and we gathered outside to play. It was silent on dark nights when we heard stories by our black rock. Gaia did not even seem to hear anything. She did not care much about my tossing, turning, and wetting the bed after my dreams with Seu Agemiro's bulls or the black vultures picking at my body. Once, as if by magic, a flock of chickens entered our kitchen. I ran to Gaia as fast as I could and stayed right beside her.

"Gaia, a bunch of chickens has just entered the kitchen," I said, pointing to the noisy animals.

I waited for my sister to jump out of bed and tell me to quickly close the door to trap the chickens at once, as we always did. Nothing happened.

Me deixa, Leda—"Leave me alone, Leda," was all Gaia said. She did not even look at me. I knew something was terribly wrong with her.

Gaia stayed in the dark room for basically her entire pregnancy. She gave birth to a baby girl under the care of Dona Antonia, the midwife in the neighborhood, and with Mother's assistance—in the same way that in the past Mother herself had given birth to all of her children, with the assistance of her mother Silvina. Mother put wood on the fire, water in the tall kerosene can, and charcoal in the *fugareiro* by the kitchen door. Then she sent her younger children out of the house to prepare for the baby to arrive. She put lavender on our black table, and she stayed close to the midwife and my sister. There was no chicken cooking for Gaia or *meladinha,* the herb infusion, nor money in the house for the honey and *cachaça.*

Knowing Gaia's physical and mental condition, Mother predicted a very difficult delivery of her first grandchild. My mother had experienced similar deliveries of her children in the past. So, she incensed the house by walking around with a tin can, then she took her rosary, knelt down, and prayed fervently to Saint Rita of Cassia, the Saint of the Impossible, to intervene and promised the saint that she would name the baby after her if it were a girl. Gaia delivered a pretty baby girl named Rita de Cássia.

Ua's old girlfriends from Flowers Street brought Rita clothes and sometimes milk. Neighbors stepped in to help Mother, who dug holes in the ground next to the bed I shared with Gaia to build a *tarimba*—a cot made with four pieces of wood dug into the ground and sturdy pieces of vine attached horizontally between the legs. She fed Rita manioc farina cooked in water and sugar when we had no milk and Gaia's breasts dried quickly. My sister did not regain her spark after the birth of her daughter. The grief, shame, and sadness crashed her spirit. The family never heard from the father. Mother decided to raise the girl herself.

Two years after Célio and Tatai had left for Salvador, Fernando followed them. Our cousins, who lived in the city, promised Fernando a job in the cafeteria of the giant Brazilian oil refinery, Petrobrás. Soon after Fernando started working, he sent us a big wooden box full of food. We walked to the train station to retrieve the *cantina,* as we called it, after Seu Pedro, the older man who worked at the train station, had walked to our house one afternoon. He knocked on our door, and we were surprised to see him.

"There's a big package from Salvador at the station for you," Seu Pedro told Mother.

We dashed to the station like lightning, way ahead of Seu Pedro, to get the box and took turns carrying it home. It was heavy. Once home, we removed the nails from the edges and found goods we had never seen before: a can of peaches; banana and guava paste, all three flavors in one colorful can arranged in triangles; oatmeal; cornmeal; canned ham and black beans; powdered milk, chorizo, and cans of sardines. Our amazement and delight were boundless. We were careful with the food that Fernando sent us. I ate my portions very slowly, savoring each bite, one at a time, as if imprinting its taste in my memory so that I would remember it long after it was gone and hunger struck again.

At the end of the month when there was nothing left from our cantina and no knock at our door from Seu Pedro telling us that there was a box waiting for us, we walked to the train station anyway, full of hope, when we heard the Maria Fumaça noisily approaching. We wished that our *cantina* would arrive that day, and when we did not see the wooden box being unloaded from the wagons, we looked for Seu Pedro and asked him many times in many ways.

"Did our *cantina* arrive today, Seu Pedro?"

"No. Not today, children."

"Are you sure, Seu Pedro?"

"Sure, children."

"Look again, Seu Pedro, to be very sure."

"Fine, but I know nothing arrived for you today."

And we asked Seu Pedro to check again and again to see if, by any chance, our *cantina* had been left unattended. We asked if he would please check someplace else and double check carefully, for it could have been left in a hidden corner. With the patience of a saint, Seu Pedro understood us and calmly replied that it would not be possible for the big box to be lost, for, like Saint Peter guarding the Gates of Heaven, he was in charge of his station and was careful about every delivery. He helped us check every corner of the small station. We found nothing and walked home slowly, empty-handed and with empty stomachs.

Fernando was not consistent with our *cantina*. I could not understand why. It came some months but not others. Sometimes it arrived every month; other times it took months to arrive, and the quantity was much less. But we would often walk to the train station, and always full of hope.

During one of those long barren stretches of running to meet Maria Fumaça at the station and walking back empty-handed, my brother Raimundo, the one born after me and Eduardo, made an unusual announcement. Raimundo weighed just ten kilos, a little over twenty-two pounds, at the age of ten. Sitting on Mother's black rock, sucking his thumb quietly as he always did when he was hungry, Raimundo heard the whistle of the engine as it approached the station. He pulled his thumb out of his mouth very fast and loudly declared, "I saw a praying mantis enter through the door and exit through the window. The *cantina* is coming today."

As soon as Raimundo made this unexpected revelation, I dashed through the door with Eduardo to meet the approaching train. Maria Fumaça had indeed brought our *cantina* that afternoon. Raimundo's prediction had come true. With Seu Pedro's help, Eduardo and I carried the wooden box home and opened it in no time. From that day on, every time that we heard the train approaching, we would look at Raimundo and wait for any sign he could interpret, as he sat quietly sucking his thumb. But there were no more praying mantises entering the door or exiting through the window or any other omen Raimundo could discern. We then resumed going to the station at the end of the month, hoping for the *cantina* from the capital.

With my older brothers living in the capital, Ua starting a family of her own and Gaia with a child, Mother thought it would be better to move the rest of the family to Salvador where we could start a new life. It became exceptionally difficult for her to feed the six of us left in Castro Alves. The resources were scarce, and she did not have any alternatives.

There was not much Mother could do to feed us without my older siblings. The money Miriam hid in her underpants' pocket from my aunt's cash register, the infrequent *cantina* from Fernando, the help from Ua, and the diminishing bra and panty sales were just impossible to live on. Mother's sewing dwindled, for people bought just one garment at a time. They bought a new piece only when the old one had become too worn-out or tattered. There was only so much our neighbors and townspeople could buy. The neighborhood was very stable; not many people moved in or out. Mother's couscous business also became unprofitable after a while.

One of Father's nieces, Angela, who lived in Salvador, offered to rent Mother a house that her husband owned in the city. Mother accepted the offer without seeing the house or knowing the location. Fernando agreed to deduct the rent from his paycheck. She left town with Gaia, the baby, and my three younger brothers, Eduardo, Raimundo, and Wilson on a bus early one morning. I stayed with Ua to finish fifth grade.

It was 1963. I said goodbye to the neighbors, to our house and backyard. The house was sold to Seu Galdino, the man who fed me bananas and a candy sucker. He later demolished it. In order to finish the school year, Miriam and I moved in with Ua and her family to a new house they rented on 13th Street, a long and narrow row of houses attached to each other with a very small backyard behind the busy market. The house had a raw sewage ditch running through the kitchen and the living room all the way to the bigger underground pipe in the street. I dreamed of fixing the open cement canal that ran through Ua's kitchen, eliminating the terrible stench it left throughout the house, the same way I dreamed of fixing our doors and kitchen on Paramirim Street; of building a fence around our house, to protect us from the bulls, and of planting an orchard.

In her new house, Ua took care of her daughter, son, and a third child, a boy who only learned to walk at the age of three. My sister sat him on a chair next to her so she could watch him while she sewed. At the end of the week, she had enough money to take her basket to the market, where she bought the smoked meat her husband liked: snake, armadillo, and all species of lizards and birds. Ua prepared the new delicacies and her husband came home and ate them with gusto. I learned to like them and looked forward to eating the smoked snake that Ua cooked.

In my new school on Jail Street, I met girls with shiny shoes, long hair, pretty dresses, and books. They always brought snacks to school to eat at the *merenda*, our 10 a.m. break. Some shared their delicious cakes and pastries with me. I was skinny, shy, and quiet and always sat in a corner of the room, away from everybody. It was my first encounter with well-groomed girls, other than my Great Aunt Zibina's granddaughter, Lia. I played with Lia, and she gave me bananas and guavas when I walked to their house on Flowers Street.

Our teacher, Dona Rita, became angry with my classmates whenever they interrupted her with too many questions about the math problems, language diagramming, or other topics they didn't quite understand. I did not have any books because Ua had little money. I sat quietly in a corner, and in most cases, I understood the teacher's explanations and started helping my classmates. They started gathering near me when they needed assistance. Two other girls in the class, Ceci and Jussara, also understood math and language well. We teamed up to help the rest of the group solve any complicated problems.

After that, I started making friends and visiting their homes around 3 p.m., when the maids served their afternoon snacks. I was not as well dressed and groomed as my new classmates. My hair was curly, bushy, and untamed. Gaia used to wet and roll it into long and pretty curls. Ua sewed one or two dresses for me when there were some remnants. When I arrived at the nice homes to play with my classmates, the mothers did not seem to mind, or even notice, my presence. It was often the maids who answered the door when I knocked. But one afternoon, when I walked to the big houses on Church Street to play with one of my classmates whom I often helped with language and math, her mother answered the door. She looked surprised to see me.

Then I overheard her reprimand her daughter, "This house is no orphanage or a place for beggars. They belong on the street."

I was deeply hurt, surprised and disenchanted for a long time. I wanted to cry but held back the tears and stayed quiet. To my surprise, the classmate continued playing with me at school, and I continued to help her with math, but never returned to her house.

On Paramirim Street, we were one of the poorest families in the neighborhood, but I never felt any different from the other children. We were all poor with only a slight variation—some of us ate a little every day while others went hungry for days. In addition, people knew Mother and her children, and they tried to help us when they could.

In December, when the school year ended and it was time for graduation, the teacher sent Ua a note explaining the details of the ceremony and the special dress that I needed to wear. I imagined my sister would have made the dress for me, as she always did in the past with her remnants. The material chosen for my dress was expensive. I remember Ua saying she could not afford it. By this time, Ua had three children and sewed until late every night to help her husband with the expenses. One morning I saw her remove the accumulated black soot from her nostrils left by the kerosene light.

I wanted to go to the party and receive my diploma with my classmates. I asked both Ua and my teacher if there was any other type of dress I could wear to attend the graduation party. They explained that all of the girls were to wear dresses made from the same material because graduation day was a very special day. So, I did not go to graduation. The next day I listened to the very classmates whom I had tutored in math tell me how happy they were to receive their diplomas and hugs from their parents. The morning I received my diploma, there was no one there to congratulate me. It enrages me now writing about it. Soon after my graduation, Ua put me on a bus to join my family in Salvador.

Part II: Salvador—The Redeemer

When people lack a critical understanding of their reality, apprehending it in fragments which they do not perceive as interacting constituent elements of the whole, they cannot truly know that reality.

Paulo Freire, *Pedagogy of the Oppressed.*

14. Nymph of the Waters

One early morning in December 1964, Ua accompanied me to the bus stop in Castro Alves and asked Seu Vadinho, a well-known bus driver, to watch over me. I was leaving to reunite with my family in the capital. I carried the few items of clothing that I owned packed in a plastic bag and tucked under my seat in the back of the bus. It was my first time on a bus to venture out of town. I was fifteen.

December is summer in the tropics, when the intense sun rises at 6 a.m. and brightens dark corners throughout the day, soaking up any accumulated moisture. After an hour-and-a-half on a bumpy dirt road, we crossed over a pristine river on a tall, old bridge connecting the picturesque twin towns of Cachoeira and São Felix. The bus continued on a trail of twisted roads before stopping at a cafe. The passengers rushed out to stretch and purchase a quick snack. I stayed on the bus because I didn't have any money. If Ua had had any extra cash, she would have given me some.

When the bus arrived in Salvador, Fernando met me at the station. I followed him to other buses that would take us home. Salvador is the oldest city and the first capital of Brazil, founded on a peninsula by the Portuguese in 1530. Our house was in an area called Ondina—Nymph of the Waters. The neighborhood, on the coastline of the Atlantic Ocean, known as the Orla Marítima, was not far from the commercial center of the city and the elite suburbs.

Gaia met me at the front door and led me inside. The house was cold and damp. Thin drops of water slowly slipped down the walls; dark spots of mold could be seen on the ceiling and in the corners; a steady dampness permeated the cement floor; a cool breeze laden with saltwater streamed through the back door. You could hear the murmur of the wind and the water, a constant hum that filled the air.

I looked at Gaia in puzzlement. "Where is all the wind and water coming from?"

"There's the ocean behind the house." Gaia looked at me impassively. "The tide is rising now. Let's go see it."

"There is an ocean in the backyard?" I asked.

"Yes. And you have to see it. Come with me," she said.

Gaia led the way. We walked outside to the left past two small houses and followed a narrow alley where large pipes were covered with layers of dirt. In front of me was a large body of water, almost as blue as the indigo water in the aluminum basin that Gaia used to rinse our clothes in Castro Alves. I was looking at the Atlantic Ocean, which extended like an infinite blue lawn in my new backyard, dotted with black rocks along the shore. Waves hit the rocks and splashed high into the air before crashing down on the shabby houses built on the thin stretch of land. The white foam drummed and sprayed on the tin roofs, invading some of the houses and turning the dirt floors to mud.

After the high waves receded, the low tide revealed a new scene, massive amounts of human feces. Raw sewage from the Ondina area covered the narrow beach and extended onto the rocks behind the shantytown. I soon found out that the schools and homes across the highway in front of the houses pumped the raw waste into the ocean through the pipes that I had seen on the ground. The sewage from our shantytown also gushed out of the tubes that were embedded in the stone walls that provided shanty homes limited protection from the powerful waves.

Human waste splattered onto the beach. The stench made breathing difficult. Every time I drew near, I held my breath and pinched my nose shut. The stink was far worse than anything that I had ever experienced, even more dreadful than the air in our backyard in Castro Alves where dead animals and feces lay scattered on the hot ground. Sewage came fast and piled high on the moist ocean beach until waves came in and swept it out to sea.

That first afternoon, I kept returning to admire the blue ocean. The warm water, the tides, and the incessant coming and going of the melodious waves mesmerized me. It felt like magic. I ran down the narrow alley, past the homes to the shore, where I would stand and marvel at the enchanting body of water. I skipped to avoid the tar balls trapped in the sand. I first reached the small rocks and then the black rocks that appeared tall and naked after the high water had receded. I saw a stretch of clean beach in the shape of a quarter-moon away from the homes and free of the waste and trash. I faced the ocean and stood on the warm sand. I dug in my feet and watched the waves coming, going, and coming again.

Waves covered the sand with a blanket of foamy water in a

rhythmic dance. Once, as I watched the frothy waves, the image of the foaming and stomping bull that I had left back in Castro Alves flashed in my mind. I stayed put on my warm spot. The ocean's spattering of foam was music to my ears and warmed my heart instead of the fear the black bull had spawned. The bubbly waves flooded me with wondrous possibilities. I was in awe.

I waded in the ocean to meet the waves and to fill my cupped hands, over and over again. I splashed the water over my body. I preferred to bathe in the ocean under the bright sky and hot sun. The small open alley between our house and the one immediately behind us, which is where we washed up, was always dark, muddy and smelly. My family used a bucket. We scooped small cups of water to clean ourselves. Although the ocean water left my hair extremely dry and frizzy and my body covered with white spots from the salt, which I later removed with a wet cloth, it was a welcome change from the dirty area behind my house. I always felt free in the open air.

From where I stood on the sand, I could see ships on the horizon. I didn't know what they carried or where they were going. I imagined that they were transporting goods from Brazil to be sold in other countries. They moved slowly in a straight line. My eyes followed them. The large ships soon became smaller and smaller in the distance, and if I took my eyes off them, it took a long time to find the small specks again. Sometimes the ships disappeared from sight altogether. I imagined myself on those ships, going somewhere, though I didn't know where. I imagined meeting with the sun that always rose and brought me hope. At dusk, the yellow sun would leisurely descend to meet the horizon where the large ships had been. And when the flaming sphere reached the ocean's edge, it quietly rested there, dispersing its rays to mingle with the ocean, sky, and clouds, forming a mixture of shades and colors that I couldn't take my eyes off. As night fell, the ribbons of color slowly dissipated in the sky, where dark clouds took over.

Our house in Salvador was on an *invasão*—invasion, as people called a piece of land that was occupied illegally. (The term *favela* is now generally used to refer to these impoverished areas.) The Ondina invaders had built dwellings on vacant land approximately three miles long. As far as anyone knew, no one owned the property. The site was central and appealing. It was near the comfortable homes across an extremely busy and dangerous highway where most of the dwellers could find work. The settlement grew slowly, as one family at a time moved in and built wooden or cardboard or tin shacks, sometimes overnight. They would wait and hope for conditions that would allow them to build a better house. Eventually, a small village was formed by the shacks huddled tightly together. These shacks, in most cases, shared common walls. People utilized every bit of space that they could call home. They built in front, on top of, or behind each other. For many residents, there was no infrastructure of any kind—no sewer system or running water, no electricity or any other service. But in the shantytown, people felt that they could have a roof over their heads.

These people had come from every corner of the city and the state of Bahia, from many small towns, in search of a better life. After moving from place to place around the big city, living under bridges, sleeping in train stations or on the streets, some with young children and no means to survive, they would find their way to Ondina, either by accident, having stumbled upon it, or by word of mouth. They would land on this stretch of land between the highway and the ocean and build their shanties.

We lived in a brick house that was painted a faded yellow on the outside. Our two front windows and one door were painted green. They were old, full of holes, and had broken latches. The waves sprayed the back wall of the house at high tide, and water seeped in, leaving the ground and walls permanently wet and cold. The house directly behind ours received most of the impact of the wind and waves during storms and sheltered our house somewhat, especially during the month of March, the end of summer in the Southern Hemisphere, when the ocean tide is high and feared.

Other homes in the shantytown were also made of brick and cinderblock. They displayed the same dilapidated and unfinished look. They had been constructed in a hurry with shoddy materials. Some had partial roofs and partly finished and unpainted walls. Others had stone foundations yet only one finished room where a large family could gather. Still others were wooden and cardboard shacks that never progressed beyond the beginning stage. For them, better times never came.

Our house was more or less in the center of a corridor of homes.

To leave the shantytown from our house you had to either walk up a dirt slope to the right or climb six or seven stone steps directly out our door. There was a small empty lot directly in front of the house, just before a treacherous two-lane highway where heavy traffic flowed in both directions, day and night. My entire family, except for Ua, who stayed in Castro Alves with her family, lived in the house. Five of my brothers shared the two twin-size beds in the front bedroom facing the highway. Mother kept the window in the front bedroom open during the day to dispel the bad odor emanating from Fernando's infected ears. Célio, the brother who had turned to drinking, slept on a cot in the back room with the women in the house. I slept on the cement floor in the second bedroom with Mother, Gaia, Rita, and Miriam. To make my bed, I laid a straw mat on the floor of a built-in closet whose wooden doors and frame the termites and humidity had destroyed. The open entryway of the house led to a small living room and a kitchen. The kitchen had a propane gas stove and a permanently stained and dirty sink with a faucet but no running water. There was no refrigerator. A stomach-churning stench came from a small bathroom to the left of the kitchen.

The sewer pipe from our bathroom, like many others in the shantytown, ran underground, ending in the stone wall behind the houses, facing the beach where all the waste was dumped. During high tide and storms, the waves often hit the back wall, sending water through the open pipe. The storm water flushed the remaining waste in the pipe right back into our toilet bowl, which would overflow onto the bathroom floor and run into the kitchen. The women would rush with a broom to clean the waste flowing on the cement floor. They would run down the alley to fill our empty kerosene cans with ocean water to rinse the floor and the toilet.

But our efforts were futile. The toilet bowl was too old. It had a thick black crust that was impossible to remove, no matter what we did. Even during low tide, our toilet was always plugged up and nauseating. We would dump a large amount of caustic soda in it. Nothing helped. There was never enough water in the house to flush it. The walls around it were moldy and cold, and the floor was always wet. At low tide, we often had to leave the house, walk down the narrow alley and to the beach to relieve ourselves, like most people in the shantytown. At high tide, we relieved ourselves in empty buckets or in bundles of newspapers we had gathered. We walked with the packets in our hands to throw them in the ocean water.

We often fetched our drinking water from our neighbor, Seu Amado, one of the very few people in the shantytown who had running water in his house. (I imagine he had the pipes connected illegally from the main pipelines by the highway since his house was just behind the road.) Seu Amado let other neighbors come and fill their cans with fresh water. We would fill our containers in Seu Amado's bathroom and walk through his house, carrying the cans home on our heads. Other neighbors trekked up and down the small alleys with their water. There was also a well on the beach behind the home of Dona Santinha, one of our neighbors. This well provided most of the dwellers with their drinking water.

I liked looking at the well and often walked alone to fetch our water. I leaned my body over the edge to watch in amazement the bubbling flow of water spring from the ground, surrounded by sand, rocks, and saltwater. I thought that the water would be salty, but it was sweet. It spun around and around and slowly filled the well. I could see my face reflected in the clear water. The image of my face moved up and down, getting bigger and smaller. Then other women would gather around the fountain with their pots and cans under their arms. They took turns throwing their heavy buckets into the well to fetch the water to fill their containers. The women walked home on the sand and rocks, carrying the buckets on their heads, their bodies swaying. I waited by the well for everyone to leave and leaned my body over the edge once more to watch the well refill. I saw the reflection of my face bounce in the water again, small at first, then bigger and twisted.

Our neighbors kept a heavy wooden lid on top of the well and secured it with large rocks to protect our drinking water from the waste, trash, and the ocean's salt during high tide. But the wind and waves often hit the lid and blew it away. The ocean water would penetrate the well making the water salty and undrinkable. If we ran out of water and Seu Amado had already given us some water for the day, we had to wait for the waves to recede and for fresh water to refill the magic fountain, flowing from the beach floor in the midst of salt water, sand, rocks, trash, and sewage. If the waves had found their way into the well, it took a few days for our water to taste good enough to drink again. In that case, there was no other choice but to drink the *agua salobre*, salty water as we called it, the potable water mixed with water from the ocean.

During the high tides in March, the ocean roared, and powerful waves disrupted people's lives. The water entered a number of houses, causing panic and harm. The storms shook the dwellings and cloaked them in frothy water that found its way into every corner. The ocean water soaked the walls and floors, causing pots and pans to fall from the shelves, tables, or stoves. People ran for shelter to neighbors' homes that were a bit farther away from the ocean's wrath. Only the occupants who were protected by other houses escaped the storm's fury.

After the tempest, the women patiently carried their wet mattresses and dripping clothes outside to dry on makeshift clotheslines. In a short time, the sun absorbed the puddles of water left on the dirt floors and dried the items hanging outdoors. The ritual would repeat itself. Once the sun had baked the mud, the women carried their things back into their homes and arranged them in their original places until another high tide came, swamped their dwellings, and forced them to carry everything outside once again to dry in the sun. The men tried different ways to protect their homes, but there was no wood or other barrier strong enough that was capable of preventing the stormy waves from destroying their houses again and again.

Very few dwellings in the *invasão* had services of any kind. Daring men bravely climbed up the electrical poles that housed large and noisy transformers to attach the wires so they would deliver electricity to their homes. Most often, the electrical connections, made at dusk or in the dim light of dawn, went unnoticed. Thus, there were no bills from the power company. Dark homes suddenly became bright; all was well, big smiles and happy faces. The electric company could not seek retribution for the illegal operations. For one thing, the utility had no record of service orders and no names or addresses for their new customers. For another, it wasn't easy to mail a notice to a dweller. There was no official recognition of these families' residences. They had come from the dark corners of the city, from the shadows of society, nameless and faceless. In this way, they also escaped all bills, forms, official warnings, and threatening correspondence.

At the same time, though, some occupants paid a high price when connecting the electrical wires to the high-voltage power lines. As soon as a new family moved in, the father would readily climb the electrical poles with wires wrapped around his shoulder and arm and a clipper in hand. Sometimes, in the process of making the connection, something would go wrong. A false step and spark of electricity filled the air, as if a show of fireworks had gone haywire. The man would fall to the ground in a flash, as if struck by lightning, landing hard, like a sack of potatoes, charred beyond recognition.

Loud screams and panicky cries, voices of pain and despair would reverberate in the air. The faces of the once-thrilled circle of spectators waiting for the magic link that would brighten a home turned dark and lifeless. The curious gathered to watch while desperate family members ran over to shake the charred body in complete disbelief. Electrocution happened in a few seconds. Whenever this occurred, I would run to the backyard, if the tide was low, skipping over the waste on the beach to reach the clear water far out where I would sit on a rock and admire the Atlantic Ocean. Or I would cross the highway, if the tide was high, to a wooded area where I saw greenery. The sobbing and laments tormented me.

But in the shantytown, the practice of connecting electrical wires to the light poles never died. It was the only way for most residents to bring electricity into their homes and some light into their lives. The electric company was aware of the illegal connections and the deaths. From time to time, it sent out a crew to disconnect the wires, but to no avail. The electricity would be reconnected soon after the crew had left. A newcomer would also resort to the well-known practice. One dim light in the center room of our house was our *gato*. I often studied under the streetlight in front of the house, by the highway, when there wasn't time for me to do my homework in the afternoon. Our light was too weak for me to do my work.

Many people lived in the *invasão*. I would estimate over 1,000, in a stretch of maybe a little over three miles, with shacks piled closely together. All of the dwellers shared a somewhat similar story. To the left of our house was a one-room shack where our neighbors Gerardo and Mira lived with their baby Nataniel. Gerardo was light skinned, quiet, short, and stocky. I always heard him forcing the front door closed early in the morning when he left the house. Mira was short and thin. She wore her blonde hair in a bun and stayed home to care for her son. The nights Gerardo came home drunk, and there were many, he beat Mira. She cried like a baby and screamed for help. Mira's crying and yelling at night would wake up Nataniel. It was impossible to fall back asleep. Fernando devised a way to stop Mira's agony and ours. He led us outside at night and told us to find rocks, bricks, wooden sticks, or whatever we saw and instructed us to gather at Mira's front door and bang on it hard with what was in our hands.

"Stop beating Mira, Gerardo," Fernando told us to say while repeatedly drumming on the door with our improvised weapons.

"We won't stop drumming on your door until you stop beating Mira," we said in unison.

Most nights Gerardo would stop the beating, and we would go back to bed. One night, Gerardo stumbled out of his front door to confront us. He lunged at Fernando. Fernando threw a brick at Gerardo, striking him on the forehead. We left Gerardo bleeding on the ground and ran down the dark alley toward the beach. We remained quiet for a while before sneaking back into our house. I was afraid Gerardo was dead and wondered what would happen to Fernando. But in the morning, I heard Gerardo slam his front door closed as he left the house. For once, I was relieved that he was alive.

In the morning, there were dark bruises all over Mira's face and arms. I approached her and tried to talk, but she never looked up while doing her laundry or watching Nataniel, who sat on a straw mat in the narrow area in front of her house. Some days Mira stayed inside to avoid any contact with me. She knew that her sadness worried me and that I wanted to help her desperately. She would see me sitting on the stairs by Mother's papaya tree waiting for her to come out of her house so that I could talk to her and hold Nataniel a little. I wished I could move Mira and Nataniel far away from Gerardo.

Gerardo's beatings would stop for a few days and then resume even more violently than before. One day, I saw a smile return to Mira's face. Her belly, I noticed, had grown and her smile widened. She was pregnant with her second child. One morning, Nataniel would not stop crying. Mother walked over to see him. She found

Mira sitting on a corner of her bed in a puddle of blood, holding Nataniel and crying. She had lost her second child during a long night of beating. Gerardo continued abusing Mira. No yelling or hard knocks on the door at night could stop him. In the morning, when I heard him leaving the house, I wished that he were dead many times over. Mira's smile disappeared permanently. Her desperate cries in the night and the marks on her body persisted throughout the time I lived in the shantytown.

One of our other neighbors, who lived with her husband and many small children in the house directly in back of ours, facing the ocean head on and contending with its fury, had a beautiful teenage daughter named Dulce. Dulce had a curvaceous figure, long black hair and deep green eyes. She was the prettiest girl I had ever seen. I never missed the opportunity to look at Dulce. One day she told us that she was going to be a model. Soon after, Dulce took a bus to Rio de Janeiro and later sent money and a letter home to her mother, Dona Neli. Dulce announced her plans to come back and move the whole family from the shantytown to Rio. Dona Neli walked around carrying the letter. She read it to the neighbors and repeated the sentence that would turn her life around: "Move out of the *invasão* to Rio de Janeiro." Soon after, Dona Neli left with her husband and their many children to live in a furnished apartment with Dulce, the model. I wondered what models did and where Rio de Janeiro was. I was fifteen and had not yet seen or held a map of Brazil in my hands. We never heard from either Dulce or Dona Neli again.

Dona Tidinha and Seu José lived to the left of our house on the way to the beach. Seu José came home each day in the late afternoon carrying bread in a brown bag and groceries wrapped in newspaper. Dona Tidinha sewed, washed, and cleaned her house. Once I started school, I often walked by her house with my books under my arms on my way to study on the rocks by the clear water. As soon as she saw me coming, Dona Tidinha leaned out the front window and signaled to me. She bent her head down to my ear and asked in a whisper, "Have you eaten anything today, Leda?"

"No, I haven't," I answered in the same soft voice.

"Come in the house," she said.

I approached Dona Tidinha shyly. She quickly closed the window and door behind me.

"I don't want anybody in the neighborhood to see you coming in my house and think they can do the same," she said. "I don't have enough food to feed everybody," she added.

Without saying much, Dona Tidinha told me to sit down at her small table, and she put a speckled ripe banana and a piece of bread in my hands.

"Eat it, and don't tell anyone that I give you anything," she repeated. "God knows I don't have enough to give if others come knocking on my door."

"I won't say anything to anyone, Dona Tidinha," I replied.

I held the banana in one hand and the hard bread in the other, and I took one bite of the banana and one bite of the bread. They tasted good together. I chewed them, and food soothed my empty stomach. Dona Tidinha watched from her seat across the table. Neither of us had much to say. She remained silent, watching me while I finished chewing the last bite of banana and bread. I liked that about Dona Tidinha, her quiet way of feeding me. I got up and walked toward the door after eating. When I looked back, I saw Dona Tidinha watching me while I skipped over the fetid sand and the small rocks, pinching my nose tightly with one hand while holding my book with the other. I reached the tall rocks and sat down to study.

Dona Bete lived along the small dirt slope a few houses below us. People called her *Bete Seca*—Dry Bete due to her extreme thinness. People believed she could be blown in the wind like a piece of straw. She walked by the empty lot in front of our house every morning with her daughters, Laura, Lena and Lili, and a small son. They crossed the highway to enter the neighborhood of good homes, directly opposite the shantytown, where they begged from house to house. They walked back late in the afternoon with bags in their hands, their bodies contorted from fatigue and the heat. Some days the family rode the bus to the city, to a place called Pelourinho, a popular historic tourist spot, where they spent the day begging. The family used the same method Fernando had used in Castro Alves: wrapping pieces of bloody cow lungs on one leg and limping around, pretending to be crippled.

In an unfinished house across from our neighbor Dona Tidinha lived a woman named Maria with her husband, Seu José, their five girls and three boys, her parents, Dona Nenê e Seu Augustinho, and her brother, João. One day, Maria came to our house seeking help. She said her husband had come home with an incredible headache. I went to the house and found Seu José lying on the ground, writhing in pain. I rushed out to stand by the highway to flag a car for help. A driver stopped, and after I explained the situation, he drove Maria's husband to the public hospital, where he died of a brain tumor a few weeks later.

Seu José left Maria with eight children and no money or other resources. I fell in love with Maria's four beautiful young daughters and went over to their house to brush their long dark hair. I felt connected to Maria and her daughters, Marta, Marli, Susana, and Mónica, maybe because we shared the same space and struggles. I could not wait for a chance to be at their house. I only stopped coming when one of Maria's brothers, João, wanted to date me. I had no interest in dating. The move to Salvador was overwhelming enough for me.

The two-lane highway that ran in front of the *invasão* was treacherous day and night. When I had to cross the road to go to school, I would stand in front of our house and look both ways until the cars were so far away that they appeared small. I ran across as fast as I could. Gaia warned me to be careful because the cars traveled at high rates of speeds and would never slow down or stop for anyone. In our culture, the automobile had the right of way. Accidents and deaths on the highway were daily occurrences as cars and buses struck people from our shantytown. Few survived. One day, a bus traveling at high speed ran over Dona Nenê, Maria's mother, who often crossed the highway to gather herbs in the wooded area and to lay her clothes to dry on a stretch of grass behind the road. She later died from the injuries.

Another day, a bus threw Seu Isaías, another neighbor, into the air like a ragdoll. He was thin, crippled, and lived a few houses down from ours. His body bounced on top of a car in front of the bus that hit him and landed on the hot asphalt. I had seen Seu Isaías walk home on crutches alongside the road in the evening. I saw him in the morning the day he was killed. Seu Isaías had been on his way home after a long day of begging.

A bus traveling at high speed also killed two other neighbors, Seu Sebastião's wife and Seu Pessoa, while they were crossing the road. And when my sister Miriam did not come home from school one afternoon, Mother worried. A neighbor later knocked on our door to tell us that she saw a driver take Miriam to a public hospital after a car hit her as she got off the bus. I rode the bus with Mother to visit Miriam. She survived but had many stitches on her head and a broken arm. The day Miriam walked to the bus on her way to the hospital to have the stitches and the cast removed, a car hit her again. And again, Miriam survived with only a few scratches.

Most of the women in the *invasão* were laundresses. They crossed the busy highway to dry their clothes in the empty lot across the road, balancing a basin of clothes on their heads and a child on their hips. In addition to washing their own clothes, the women earned a living doing the laundry of those who lived in the nicer homes. The women were often hit by cars and tossed up in the air, like toys. Bodies and basins full of clothes landed in all directions. Their bloody and broken bodies would remain under the hot sun for hours until an ambulance eventually appeared to gather the pieces and cart them away.

On weekends and holidays, the ocean that growled in the backyard offered the dwellers some leisure time. They gathered at the small semicircular beach and lay on the sand to relax and enjoy the sun. Some went into the water, sometimes venturing too far out. A strong wave or a sudden underwater current could take a swimmer by surprise, like a sea monster, and suck him into the deep waters. Many times, a cry for help failed to summon a brave soul to save the bather, who, after bobbing up and down, disappeared from sight. The body reappeared on the beach a few days later, bloated and disfigured from swallowing the water and drowning and from the vigorous shuffling of the waves.

If I was around and heard the desperate cries for help, I covered my ears and ran away. I crossed the highway and walked up the long, steep hill behind the nicer homes where I found a place to look at the flowers that grew wild in the area, including birds of paradise. I would sit on a log behind a fancy restaurant on top of the hill and admire the plant's tall stems, long leaves, and vibrant red, yellow, and blue flowers that looked like a bird's head. I looked at the flowers for a while and imagined them freeing themselves from their stems and taking off as if they had suddenly turned into real birds. I closed my eyes. In my head, I envisioned myself transformed into a colorful bird, flying away to a distant forest with countless tall trees, where I could drink water from fresh streams, eat fruit, and skip from tree to tree.

My mind's eyes saw how peaceful paradise would be. The place that I imagined had no highway or turmoil. My neighbors sunbathed in calm waters while looking at the birds of paradise circling around in perfect harmony. The thoughts soothed my soul. I walked back home with the red, yellow, and blue flowers I had been staring at for so long stamped on my memory. Everything I saw on my path suddenly turned into the bright colors of the birds of paradise. I forgot about the death of a neighbor for a while, at least until the ambulance came to retrieve the body or it washed ashore the following day. If I couldn't run to my spot at the top of the hill to visit the birds of paradise, I covered my ears and stayed on my straw mat in the narrow alley in front of my house.

There was another commotion in the *invasão*. When the neighborhood children heard it, they would race to the edge of the highway where they watched a procession of black cars with small flags flying on their sides. From the steps in front of our house, I imagined that important people were riding in the gleaming cars because the windows were always closed. A procession of attentive police officers rode alongside and led the way with loud horns, whistles, and blaring sirens. The parade of cars went by in a flash, and I wished that they would slow down so that I could admire the cars and motorcycles and enjoy the show a bit more.

Throughout April 1964, after school started, trucks with cannons and soldiers often went by on the highway. The children weren't thrilled to watch them, and some mothers kept them behind locked doors. They were afraid. They scared me, too, and I stayed away when I heard the roaring noise of the big machines approaching on the tar road. No one in the neighborhood knew where the war apparatus was coming from or going to; no one had any idea of what was happening in the national arena. Our daily survival occupied our bodies and minds. It was only years later that I learned that the military display that we had witnessed was the Brazilian coup d'état, the military takeover of the country that lasted until 1985. My siblings vividly remember the uproar on the highway, but they still do not realize the full extent of the event. We were oblivious to history unfolding before our eyes.

Gaia often crossed the highway with our aluminum basin on her head to wash our clothes on the vacant piece of land. Her lean figure stood by the road for a long while, the cars zooming by, her head turning left and right and then left again to quickly judge a safe distance between herself and the fast-approaching cars. Gaia, like the other women, also carried our clothes to wash by the well on the bottom of the beach during low tide.

When Gaia first arrived in Salvador and saw the body of blue water in our backyard, she thought that the days of having to walk long distances to find water to wash with were gone. But when Gaia took the basin full of clothes to the beach and went to fetch the ocean water for the wash, a neighbor approached laughingly and explained to Gaia what everyone already knew about the ocean.

"This isn't like a pond or a river," the neighbor said. "This is the Atlantic Ocean. The water is too salty. It's no good for washing, drinking, or anything of the kind. It'll cut right through the soap and destroy your skin and the clothes if you try to wash them."

"Oh, what a waste," Gaia responded.

After that, Gaia took the clothes across the road and fetched water from the well on the beach. Our clothes lay on the rocks by the ocean during low tide or on the thin grass across the highway, like a patchwork quilt blowing in the wind. In the process, the wash accumulated more dirt and dust from the road than bright rays from the sun. I often crossed the road with Gaia and longed for our time back in Castro Alves, where we walked to the woods to find clear water to wash our clothes.

Life in Salvador was noisy and distressing. The ocean rumbled in the backyard. The cars zoomed by on the highway. The neighbors cried in painful times. My life was hard in Castro Alves, but I never ran short of places to walk to. I often ached for the trips we took to the woods in December to eat wild berries and to gather the green foliage for Ua's *presépio*. I longed for the early morning walks to the dairy farm to drink milk and the gathering of fruits to bring home. I could still smell the cooking and roasting of caju nuts in the backyard. I wanted to walk around the neighborhood again with my friend Creusa. Above all, I missed the stories my mother and siblings would tell on dark nights and the songs and games we sang and played under the sparkling moon. I even missed the quiet spot where I slept off my hunger. I felt incredibly disconnected from my family and from nature in Salvador. I was extremely lonely and caged in a fetid house between a rock and a hard place—with a powerful ocean in the back and a dangerous highway in the front. The samba of survival became mine, and I was united with it. I danced to the rhythm that circumstances dealt me. I followed my instincts closely, determined as ever to make it through.

15. Paralyzed Papayas

My father's niece Angela married Odilo. Odilo owned a cleaning supply business, and he was also our landlord. When Odilo's business was doing well, he hired Tatai to sell his products at restaurants, cafeterias, hospitals, and door to door. Fernando paid our rent, which was deducted from his paycheck at Odilo's demand. Soon after I arrived in Salvador, Angela began visiting our shantytown. I first saw her one afternoon walking in high heels and arm in arm with a tall black man she called her chauffeur. Her chauffer had parked the car in the empty area in front of our house. He guided Angela through the uneven dirt path and stone steps, then returned to the car to stand beside it, waiting for her to finish. Mother was surprised. She had not seen Angela since moving to our house, which she found with Angela's help. We did not have a table or any chairs. Visitors had to sit outside on the steps leading to the empty lot or on one of the two beds in the front bedroom.

Angela, happy and glamorous, with charcoal black hair and a tight-fitting flowered dress, could not sit on the front steps, so Mother opened the window and guided her to the front bedroom where they sat on a corner of the bed and talked. After a while, they said goodbye, and Angela walked toward the door. The chauffeur hurried to take her hand and walk her to the car. She sat in the back seat as they drove away, her hair blowing in the wind.

A few weeks passed. Angela came back, this time on the city bus in mid-morning and talked with Mother again for a while. From my straw mat on the corridor by the window, I heard Angela laughing. And when it was noon, and she realized that we had nothing to eat in the house, she handed Gaia money to buy food at Seu Jacinto's store, a small front room in his shack where he sold fruits, vegetables, eggs, dry goods, and liquor. Gaia made lunch, and Angela ate with us, talkative and happy. By mid-afternoon, a white van parked in the empty lot in front, and a blue-eyed, tall, handsome Spanish man named Mauro walked in the house and asked for Angela. She introduced him as her friend and whispered something in Mother's ear. Soon the two walked into the front bedroom and talked for a long while sitting on the bed. Mother ordered us to stay away, and I heard their whispering voices. At dusk, Mauro drove away in his van, and Angela walked alone to take the bus home.

Angela came again to meet Mauro at our house another afternoon. This time Mauro walked in carrying a large box of pastries that he had made at the bakery where he worked. Once again, they talked for a short time in the bedroom, then walked with Gaia to the bus stop to go to the remote beaches where the three spent the rest of the day. The couple chose to ride the bus instead of taking Mauro's van because the van belonged to the bakery. It had big blue and red lettering with yellow and white pictures of pastries. Mauro was afraid to be seen driving in daylight with women in the van. Gaia talked about Angela and Mauro spending their time at the beach holding hands, rolling on the white sand, and bathing. My sister maintained her distance from the pair and later joined them to eat at a local restaurant. They rode the bus back to the house at sundown.

Angela returned to our house many more times. I imagine she felt safe meeting Mauro there. She knew no one would think of our house as a place for a rendezvous, and we would not mention it to anyone because Mother was thankful to Angela for convincing her husband to rent the house to Fernando. They rode the bus to the beach with Gaia each time until Angela became pregnant. Then their encounters at the house and at the beach became less and less frequent until they stopped altogether. I did not see much of Angela or Mauro after that. I missed her cheerfulness, the food that she sometimes bought, and Mauro's pastries. Gaia reminisced about the long bus rides to the beaches and the wonderful foods that she ate at the restaurants. Angela had a baby girl, who my family said looked just like Mauro.

Miriam, who was eighteen, enrolled in classes to become a schoolteacher. The days Miriam arrived home after a long bus ride from school and found nothing to eat in the house, she went directly to bed to sleep off her hunger, wearing her white and blue uniform. She had no energy to change out of her school clothes. One hot afternoon when Angela came to the house and saw Miriam in a deep sleep still in her uniform, she asked my sister to move in with her family for a while. I did not see much of Miriam after that. She spent most of her time with Angela and her family. They lived a distance from us, in one of the elite suburbs. My sister had a pretty body and face. She was outgoing and enjoyed going to social events at the clubs with Angela's two elder daughters and taking part in the celebrations they organized.

Miriam seldom came home. When she did, she showed up late in the afternoon in the company of Angela's well-kept daughters and the chauffeur who parked the car in front of the house and stood waiting for them. As soon as the black car stopped, I looked up from my straw mat by the window and saw Miriam and the girls open the car door and run down the steps to the house. I looked closely at them as they came near.

"Where's Mother?" Miriam asked.

"She's resting," I answered.

I did not know where my sister and our stylish cousins came from or why they were always in a hurry. Nor did I understand why Miriam asked about Mother. She knew that our mother always rested in the afternoon. They headed to the bedroom to see Mother and toward the bathroom. Miriam seemed to have forgotten that our toilet was always plugged up. She turned away and directed the girls to the smelly and muddy narrow alley where they pulled down their panties and urinated. We also relieved ourselves in the alley whenever the bathroom was badly flooded and the caustic soda would not work, or if the night was too cold or wet. We resorted to using the alley when the water was too high to head to the beach.

Miriam's visits never lasted long. After kissing Mother and peeing in the alley, she would climb the stairs to the parked car, jump in the back seat, and slam the car door. She never looked back at me. The chauffeur drove away with the same lightning speed with which they had arrived, only to reappear several weeks later.

The car mingled with the other fast cars on the congested highway. As I watched the car disappear, I sat back on my straw mat, wishing there was some place for me to go so that I could come back to the shantytown only for a very short visit to pee and kiss Mother. I would be in and out of the house fast, the way Miriam came with our cousins.

I was feeling lonely and disconnected and became more introspective. My isolation and silence were painful. I lived inside my head. Ua had stayed in Castro Alves; Miriam spent most of her time with Angela and her family, and I did not know how to talk to my brothers or Mother. She did not say much, nor was I able to tell her anything. She cooked vegetables, or fish when we had some, or washed our clothes when we had soap. Most of the afternoon, Mother was tired and rested in the front bedroom. I wanted an active mother, someone to converse with, feed me and buy me books. Gaia had left the house to live with the neighbor Dona Lucinda and her son, Zeca. My brothers were out most of the day either working or searching for something to eat or do.

Sometimes I felt so painfully lonely that I thought something was wrong with me. I wanted to skip the fetid sand and the small rocks in the backyard to reach the tall rocks. There I could find a cave close to the blue water and hide forever. I wished that the ocean water would recede so that I could reach the large black rocks that were farther out. There I could stay quietly in my cave, and no one would find me. And if the high waves came, I would close my eyes, and ride them to a calm, distant, and clean place where I would have food to eat, friends, and be able to study.

One day, I learned about Miriam's glamorous life when I overheard Tatai telling Mother about Angela's furnished apartment, complete with maids and cooks who prepared tasty food. The girls wore pretty clothes and had a seamstress to sew colorful costumes for the street dances and parades at the social clubs during carnival time in February. Angela organized dances and make-believe weddings with popular theme fashions, live music, and food for the St. John's festivities in June. Miriam and the girls competed for the best prizes and won many times.

The much-revered New Year's Eve celebrations, the *Reveillon*, at the social clubs were extravaganzas that lasted from dusk to dawn. Once, Miriam and Tatai spoke to Mother about the time they danced with Angela's group at the club. They described the trips they took to the famous enchanted lagoon on the shoreline called *Abaeté*. At the lagoon, under a silvery full moon, lovers, poets, and musicians gathered with delight and found inspiration among the white sand dunes, the shimmering water, and the palm trees.

I dreamt of Angela's social clubs, the festivities, and the *Abaeté* Lagoon. I felt that they were part of another universe I did not belong to, a fantastic world so near yet so far. From my straw mat, I imagined my skinny body covered with glimmering costumes, parading on the streets to loud music and dancing day and night during the carnival. In my dreams, Tatai escorted me to the ballroom. I was the Columbine, he the Harlequin. We danced the entire time. All eyes were on me.

During the entire time I lived in Brazil, I never visited a social club. I did not belong to the elite upper class nor did I live with Angela's family. Besides, I was not considered pretty enough to gain Angela's attention as Miriam had. The closest I came to a social club was when the mayor of Salvador removed the "invaders" from the shantytown in Ondina and relocated them to another slum close to an hour away by bus, in a place called Boca do Rio. There, I saw the Portuguese Club, across from the bus stop on the ocean side. It was surrounded by barbed wire and tall walls, topped with sharp and shiny pieces of broken glass shining in the sun. They prevented trespassing.

In our house, Mother cleaned and did what she could. She would do my brothers' laundry when Gaia moved out and cared for Rita, Gaia's young daughter. Mother moved slowly due to the bulging varicose veins in her legs and rested when she was tired. My older brothers were either working or looking for a job, and my younger siblings were never around. The youngest one, Wilson, eight at the time, attended a public school across the highway.

One afternoon during the school year, a couple of male teachers appeared at our door with Wilson in their arms. My brother was weak from lack of food and had fainted at his desk at school. At first, the instructor thought Wilson had fallen asleep but realized he was unconscious when he did not wake up. One teacher told Mother that my brother might have a case of hookworms and recommended that she go to the pharmacy to buy some purgative. Mother knew better and disregarded the teacher's advice.

Instead, Mother sent my brother Raimundo with his fishing rod to the ocean to catch a fish or two so that she could feed Wilson. She then climbed the front stairway to the top of the papaya tree that she had planted on the left side of the house at the corner of the steps that led to the road. Mother's papaya tree was one of the very few that grew in our shantytown, thriving among dry and unhealthy palm trees. She picked some green papayas, peeled and cut them into cubes and made a stew with thick yellow palm oil for Wilson to eat until Raimundo could return with the bluefish that she was sure he would catch. Raimundo had become a good fisherman.

Mother had planted her papaya tree from a seed when she first arrived at the capital. The tree received lots of rain and sunshine. It grew tall, but during the time it took to begin bearing small white flowers in the shape of stars and fruits, I never saw a papaya grow long enough to mature and ripen. Mother had no choice but to always pick the papayas when they were still green. I wondered how big Mother's papayas would have grown and how sweet they would have tasted if they only had a chance to grow. She picked the young and green fruit to make a stew to feed us when everything else failed, and when she knew that we had been hungry for a bit too long.

When I think of Mother's papayas, I see her children as being in a similar situation as her tree. The tree received abundant sunlight and rain; it absorbed enough nutrients from the terrain, although sandy and salty; and it grew, though the flowers could never fully develop into mature fruit. Mother was always forced to pick her young papayas to ease the hunger of her children, who never had the opportunity to grow and develop their potential as deserving human beings. The lack of food, schooling, guidance, and basic needs from the time Mother's children were born never gave them a chance to mature and to develop as fully as nature would have allowed.

In spite of the many difficulties in Salvador, we experienced less frequent stretches of hunger than we did in Castro Alves. Since the family had dispersed, there were fewer of us to feed during the day. Though inconsistent, my older brothers brought some food home. The males living in the shantytown improvised small bombs and threw them in the water by the small beach a short distance away from the houses, in the spot where people bathed. As soon as we would hear the loud explosions and the cry of *bomba*, we would rush with empty containers in hand to collect the silver sardines that the powerful explosions had washed to the shore. We piled the fish, still trembling, in our pots and pans and took them to the small puddles of saltwater between the big rocks to clean them. Once finished, we would carry the sardines home and Mother would make a fish stew. Sometimes it would be the only food we ate that day.

My older fun-loving brother, Tatai, helped the family, but not consistently; he was often unemployed. He left the house early in the morning to look for work and came home late at night after visiting with his girlfriend who lived in the Cidade Baixa, far away in the lower part of the city. My brother Célio had a steady job, but he spent most of his money on liquor. My three older brothers were our basic source of provisions, and whenever they failed to give us enough food, we went hungry.

A bus stopped in front of our house to take Fernando to work at Petrobrás, the giant oil company on the outskirts of the city where he worked as an aide in the cafeteria. On the days that we went without eating, we got out of bed at midnight when Fernando arrived, to eat the leftovers he brought home in aluminum containers and wrapped in newspapers. On his days off and at the end of the month when he got paid, Fernando disappeared from sight only to reappear days later, drained, dirty, penniless and putrid. He spent his month's pay at the brothels. In just a few days, my brother wasted everything he had earned in an entire month. His pockets were bare. I did not understand Fernando's whereabouts very well, but later in life, I realized what he had been doing. I came to understand why the cherished *cantina* in the wooden box full of food that came in Castro Alves was always late, if it arrived at all. My brother's heart was in the right place; however, his troubled mind and upbringing contributed to his irresponsible and disturbing behavior.

Around that time, Fernando became sick with infections, and aches and pains that were caused by his venereal diseases. In addition to his rotten ears, Fernando had acquired a rotten penis. The pus from his ears dripped down his neck and soaked his shirts. The secretions from his penis drenched his underwear and pants, ran down his legs, and dripped on the cement floor. Fernando smelled bad in two places. Sometimes, he stayed out of work for days and limped around the house. To dress his wounded penis, he would pull down his pants, sit on the edge of his bed in the front bedroom where he slept and hold it in one hand, carefully rubbing iodine over it with the other. He would wrap it gently in white gauze like a mother caring for a newborn baby. Fernando reminded me of the men dressing their birds' red heads after cockfights in the neighborhood. He walked around slowly, legs apart.

Mother worried about my brother's infections and tried to remedy the pain with her herbs. The thought of her younger daughters catching Fernando's disease troubled Mother deeply.

"For God's sake, stay away from Fernando and don't ever touch his pants or underwear," she often reminded Miriam and me.

"If any of you catch his terrible diseases, I won't know what to do anymore," she said.

Mother tried hard to cure Fernando's infection. She sent me to the woods across the highway and up the hill to find *mastruz*, the bitter cress she used to cure everything. She believed the herb would kill whatever was ailing Fernando. I crossed the highway past the nice homes and went up the hill to gather *mastruz*. I later walked back with a bunch of herbs tied in a bundle over my head and handed them to Mother, who waited outside the house. She added the *mastruz* to water in our kerosene can. She boiled the water over a crackling fire built over three pointed rocks arranged in the shape of a triangle. She stood beside the smoky fire in the small dirt strip in the front of the house by the left of the steps where she had planted her papaya tree. Mother picked up Fernando's caked underwear from a pile with a long wooden stick and threw them into the boiling water in the kerosene can. The underwear that was too smelly for Mother to handle was put in a different pile to burn in the fire. Fernando's underwear turned dark green as soon as it hit the boiling water in the kerosene can and mingled with the bitter cress that went popping up and down in the bubbling water. Mother kept turning them around and around with her stick as if stirring beans in our clay pot with a wooden spoon. I stood by Mother's side but away from the underwear and gathered more scraps of wood to add to the fire and to the new one that she built to rinse the garments. It took a long time to boil Fernando's underwear, and the smoke got in our eyes and throat.

Mother stepped aside to wipe her tearing eyes and clear her throat. She looked at me by her side. In a low, calm voice she repeated another of her favorite sayings that meant that conditions could change and that no situation in life lasts forever, *Nem todo tempo cavalo caga no meio da estrada*—Horses don't always crap on the road. She returned to tend to the fire, transferring Fernando's green underpants to the other kerosene can of boiling water over the second fire. She wanted to kill the germs and bleach the garment that was completely green from the *mastruz*.

Over two years, Mother built many more fires in front of our house whenever the caked underwear piled up. I crossed the highway many afternoons and walked up the hill to the woods to gather *mastruz*. But Fernando continued his visits to the city's brothels until he finally lost his job with Petrobrás in 1967. He had failed to show up for work too many times. I doubt that he was ever completely cured of his sicknesses.

Thinking of my mother now, I embrace and carry her away from that fire, away from Fernando's underwear, away from that house, and away from all her suffering. In my mind's eye, I set Mother on the side of our house on Paramirim Street, where she was happy making lace with singing *bilros*. And I set Mother on a throne so high she can touch the sky.

To the right of our home was a black adobe house attached to ours. Our neighbor Dona Lucinda and her son Zeca lived there. Zeca was a 6-foot-tall, thin truck driver in his 30s. I always stared at his face when he spoke. He stuttered badly, opening his mouth wide and rolling his eyes. His lips trembled repeatedly while touching each other, and for a while you could only see the white of Zeca's eyes. When his lips stopped moving, the words would suddenly burst out, one syllable at a time, followed by long pauses, loud explosions of air, and shortness of breath. It looked like he was having a heart attack.

In the evening, Zeca came home and parked his dump truck in the square empty lot out front. On weekends, some of the many children he had fathered—and left behind with their mothers to raise—gathered at his mother's house for a visit. He took his kids for a ride in his dump truck. The weekends when no one came, Zeca would walk past our house to spend his day drinking at Seu Jacinto's store at the end of the corridor of homes. He came stumbling past our house in the evening, drunk and mumbling his words.

Gaia befriended Zeca's mother, Dona Lucinda, who seemed very ill. The two women spent afternoons in her house chatting, sewing, or doing chores. One afternoon, Gaia told Mother she was helping Dona Lucinda gather *capim-santo*, holy grass—a tall, sweet herb used to cure colds and other infirmities—in the woods up the hill. The two women walked past our house in the afternoon on trips that lasted until dusk. Gaia wore her pretty black hair down and her one flowered dress, which raised Mother's suspicions.

"What the devil kinds of *capim-santo* are you and Dona Lucinda looking for that take the whole afternoon and into the evening, and you need to wear your best dress, Gaia?" Mother asked one day.

"Dona Lucinda can't walk very fast, Mother. It takes her a long time to move. She coughs a lot, gets tired, and needs rest. I wore my dress because all my clothes were dirty," Gaia explained.

One sunny afternoon when Gaia left with Dona Lucinda to gather *capim-santo*, a young man in the neighborhood saw my sister entering Zeca's dump truck parked by the road and told Fernando. We soon found out that Gaia and Zeca had been secretly meeting in the woods instead of gathering herbs with Dona Lucinda. Fernando got angry with Gaia and they started fighting.

"What do you want with Zeca, Gaia? This drunk will leave you for another woman as soon as he gets you pregnant the way he has done to many other women. Don't you see that?" Fernando asked.

"This is none of your business. This house stinks too badly. I'm tired of it and don't want to stay here anymore. I will do as I wish," said Gaia.

"For you to do as you wish you should live under your own roof and not under the roof I pay for. You should leave this stinky house soon," demanded Fernando.

"I will," Gaia replied.

After a few more fights, Gaia wrapped her good dress and her few belongings in a bundle tied in a knot, a *trouxa*, and walked over to Dona Lucinda's house. She never came back. Her firstborn daughter, Rita, stayed with Mother. Zeca did not want the girl to live with them. She was white. He was black. I did not see Gaia for a long while, even though the houses were attached. She kept to herself. The first time I saw her after she had left was when she was carrying a big aluminum basin full of clothes on her head and walking toward the empty lot across the highway to dry them. Her eyes were downcast when she passed our house. Her figure was rounded.

Gaia was pregnant. She soon gave birth to a child and more births followed, one after another, just like Mother. Dona Lucinda's house had dark walls, unpainted adobe, and dirt floors. I went there to see Gaia and her newborn, a tiny baby boy who was wrapped in a cotton blanket. His eyes were closed. He had difficulty, Gaia said that the child had not cried yet, not at birth or afterward. He did not want to eat and died a few days later. Gaia wrapped the body in a white cloth and carefully set it in an old shoebox, which she gave to Zeca to take away. Zeca went up the dirt ramp. He set his deceased son next to him in his rusty dump truck and drove away to Nina Rodriguez, the public teaching hospital in the center of town that received the bodies of the indigent. There, Zeca left his dead child for the medical students to study.

Soon after, Gaia was pregnant again. She gave birth to another boy, who lived only three months. She had a girl who survived although she was also born malnourished. My sister was now as thin as a rail and continued miscarrying Zeca's babies. Her once flattering figure had lost its shape. She looked like a walking stick. Her smooth skin gave way to premature wrinkles. I watched her contagious smile fade away little by little. I stopped visiting her and the children altogether. It pained me. I could not do much for Gaia. Zeca, I later learned, had tuberculosis, syphilis, and other venereal diseases.

Célio worked for the City Department of Transportation, a job that he found thanks to the blonde lady who used to give Mother food on Saturdays in Castro Alves. Célio started his day early in the morning. In the afternoon, he would come home drunk. His co-workers dropped him off in front of the house. He always carried a piece of cow liver wrapped in blood-stained newspaper under his arm. Célio stumbled out of the truck, down the dirt path to the stairway. When he entered the house, he headed straight to the back bedroom and opened an iron frame cot, where he slept the rest of the afternoon, with the bloody cow liver nearby.

In the evening, Célio would wake up from his deep sleep half-drunk, unbalanced, vulgar, and mean. Hands shaky, legs wobbly, and his face red, my brother picked up his half-wrapped piece of cow liver from the cement floor and headed to our kitchen. He planted himself by the sink to sharpen the knife to filet the liver, rubbing the blade back and forth alongside the cement sink top time and again. He looked at the rest of us out of the corner of his eyes. Under his breath, he mumbled words of rage. The image of the immovable foaming bull in Castro Alves came to mind. Célio was the fairest of my siblings, with hazel eyes and, because he worked outdoors year-round, his hair turned golden blond, his skin tanned, and his nose was red from the effects of the sun and alcohol.

Some days, Célio wobbled home with his cow liver, stumbled through the front door and fell asleep on the cement floor. After a few hours, he awoke still half-drunk and searched in his pocket for his wallet in frenzy. He turned violent, yelling and calling the rest of us miserable starving thieves—like what the neighbors in Castro Alves used to call us when their chickens disappeared. My brother claimed that we stole his money. I do not know if anyone in the house took Célio's money, but I remember Mother mentioning that my brother rarely gave her any part of his paychecks. He spent them on alcohol and his cow liver.

On most days, my brother Tatai left the house early with a toolbox in hand. He traveled around the city servicing the cooling machines for tropical drinks in cafeterias and restaurants. When he did not have cooling machines to fix, Tatai worked at odd jobs, mostly cutting and delivering glass for a factory. When Tatai did find work, he helped Mother with money left after he paid his expenses.

My brother Eduardo learned to drive and worked maneuvering cars in and out of a small parking lot in the city. He brought money home when he had some. Our youngest brother, Wilson, continued attending the public school across the highway in the good neighborhood, where he endured many more fainting spells. The second youngest, Raimundo, who had left school in the fourth grade, helped Eduardo maneuver cars in the parking lot.

In our house, no one had much to say about anyone else's fate. Our lives were like Mother's papayas, picked before they ripened, or like dry leaves fallen from the tree and left to the mercy of the wind. Any direction the wind blew, we went with it. We didn't have the luxury to make choices. We had no control over anything. Our lives were determined by our living conditions and whatever trap we fell into. We were doomed to remain there, without help, without guidance. Our basic needs were never met. We received no public services. Everyone in my family knew this unspoken truth, and everyone accepted it. No one talked about it. No one rebelled. No one asked questions. All went the way of the wind.

16. Across the Highway

Around the time the school year began in March, I worried whether I would ever be able to go to school again due to my living in the *invasão*. One afternoon, I heard a loudspeaker attached to the top of a van blasting music across the highway. Then a voice came on to announce the opening of a new school in the affluent neighborhood.

I jumped up from the front steps where I sometimes sat to look at Mother's papaya flowers, and I ran inside to tell her the news.

"Mother, I'm going to follow the car with the loudspeaker," I said. "I want to ask the driver about the new school."

"I'll come with you," she replied.

Mother seldom left the house, but to my surprise she took my hand and we crossed the highway. She was a stocky woman with thick varicose veins and could not walk quickly. I let go of her hand and ran ahead to catch up with the car driving circles around the nice neighborhood, tossing colorful paper into the air. I caught one of the pamphlets.

The following morning, Mother and I crossed the highway again to look for the address of the Social Institute of Bahia. The school building was small, with cement walls designed in a way that allowed you to peer inside if you bent your head to look through perpendicular openings. There were only a few rooms, a spacious yard, and a banana plantation in the backyard. Mother and I went inside and sat in a small office before meeting with the principal, Dona Maria Alice. She told Mother to send me to school to be tested the next morning. I awoke with the sun and hurried to school. When Dona Leonor, the assistant to the principal, told me that I had passed the tests and would receive a scholarship to attend, I was thrilled. There were seven girls and one boy in my class.

At fifteen, when I headed into the first year of secondary school, I was skeletal, introspective and shy. At that time, the Brazilian education system consisted of five years of primary school and seven years of secondary, split between four years equivalent to middle school, and three years of high school. Students could opt out of high school and attend a technical institution of their choice.

Soon after I started secondary school, my older brothers bought me my first book. Mother returned to waking up early in the morning to make couscous to sell from our windowsill. But her efforts were not successful. I arranged the unsold slices on a plate covered with a damp white cloth and went knocking on the neighbors' doors to try to sell them. My older brothers contributed what they could. With the money, I rode a bus with Fernando to buy some school supplies as well as fabric for my uniform. Mother sewed a white blouse for me, a navy-blue skirt for class, and, for physical education, a pair of blue shorts with tight elastic on the legs. Every Wednesday, I would wash my single white blouse and a pair of socks.

In my eyes, my classmates were well groomed and polished. I would not know until later that they came from the middle-class because by comparison to them I was poor. Most of the girls were talkative, had bright smiles, white teeth, and more flesh on their bones than I had on mine. I felt as if my classmates and I came from different planets, though some of them came from very modest backgrounds. Everything was foreign to me. The many emotions I experienced at once overwhelmed me. I felt little, unclean, ugly, and too short. I cried in class once and hid in a corner. In Castro Alves, I had learned the importance of one's looks when the mother of one of my classmates rejected me because of my appearance. In the Brazilian culture, girls strived to be attractive, even the poorest ones. If they had only one dress to wear, they would wash and iron it before putting it on. Girls always wanted to look good, often wearing high-heeled shoes and stylish hair styles. I did not have the luxury of worrying about buying things to make me look attractive; I did not have money to buy food to put in my stomach.

Although being around my classmates was painful at first, I continued going to school, wearing my white blouse, navy-blue skirt, white socks, and black shoes uniform. I learned to turn away when the girls approached. I looked down when their eyes met mine. I was only able to look at them from a distance when they were not aware of me. My body was skin and bones, my hair dry and bushy from the saltwater. I tied it up in a bun most days. My shoes did not shine like my classmates' shoes.

The school principal, Dona Maria Alice, taught religion, ethics, and French. We would walk to a small chapel in the back of the building to pray and sing the French prayers and songs that we had learned. She accompanied us with her guitar and beautiful voice. We read and discussed books, such as Saint-Exupéry's *The Little Prince* and Valfredo Tepe's *The Meaning of Life*. Dona Maria Alice reminded us that our bodies were Temples of God and that they should be respected as such. In life, she taught us, a simple sentence sums up what a person should expect from others: "One gives what one has." She would remind the class that in life, "The essential is invisible to the eye," meaning one should search for the essence in people, not the superficial.

We learned about many historical figures and dates, from the Egyptian pharaohs and the Babylonian King Nebuchadnezzar, to the Athenian and Spartan wars. On Fridays, our teacher, Dona Cremilda, called our names for a weekly oral quiz called *sabatina*. I always became excited and could not wait for my turn to stand in front of the class and spell out the facts and the dates that I had memorized from my history book. I wiggled in my seat wanting to shout the answers my classmates had failed to give, or to offer minor details they left out. Dona Cremilda always looked my way and reminded me, "If you yell out any part of the answer, you'll have to leave the room and sit outside until the *sabatina* is finished."

I did not want to sit outside, so I sat quietly in my corner waiting for my turn to recite the answers to the question Dona Cremilda asked me. I liked history and could remember the exact pages in the book where I had memorized the lesson.

"A good memory you have, Leda," Dona Cremilda would say with a smile. "You're a learner."

Our Portuguese teacher, Dona Regina Helena, diagrammed and analyzed sentences on the board. We gave presentations about the African influence on the Brazilian culture, performed some dances in her class and memorized Portuguese sonnets by Luis de Camões, which we recited standing in front of the room. My favorite was Sonnet 29, in which a shepherd named Jacó was required to serve Labão for seven years with the promise of securing the love of his daughter Raquel. But instead, Jacó was given her sister Lia at the end of his service. After serving seven more years, the lover lamented his misfortune and said that he would serve longer for his beloved Raquel if life weren't short and love everlasting.

Dona Sara, a tall, strong black woman with a kind deep voice, taught math. She began every class by telling us to pay close attention so that we could learn "the first time around and not many times over." She wanted us to correctly solve the problems, so that she did not have to repeat her explanations. I learned to like math and love Dona Sara. One day, the school asked Mother to come for a conference. Dona Sara told Mother that I understood math problems and that she did not have to explain them to me a second time. When Mother told my siblings what she had heard from Dona Sara, they said nothing. They did not even look at me and soon were gone. Survival was the main concern for my siblings. Education, with no immediate reward, was a hard road to travel. Their reactions did not bother me then because I was growing apart from my siblings. I now understand that my family was mostly concerned about finding food and meeting the very basic necessities, such as food, water, sanitation and electricity.

In the years that followed, I did not have the money to buy the required books for most of my classes. I worried that I would not be able to retain the information from my classes to pass the test and exams. After I became more comfortable around my classmates, one of them, a pretty black girl named Olga, who lived in a small house on a hill, offered to lend me her books. I graciously accepted her offer and sometimes took her books home ahead of a scheduled exam. Most of the time, I sat in the corner of the room and paid close attention to the teachers so that I wouldn't have to borrow Olga's books.

When some of my classmates did not understand a math problem or had trouble with the French *Passé Composé*, they would gather around me for help. I explained the subjects in a way that they understood and soon became the unofficial tutor anytime something was unclear to the group. I remember one classmate in particular, a girl named Eraldina. She had left her family in the interior of the state and moved in with an uncle to help raise her cousins in exchange for room and board and the opportunity to attend school. In addition to doing the housework, Eraldina also tended to the family's small store attached to the side of their house. She would come to school unprepared and tired and had difficulty understanding the French verb tenses. Eraldina slowed down the class and made the teacher unhappy. I started helping Eraldina, and she occasionally brought me an extra snack.

In my second year at school, the black holes in my front teeth grew bigger. One afternoon, I walked to see a neighbor, Dona Tidinha. She used to give me a banana and some bread whenever I passed her place. I asked Dona Tidinha if she had pieces of cotton. She handed me the cotton without asking questions. I hurried to stand in front of a small mirror Miriam had hung on the wall by a side window in the center room. With the tip of my fingers, I carefully filled the cavities in my front teeth with small pieces of cotton. Every day, when I spoke, I only slightly opened my mouth. I tried to keep my upper lip snug to my teeth to keep the fillings in place. I often rubbed my tongue against the cotton in my teeth to make sure that it was still covering the black holes. But I was only able to speak briefly before the cotton would fall out. I had to either run to the bathroom or lower my head on the desk to recover the cotton and put it back in place.

Toward the end of the school year in November, one day I had to stay home with a swollen face after a night of crying due to an excruciating toothache. To my surprise, two of my classmates who lived in the nicer neighborhood, Enaide and Vera, who were inseparable friends, crossed the highway and stood by the empty lot calling my name. When I heard their voices, I came to the window keeping both hands in front of my face trying to hide my disfiguration. I had an elephant face. I looked at the two girls in their white and blue uniforms, carrying their books under their arms. Enaide looked at my face.

"Leda," she said, "the teachers gave us our final grades today. You passed French without needing to take the final exams."

"Why weren't you in school today?" Vera asked.

"I have a toothache and couldn't go. I'll go tomorrow," I said.

After taking another quick look at me, my classmates said goodbye, turned around, and crossed the highway to walk home. I stayed at the window watching them until their figures disappeared in the distance. I felt a tremendous sense of relief that they were gone and that they had not walked down the steps to my house. The few times I had to stay home from school and the girls came to give me important news about missed assignments, I would run to the window or meet them out front when I heard their voices. Deep inside, I knew that my classmates would not enter our house, but I always feared that they would forget to stop at the empty lot and call out for me. I knew they knew how bad things were at my house. The living conditions of the *invasão* were well known. But my biggest worry was that they would find Célio sleeping on the floor with his cow liver nearby and his private parts exposed, after having come home drunk and passing out before he could reach the rear bedroom.

My school added more students each year. Some pupils came from the nicer homes in Ondina, others from distant elite suburbs. When they fell behind in their schoolwork or were having difficulty with certain subjects and their mothers asked the assistant principal, Dona Leonor, for help, she recommended me as a tutor. I went to their homes to help their children for an hour or two after school. Sometimes I would spend the entire afternoon at the students' homes, tutoring the entire family in many subjects. I don't remember how much I earned working as a tutor. But I earned enough to pay for some of my books, school supplies, and transportation. I also helped Mother buy groceries and paid for Rita's schooling and books.

I didn't dare ask any of the well-to-do mothers to bring their children to my house for tutoring. With Célio's drunkenness, Fernando's diseases, the lack of furniture, and the horrible stench, it was hard to imagine inviting anyone into that kind of environment. One day, I found out that a mother and one of my students knew where I lived.

"Carlos and I saw you in front of the *invasão*, waiting to cross the road one morning when I drove by. Do you live there, Leda?" a mother asked.

"Yes, I do," was all I said, and I lowered my eyes.

She was silent and left the room.

Soon, I started helping different students, including ones who lived in small shacks in hidden wooded areas, as well as the wealthy ones who resided in the nicer homes surrounded by tall walls and catered to by servants. The mother of a student named Lourdes approached me once as I was leaving school. She asked if I could help her daughter with math. I said that I could. The next afternoon I walked a short distance from our shantytown to a wooded area where they lived in a shack surrounded by mango and banana trees. I sat outside on a bench with Lourdes in the shade of the leafy trees and reviewed the math that was giving her trouble. We studied for a while and when I got up to leave, the mother approached me and paused for a while, as if looking for a way to express unpleasant news.

"I can't pay you, but I'll walk home with you and give one of my ducks to your mother as a present," she finally told me.

I told her not to worry, that I liked helping. Nonetheless, she walked into her backyard and lifted the large duck that had been tied up. She walked home with me and Lourdes carrying the bird for Mother, which we had for lunch the following day.

When I tutored students who lived across the highway in the good neighborhood, I walked to their homes and met their maids at the door. I would first sit in their living rooms and then in their dining rooms after the servants had cleared the tables. At first, the mothers arranged for me to tutor one youngster in the family who was having difficulty in math or another subject. After a while, I was often asked to tutor other members of the family who might be showing weakness in French, Portuguese, history, or geography. Before explaining the subjects to the students, I usually spent some time reviewing their notes and tests or going over the material in their books. Some students were close to my age; others were a bit younger or older.

My school day began at seven in the morning and ended at noon. After classes, I walked home across the highway. Once home, I would change out of my uniform and cover the black cavities in my front teeth with pieces of cotton. If we had any food, I ate and walked back to stand by the highway again, looking right and left, left and right, waiting for a chance to run across to the nice neighborhood without being hit by a car. Some days, when I left the house without breakfast in the morning, ate no snack at mid-morning, and arrived home at midday to find nothing to eat, I wanted to snuggle on my straw mat in the back room and sleep to kill the hunger. Instead, I crossed the highway and walked to the students' homes to tutor them.

I sat in the quiet living rooms adjacent to the dining rooms and waited for the students to finish their noon meals, the biggest meal of the day. The loud voices talking over lunch, the silverware jangling, the passing of plates, and the busy maids walking back and forth carrying the forgotten items to the table kept me alert. The smell of food would arouse fantasies. I imagined myself sitting at a table with plenty of food, eating as much as I wanted, savoring it slowly one bite at a time.

Dona Terezinha was the mother of one of the first students I would cross the highway to tutor. One day, she walked into the living room and saw me sitting quietly on her white sofa. I sat with my hands together and my head down. My skinny body sank into the fluffy seat while the food fantasy danced in my head. Dona Terezinha seemed surprised to see me in her house when most students were at home eating lunch or resting after their noon meal. First, she looked at the clock on the wall as if to check the time I was scheduled to arrive at her home. She then looked at me on her couch as if to confirm what she saw. She quietly approached me.

"Have you eaten lunch yet, Leda?" she asked in a soft voice.

"No, I haven't, Dona Terezinha," I answered hesitantly.

Dona Terezinha walked back to the dining room where the lunch commotion had eased and called to the maid.

"Joana, the teacher is here. Set a plate for her and tell Ritinha to hurry up and get ready, take out her notes, old tests, and books and wait for Leda," she ordered.

I followed Joana to the dining room, head down, walking slowly, almost afraid of stepping on the gleaming hardwood floor. I subconsciously assumed that posture when I walked into nice homes. It was as if I felt unworthy. That feeling stayed with me for a long time until I made a conscious effort to change it. I was accustomed to walking barefoot, unkept many times, feeling different from my classmates, and not having the basic necessities. With my hands clasped between my legs, I sat and waited for the plate of food Joana went to get for me. Bodies moved in and out of the room. Others remained at the table. I sat and said nothing. The embarrassment of eating with the family made me want to disappear so that no one could see me, not at Dona Terezinha's table, not anywhere. My body sank lower in the tall chair. Joana set the plate of food in front of me. I ate it in a hurry. I believe now that I acquired the habit of eating quickly in those nice places, a habit I still have today. Food never tasted so good. Walking home that day, I wished that I could have eaten my food more slowly so that the smell and taste of it would have remained with me longer, like the way I slowly sucked the sugar candy Seu Galdino handed me back in Castro Alves.

Ritinha was a lovely girl two or three years younger than me. I tutored her in math for a couple of hours. I knew how to handle most of the difficulties the students had. They were problems I had solved in class. If the subjects were difficult or new to me, I would quickly open the books to study the formulas. I also looked over the students' notes for a short while before working with them. After my tutoring, Ritinha asked me into the kitchen to help her make *brigadeiro*, a very popular dessert in Brazil. It consists of a mixture of condensed milk, butter, and chocolate powder cooked on the stovetop until caramelized. Ritinha liked making the dessert in the afternoon after her work was finished. It gave me a chance to taste *brigadeiro* for the first time in my life. I ate it quietly. It tasted very sweet and gummy, and I enjoyed it very much but did not tell Ritinha I had not had it before.

I walked to Dona Terezinha's house to tutor Ritinha twice a week. I never worried about being hungry on the days I tutored her. I did not know until later that Joana had orders from Dona Terezinha to feed me no matter the time I arrived at the house. After a few sessions of tutoring Ritinha, she felt more confident and needed less help from me. But an older sister, Rosinha, took her place, and later I also tutored one of her younger brothers, Jorginho. Joana always brought us delicious desserts for a mid-afternoon snack.

Dona Terezinha's mother, Dona Rosa, lived with the family. Dona Rosa was blind, and a maid helped her get around. Dona Rosa knew me by my voice when I was in the house. One afternoon when I was in the kitchen making *brigadeiro* with Ritinha, Dona Rosa approached me and asked if I would take her to Sunday Mass. She explained that her grandchildren slept late and the maids were busy preparing the family breakfast. I said I would, and the following Sunday I woke up a little before six and appeared at the house to walk with Dona Rosa to the school chapel for the early Mass. I walked slowly with Dona Rosa, holding onto her arm. She was frail. During Mass, I whispered in her ear some of the priest's movements to help her visualize the routine. On the way back to the house, Dona Rosa asked me to have breakfast with her. There was the smell of freshly brewed coffee and baked goods in the kitchen. I was excited to eat the cakes, fried plantains, and boiled yams the maids had set on the table for breakfast.

I sat opposite Dona Rosa and ate the large portions the maids served me. The faster I ate, the more food they added to my plate. I no longer felt embarrassed eating at Dona Terezinha's table. Dona Rosa could not see me eating, but I still ate fast because I feared someone in the family would see me eating so much and so fast. The maids, however, seemed delighted to serve me. When it was time for me to go home, they cut and wrapped large pieces of the delicious cakes and told me to give them to my mother. After this feast, I did not hesitate to greet the rising sun with prayers on Sundays. And when the sun went down, I crossed the road again with Mother to take her to the 6 p.m. Mass.

I tutored other students across the highway. It was always the mothers who went to the school to request help for their children. Dona Leonor sent them to me. I started organizing my afternoons accordingly. On Mondays and Fridays, I might walk to one house and tutor for a few hours and go to another house nearby. On Tuesdays and Thursdays, I would tutor students who lived farther away. I rode the city bus to their homes. On Wednesdays, I tutored students who needed me for the entire afternoon. It was tiring, but I was happy to earn some money and, most importantly, to get out of the *invasão*.

As the school kept growing, I kept adding students to my schedule. I helped Dona Terezinha's two nieces when they needed assistance. One afternoon, one of their neighbors walked over while I was at the house and asked if I could teach her daughter, Lidia. I walked to Lidia's home after finishing with Dona Terezinha's nieces.

At Dona Terezinha's sister's house, the maid mentioned that she was told to feed me no matter the time of the day I arrived. However, some of the new mothers never thought of offering me lunch even though I arrived at their houses wearing my school uniform just after noon when the aroma of good food filled the air and invaded my senses. One day after I tutored Lidia, her mother handed me a bundle of loose recipes tied up in a red ribbon along with a pen and a notebook. She asked me to rewrite and organize the recipes in the notebook for extra pay. I took the bundle of crumpled and stained pieces of paper and asked Miriam, who was home from Angela's house, if she wanted the job of organizing the recipes.

"I don't want to think about food let alone write any recipe when I haven't eaten all day," Miriam said.

I sat outside on my straw mat to rewrite the recipes. I read them over, one by one, trying to interpret the handwriting. Many were dishes I had never heard of or tasted: *rocambole de batata, piré de batata, bife acebolado, bife a milanesa, bacalhau ao forno, filet mignon, lasagna*. The food fantasy started dancing in my head as I wrote the recipes in the thick notebook. It was my introduction to those dishes. I could only fantasize about eating those kinds of foods. In our house when we had food, we mostly ate beans, rice, and farina, the food staple of the region where I lived. Sometimes we ate Mother's vegetable stew with *dendê* oil, cow intestines, tongue, liver, lungs, brains, and pig's feet. We bought chicken or inexpensive cuts of beef only when we had extra money to buy them. At sundown, I carried the notebook with the recipes under my arm across the highway to give back to Lidia's mother. She gave me the extra pay. The next morning, I walked to Seu Jacinto's store to buy beans, rice, and farina.

I also tutored a girl from across the highway, Ana Maria, blonde and happy, a bit younger than me. She wore a smile on her face from ear to ear, which showed her perfect white teeth. She lived in a big house beside the school. At first, I helped her with math; later, I tutored her two younger brothers. I arrived in the afternoon, when the house still smelled of food and the plates and silverware jangled on the dining room table. Their mother, Dona Lolita, also told the maid to serve me a plate of food when I arrived.

Sometimes on weekends, Ana Maria and her family traveled to their farm in a town in the interior called São Gonçalo. They often invited me to go along. On the way back, Dona Lolita packed the small family car with the many fruits and vegetables they grew on their land. Even when the vehicle was crammed with edibles and passengers, the mother jokingly mentioned that she had no problem finding room for me. I was pure "skin and bones," she used to say, and I could easily be squeezed into any tight corner in the back of the car.

My list of pupils kept mounting as the school kept growing. One lady, who lived in an apartment in front of the school, enrolled her three children. At 10 a.m. every day, Dona Zélia walked to the school to bring her youngsters the snacks that the maid had prepared. One day, on her way into the school, Dona Leonor approached Dona Zélia.

"When you come, Dona Zélia, please bring an extra snack for this one girl we have here. All of the students eat their 10 a.m. snacks except her," she said.

"Who is this girl and where do I find her?" asked Dona Zélia.

"Her name is Leda. She lives in the *invasão*. See me next time you come, and I'll take you to her," said Dona Leonor.

"And Dona Zélia, it would be kind if you could also take Leda home one day and feed her," Dona Leonor pleaded.

The next morning, Dona Zélia carried an extra lunch to school and Dona Leonor gave it to me. I stood alone in a corner as I always did during our mid-morning snack when Dona Leonor approached me.

"Leda, this is Dona Zélia. She brought an extra lunch to school today and wants you to have it," she said.

I took the grilled cheese sandwich and the piece of cake Dona Leonor handed me and walked to the school's banana plantation, where I sat and ate the food. Later in the school year, I met Dona Zélia in the school yard again. As an adult, I have thanked her many times for that first snack, for many other meals, and for the unconditional friendship and love she gave me.

After that first lunch, Dona Zélia stood outside the school entrance after class and escorted me to her apartment for a meal with her family. After the maid had set the kitchen table, the family gathered around to eat. I shyly sat near Dona Zélia. I was uncomfortable at the family's table. But I quietly ate at Dona Zélia's home. Her children discussed their school day. Dishes were passed around. Voices filled the room. Praise was expressed for the delicious food Lourdes had cooked. I remained quiet. Dona Zélia dished more food onto my plate every time she had the chance.

Dona Zélia stood at the school's front entrance a few more times to invite me for lunch. I began wishing that she were at the school gate every afternoon to escort me to her apartment so that I would not have to worry about food. Even though I was shy, I wished that I could just walk to Dona Zélia's place for a meal all the time, even when she was not at school. The days I searched for her tall figure among the small bodies walking through the door and did not see her, I walked home. It would have been too embarrassing to appear uninvited at Dona Zélia's doorstep. In retrospect, I wished I had. I am sure she would have fed me, no questions asked.

Later, when Dona Zélia's eldest son, Zeinho, needed help with his school subjects, she met me at school. I gladly walked to their place to tutor him. I was feeling comfortable with the family and had a good reason to walk alone to the apartment just after noon. Sometimes, if I had walked home first to change out of my school uniform, the family had already eaten lunch by the time I arrived at Dona Zélia's home. But it wasn't a problem. Lourdes always set a plate of food on the kitchen table for me. I would eat alone, quietly and fast. It was always painfully awkward for me to sit at the table with the families of the students I tutored. I felt all of their eyes on my skinny body. Eating alone was easier.

When Dona Zélia's second son, Jorginho, needed help with math and Portuguese, I walked to the apartment to tutor him and later to help her youngest daughter, Márcia. I was forced to reshuffle my schedule constantly to continue serving the old students and accommodate the new ones. I sometimes walked to Dona Zélia's house to stay with her even when I was not tutoring her children. When she saw that I was exhausted from my walking to the many homes in the neighborhood, she offered me a couch to rest on and a bed in her daughter's room to sleep on at night. Leaving Mother in the neighborhood bothered me. I felt torn between eating and sleeping on a bed and knowing that she might not have eaten anything the whole day, but my need to survive guided me.

One morning, I awoke on Márcia's bed and found the sheets and mattress soaked with menstrual blood. I panicked. I could not afford to buy sanitary napkins, and I had been extra careful with the pieces of my old clothes that I had cut to use as absorbents. I washed them after use and carried extra thick ones when I slept at Dona Zélia's house. I took the soiled sheets to the maid's quarter off the kitchen and desperately tried to clean them. The bloodstains did not come out easily. I told Dona Zélia about the messy bed in Márcia's bedroom. She told me the maid would help remove the spots, and when I tutored her children, she gave me some extra money to buy hygienic napkins. For the first time, I experienced the feeling of security and comfort that Modess napkins provided as opposed to the loose rag I had used and always feared would fall from place or soil my clothes.

I confided in Dona Zélia once at carnival time my hidden desire to wear a colorful costume and dance at the celebrated social clubs. She quickly arranged for a male relative of hers to take me to a club where they were members. She took out her sewing machine and made me an outfit of vibrant strips of ribbons. She sewed the ribbons to a black top to cover my upper body and attached small golden bells to the ends of each ribbon. She also made a pair of spandex shorts to wear under my ribbon top. I proudly pinned a red flower to the side of a bun on top of my head. Dona Zélia and I waited at her apartment window for my arranged escort. Our eyes followed any figure walking toward her place. The hours dragged on to eleven, twelve midnight. My escort never came. I walked home, not wanting to stay at Dona Zélia's apartment any longer. As I walked, the golden bells on my costume jingled in the quiet of night, as the ribbons swung in the air and touched each other. The sound bothered me, so I slowed my pace. I felt abandoned and did not want to see Dona Zélia for a while. I later learned that my intended escort had drunk too many beers at the carnival and forgot to meet me.

In the summers, the school offered remedial courses for those who had failed seventh-grade math. Dona Leonor called on me to teach them. I did not receive any preparation or books or training. I remember getting up early in the morning to be at school. I splashed cold water on my face, filled the cavities in my front teeth with pieces of cotton, tied my kinky and untamed hair in a bun and ran across the highway to teach until noon.

There were many students now, all from the wealthy suburbs near and far. Some I remember well. There were Frieda and Anelise, two sisters of German ancestry, who lived near the school. They had long blonde hair, deep blue eyes, and broad smiles. Samira and Samara, from the distant suburb of Pituba, were twins with olive skin, dark hair and stunning green eyes. There was also Elizabete, another blonde, a daughter of European immigrants who had no maids in their apartment. There were Fred and Carlinhos as well, two boys from Graça who could not sit still. I explained math to them the way my beloved Dona Sara had explained it to my class: clearly the first time so that you wouldn't need to do it a second time. I continued tutoring some of these students for many years.

Again, I have no recollection of what I was paid exactly during the time that I tutored, starting with the second year of secondary school in Ondina through the fourth year, including summers. My memory is blank no matter how hard I try to remember. Maybe it's because what was really important was the struggle to keep me afloat.

I gave Mother some of the money I earned so that my younger brothers could buy an egg or two at Seu Jacinto's store and boil them for lunch when there was not enough cash to buy beans, rice, and farina. Other times, Mother was happy that she still had money left over to buy vegetables from the street vendor. As soon as she heard his chanting in the distance, she would walk up the stairs in front of the house and wait for Seu Antonio to come by. Seu Antonio was an older black man with a deep voice. He walked alongside the highway every day, pulling an underweight and tired donkey carrying two large black baskets of fruits and vegetables attached to each side. "Sweet mango… I have sweet mango today," yelled Seu Antonio. Other vendors also walked by selling fresh fish and lobsters, but we could never afford them. No one in our shantytown could ever afford the lobster the fisherman caught right in our backyard. We didn't know how lucky we were due to the unhealthy waters they bred in. The vendors crossed the highway to sell their catch in the better neighborhood.

With the money I earned, I also helped Rita, Gaia's daughter whom my mother was left to raise. I registered her at a private primary school in the nice neighborhood. I bought Rita books, shoes and a school uniform, thus alleviating the burden on Mother who had lost patience with Rita and was tired of running after her. Rita was very active and never missed a chance to run down the alley to the fetid beach, where she was not afraid to jump into the deep water.

In order to buy my own shoes and clothes, I had to ride a bus line that ended in the center of town, *Praça da Sé*. From there, I went to a commercial area called *Baixa do Sapateiro*, a strip of stores that displayed colorful merchandise on long rows of tables set outside. Music blared from the inside of the stores. The ride was long, and the bus was always packed with people. It stopped every few blocks to either drop off passengers or pick up new ones. At the end of the bus line, I walked for about half an hour down a steep hill paved with stones. I passed the boutiques that sold nice clothes but did not dare go inside. I felt unworthy of elegant places and could only admire the outfits displayed in the windows. Besides, my earnings were not enough to buy any of them. I could only afford to buy clothing from *Baixa do Sapateiro*. The items I bought, however, did not last long. Garments from the *Baixa do Sapateiro* were easily distinguishable by their poor quality. After one or two washes and drying them on the grass under the hot sun or on the rocks in the back if the tide was low, the colors faded.

17. The Return of the Syringe

By the time I turned seventeen, the holes in my upper front teeth were so large that the pieces of cotton I used to fill them no longer remained in place when I talked. My tooth decay, like many things, can be attributed to the untreated drinking water we fetched from the well at the rocky beach; to the unclean rainwater we caught in empty kerosene cans that my mother and sisters put under the roof tiles in Castro Alves; to the rusty water delivered by town trucks in times of severe drought; to the algae-infested water we fetched from puddles in the backyard; and to the leaves that we pulled from *juá babão*—a bush with foamy leaves that we used to clean our teeth when they were too yellow.

Toothbrushes and toothpaste were hardly ever used in our house. Everyone in my family, except the youngest, Wilson, and one of the oldest, Tatai, lost most of their teeth. We stopped using toothbrushes and buying toothpaste after Father died. There was never enough money to buy them, and the search for food came first. When we had extra money to buy dental cream, we were happy and squeezed every last drop of it onto our fingers to rub over our teeth. When it was finished, we opened the soft aluminum tube from the top and the sides to remove the last bit of paste before the container was discarded.

Sometimes, my rotten teeth kept me from school and my tutoring. I bought a large roll of Johnson & Johnson's cotton and stood in front of the small mirror on the wall to carefully fill every black cavity in my teeth before I left the house. However, the holes were wide, and the cotton was slimy with saliva so it would fall out of my teeth. A couple of times I gave up and didn't go to school or see my classmates. I became even more withdrawn. I did not speak, nor did I want to be seen. No one in my family was aware of my battle with the cotton and the holes in my teeth. It was not that anyone cared but rather that we all had to fight our own battles.

Though painfully discouraged, I continued crossing the highway and riding the city bus to see the students whom I tutored in the distant suburbs. When I spoke, I tried not to open my mouth too wide or too fast so that the cotton in my teeth would stay in place. My voice sounded soft, almost a whisper. When some of my students looked at me puzzled and asked if I was all right, I said that I had a headache and that it would soon go away. The more frequent and severe toothaches kept me awake; I cried at night. Often in the morning, I was left with a swollen face. Once, my face was so puffed up that it took a while for my eyes to fully open and the swelling to go down. This hardship finally forced me to stop meeting with my students.

I asked Célio if I could see his dentist. His job provided benefits that extended to our mother and siblings. Célio's health services were in the lower seaport, the commercial part of the city. We lived in the hilly, mostly residential upper area. A steep slope divides Salvador into the Upper and the Lower Town, *Cidade Alta* and *Cidade Baixa*. From my house to the dentist's office, I would have to take the green *Viação Beira Mar* bus line for about an hour. The buses were always packed with riders and stopped often until reaching the center of town, a place called *Praça da Sé*. From there, I would walk a short distance to a tall and historic elevator, Brazil's first. The elevator, called *Elevador Lacerda,* connects the upper residential area to the lower commercial section. After getting off the elevator, I would walk a short distance and ride the blue line bus for thirty minutes. This bus took me to the dentist's office.

One morning after a sleepless night, I took some of the money that I had earned and walked with a swollen face to the bus stop to see Célio's dentist. Dr. Dante was short, stocky and light skinned with hairy arms and eyes as blue as the ocean. The dentist met me in a small waiting room, looked at me from head to toe and led me to a blue chair in another small room. After he heard my story of relentless toothaches and a swollen face, he asked me to open my mouth. He took a quick look, stepped back, and with a soft voice said that my upper teeth were rotten beyond repair and needed to be extracted.

"All of them?" I asked in disbelief.

"All of them," he replied. "Your teeth are very infected. The decay is too advanced to save any of them. Take this prescription for penicillin," said Dr. Dante. "Come back when the swelling and the pain are completely gone."

I bought the penicillin and took the long ride home. In a few weeks, when the inflammation disappeared and I felt no pain, I rode the green bus and took the tall elevator followed by the blue bus. I sat in Dr. Dante's chair and stared at his blue eyes. He examined my mouth again, looking carefully at each tooth and stepped back. He came closer again, touched my teeth with his gloved hand and told me that he did not know where to start. But he would extract the teeth that he thought were giving me the most trouble, the ones most infected in the back of my mouth. He did not bother with X-rays. My case was clear-cut. My teeth had to go.

"I'll pull all of your upper teeth and have a denture made for you," he explained.

"A denture," I said.

"You'll be fine," he said.

I was silent. Tears rolled down my face.

"I'm going to numb your tooth," he said. "It'll hurt at first, but the pain will soon be gone, and you won't feel anything for a while," he added.

I nodded in agreement. I remained quiet and tense in the blue chair staring at the white ceiling.

Dr. Dante was friendly. He worked alone and whistled a soft tune when he moved around the office, taking short steps, sorting out the metal instruments and aligning them on the counter. I heard the tinkling of the metal and saw him taking a large syringe with a huge needle. It was like the one I remember seeing the pharmacist Orlando Lima use in our house on Paramirim Street when he gave Father an injection to ease his pain. Dr. Dante took a small glass container with a rubber top and inserted the syringe needle into it to draw out liquid. He held up the syringe, tapped it a few times with his finger, then squirted some of the liquid into the air and onto the floor.

I closed my eyes tightly. Dr. Dante inserted the giant needle into the front of my gum. The pain was unbearable. I opened my eyes and felt my gut clench. I held onto the arm of the chair. The dentist poked the other side of my front gum. I cringed. Then he injected the back of the tooth, one side first then the other. I closed my eyes tightly again and pressed hard onto the chair. My body tightened. I moaned and tears rolled down my cheeks. It was as if the dentist's needle had reached deep inside my very being, had touched my inner soul. Each time he pulled out the large needle to reapply anesthesia, my body shrank in the chair.

After Dr. Dante poked my tooth, I felt lightheaded and slid farther down in the chair. The ceiling and walls started dancing.

Everything turned blue in front of my eyes, the same color as Dr. Dante's eyes. I closed my eyes tightly again and felt the dentist's heavy and warm surgical pliers touch my lips. He whispered that the job was finished. I opened my eyes. For a moment, I saw the dentist holding his silver pliers and what was left of one of my rotten teeth grasped in its jaws. Then I heard the tooth clang in the metal disposal container.

Still lightheaded, holding a piece of cloth over my numb mouth and spitting blood along the way, I walked back to the blue bus line, then over to the tall elevator to take the green bus home. As soon as I got home, I went straight to my straw mat to rest. Mother brought me warm water with salt to soothe my gums and an empty can filled with sand, which she set near me so I could spit blood and water into it. Later, feeling better and very hungry after the bleeding had stopped and my lips could move, I got up from my mat to look for food. But like many other occasions, there was nothing to eat in the house, so I went back to my mat to sleep off the hunger.

I was back in school the following morning with pieces of cotton covering the cavities in my remaining upper teeth. One week later, I rode the buses and the elevator again to the dentist's office. I sat in his chair and stared into his blue eyes. I saw him take the giant syringe and needle and draw the anesthetic liquid from the container to inject around my teeth. I cringed in his chair and heard another tooth clang in the metal waste bin. Sweat saturated my clothes. I felt dizzy walking back to the bus stop with a numb mouth, spitting blood all the way to our house, where again there was nothing to eat. And yet again, I went back in school the following morning. I tutored in the afternoon, waiting to return in a week to the dentist's chair.

The next time I went to the dentist, I asked Dr. Dante if he could extract more than one tooth at a time. I explained that it would be better for me, less bus fare and more money saved for my denture.

"Where do you live?" he asked.

"At the *invasão* in Ondina," I said.

"No. I can't," he said. "You live too far, bleed too much, and look too frail for me to extract more than one tooth at a time. One tooth a week already is a lot," he explained in a half-angry voice.

My mouth quickly shrank after my upper teeth were extracted. I opened it with care when I spoke, not too wide, trying to hide my bare gums. I talked only when necessary. At seventeen, I had the mouth of an old woman. My excitement for the Friday *sabatina* at school diminished. My desire to volunteer answers disappeared. I continued tutoring because I had to earn the money to pay Dr. Dante to have a denture made for me in six months. Six months was the time he said it would take for my mouth to heal if there were no infections. For six months, I avoided people at all costs, especially my peers. Once, Ana Maria, a girl I tutored, crossed the highway to see me. I met her at the front steps of our house. She had not seen me and wanted to know why I was not around much. I looked at Ana Maria's wide smile and white teeth. I wished that I had teeth like hers. She was always vibrant and bubbly and wanted to talk, like any teenager. I had nothing to say. I had not seen any of the movies she had nor had I listened to the music she had. We never had a radio in our house. Nor had I gone to any of the clubs or beaches Ana Maria had visited. And I hadn't seen or heard of the boys she flirted with. After many minutes of silence, Ana Maria said good-bye and disappeared across the highway. I tutored her and her younger brothers in math and other subjects, but yet, I felt inferior in her presence and could not express my feelings.

I went back to Dr. Dante's office with the money that I had saved to pay for my false teeth. I sat in his chair and bit into a white compound to make the mold. My denture would be temporary, and it would have to be replaced in a year or so. My mouth was still growing, and my gums would shrink with time. The set of teeth soon would lose its grip, fall from place, and dance in my mouth.

I visited the dentist's office twice more for the fitting of my new teeth. After my last visit, I walked out of his office with a new mouth. It didn't matter how much pain and discomfort I felt in adjusting to my new set of teeth. I had to relearn how to talk. There was the irritation and the bleeding of my gums, the awful sensation of a mouth that had a foreign object in it, and the initial lack of taste. These experiences with the denture, however, could not compare to the feelings of nakedness and shame that I felt when I was without my upper teeth.

Of the hardships I have gone through in life, losing all of my upper teeth was one of the most painful and traumatic experiences.

Every time Dr. Dante attached his pliers to one of my teeth and pulled, I felt as if he were yanking some of my vital organs along with it. And each time I left his office and walked onto the busy roads to the bus stop, rain or shine, I felt dizzy and spat blood along the way. After every visit, I felt as if I had lost a part of my being, as if I'd left an essential part of me in the dentist's chair.

The walk, the long bus ride home, the straw mat where I slept, the swollen face the next morning and the students I had to tutor the following day all remain a horrible memory. At the time, I could not wait for Dr. Dante to pull all of the rotten teeth out of my mouth because my daily battle with the black holes stuffed with cotton dragged me down. But once my teeth were out, I felt tremendous shame and grief. By age seventeen, I had lost my teeth and had to wear a denture. I have had many dental implants, laser and graft surgeries since Dr. Dante pulled my teeth, and to this day, I cringe whenever I sit in a dentist's chair. On many occasions, I feel the need to explain to the dentist and the hygienist the circumstances that led to losing my teeth and the condition of the teeth that remain.

18. Grace

Eighth grade was to be my final year across the highway in Ondina at the Social Institute of Bahia because the school did not offer classes past eighth grade. It was 1967 and I was eighteen. One Saturday afternoon, I walked to school to meet my classmates to work on a project for our Portuguese teacher. While I waited outside by the tall metal school gate for the girls in my group to arrive, a blond, fair-skinned, young deliveryman from Portugal approached me and introduced himself as José Domingos. We spoke briefly. He said he lived with relatives in a house in the neighborhood and worked delivering supplies to stores and schools.

"I have seen you during school breaks," he said, then went about his business.

On my way home from school that day, José Domingos again approached me to say he wanted to continue our conversation. When I quickened my pace, he quickened his. He asked where I lived and when he could see me again.

Not knowing how to answer José Domingos, I stopped. No one had ever shown any interest in me before. I remained quiet for a while, thinking of a way to deflect his questions, then I told José Domingos that I had forgotten my notebook in the room where I met with my classmates and that I had to retrieve it. I ran through the tall gate and hid in the backyard banana plantation for what seemed like a long while waiting for him to leave. When I finally came back outside, José Domingos stood at the the gate waiting for me. The second I saw him I walked around the school building and ran home without being seen.

José Domingos was back at school later in the week, standing outside. He came up to me as I walked through the metal gate.

"I waited for you the other day, and you never came out," he said.

"I had forgotten that I had French homework and decided to do it before going home," I said.

"Can we talk a bit now?" he asked.

"No. I'm a tutor and I'm meeting a student who has a test on Monday. I have to get ready," I explained.

José Domingos offered to walk me home. When he again asked where I lived, I told him without hesitation. It always pained me to reveal where I lived. But I thought that telling José Domingos that I dwelt in the *invasão* would be enough for him to leave me alone. Instead, we walked together and stopped by the highway. I said I needed to go, and he asked if he could come back to meet me at school another time. The *invasão* didn't appear to bother José Domingos. He seemed very nice. So I agreed to see him even though I did not understand why he would want to talk to me. I did not consider myself pretty. I did not wear nice clothes. I was malnourished and underweight. No one had ever complimented my looks or anything else, except my teachers who told me that I had a good memory and was a good student.

One week later, on Sunday afternoon, José Domingos crossed the highway to look for me. I was outside on my straw mat with my books. When I saw him, I immediately stood up, tense. I did not know where to sit with him, what to say to him, or even whether I should introduce him to anyone. I suggested we sit on the steps by Mother's papaya tree, where we talked. José Domingos shared with me how he missed his family and his country. Although he loved Brazil, he wanted to return someday to Portugal, buy a house and start a family. I didn't understand until later what missing one's country meant. Nor did I comprehend his love for Brazil. I told him how I missed Castro Alves, the backyard, my friend Creusa, and the freedom I had walking into the woods to eat berries, drinking warm cow's milk in the morning, and meeting the rising sun on the way back. He stayed for a while and then left, returning the following Sunday.

Soon my classmates found out about José Domingos' interest in me. They had seen him outside the school gate at noon, waiting to walk me home. During our 10 a.m. break one morning, a classmate told me that she thought that José Domingos was the best I could hope for, meaning that I should not expect anyone better than a delivery boy, given how poor I was. I took the comment as offensive and a put-down but chose not to say anything. I was not comfortable in the presence of José Domingos, and deep inside I already felt that we should not be talking anymore. It would be difficult to incorporate someone new into my life. I was used to making my own decisions and always followed my instincts. I decided that I was not going to see the young man again.

Another contributing factor was the gold on José Domingos' front teeth, which glittered in the sunlight. I had overlooked his teeth when I first met him, but they suddenly caught my attention and bothered me. They left me feeling inadequate, thinking of my own teeth. I still longed for them even though I realized that they had been rotten and painful. In many ways, I was glad that they were gone, but I often grieved for my teeth and wondered if Dr. Dante really had to extract them all. My teeth were then and are still a sensitive issue. I was very aware of everything related to them. The following Sunday afternoon, I asked José Domingos to stop coming to school and my house. He didn't wait for an explanation and left. He didn't look back, and I never saw him again but often thought about him. I felt terribly guilty for rejecting the only person who so far in my life had accepted me and the *invasão*.

Around that time, I rode the city bus to some elite suburbs, Barra, Graça, and Pituba, to tutor the students registered at school because the youngsters I tutored in Ondina needed my help less often. The city buses never ran on a fixed schedule. I spent a long time waiting for one to come, especially in the early afternoon when students traveled to and from school and workers commuted. When the buses finally arrived, they often were so packed that they didn't stop. They sped by with passengers hanging out the wide-open back door.

When money was short, I rode the cheaper bus, called *mixto*, which was less popular and ran more frequently. People generally stayed away from the *mixto*. It carried the dispossessed and their belongings. This bus transported live chickens with their feet tied up; goats and pigs; laundry baskets full of dirty clothes to be washed and clean ones to be returned to their elite employers in the suburbs. There were baskets full of fruits and vegetables being taken to and from the market. The foul smell in the *mixto* flooded my senses and sometimes made me sick. I pinched my nose when boarding and often searched for a less crowded corner by an open window or a door until I reached my destination.

Late in November, at the end of eighth grade, Dona Leonor introduced me to another mother from Graça, who wanted to know if I would tutor her two sons, Marcos and Paulo. They had failed fifth and sixth grade, respectively. They needed remedial work in many subjects before the beginning of the school year in March. The mother explained that the boys were staying at the family's cocoa plantation in the interior of the state for the summer, and I would have to live with them during the time that I tutored them. I remember thinking what it would be like to live on a farm and have enough food to eat every day. The idea sounded good, although I had just met the woman and could not imagine how it would be to live with a new family.

My instincts told me to go. That's how it was with the decisions that I made. They were solely guided by my instincts. I had no one in my family to talk to or to ask for guidance. I was alone. Mother didn't say much about the decisions that her children made. I explained to my mother that I could save the money I would earn during the summer at the plantation for transportation to and from school and to buy my school supplies for the coming school year.

In early January, the students' mother, Dona Clara, handed me a bus ticket and a piece of paper with instructions on how to travel from Salvador to the cocoa farm in Itabuna, a town 300 miles south of Salvador. From Itabuna, I rode in a white van packed with peasants who were dropped off on narrow dirt roads that led to the villages and farms where they worked. I was dropped off at the entrance of the family's farm. A worker met me with a horse. I rode the last leg of the daylong trip to the farmhouse on horseback. The sun was on its way down behind a verdant hill. The worker and I rode for at least an hour, passing many charming cocoa bushes with green and yellow fruits growing on trunks and branches.

During mornings on the farm, I reviewed sixth- and seventh-grade math and Portuguese with my two students. When we had extra time before the midday meal, we studied history and geography. We worked at a long dining room table in the center room. I taught the two boys the subjects that I had studied the night before, did some practice exercises, and reviewed their quizzes and tests. Our study sessions usually began at 9 a.m. after the maids had cleared the breakfast table. The tutoring would end when the servants told me that they needed to set the table for lunch.

As I watched the maids scamper from the kitchen to the dining room carrying colorful and aromatic dishes, I thought of the times in Salvador when I walked to students' homes at noon and saw the maids setting dishes of food on the families' tables. I walked into this new family's kitchen and asked the maids if I could help them with lunch. They handed me dishes of food to carry, some of the food I had fantasized eating. They were the dishes I had once carefully copied down in a notebook, for extra pay, and given to the mother who lived across the highway. They were the filet mignon, lasagna, and the stew meats I only knew by name. Now I held the steaming plates in my own hands; they were like a dream come true.

For the first time in my teenage years, I experienced what it was like to eat every day. I stopped thinking about food and felt a sense of accomplishment and empowerment, as if I had won a hard-fought battle or had discovered gold. At that moment, I thought that I could live without hunger and that the food that I had often imagined had become a reality. During the months of January and February when I lived on the farm, the food fantasy completely stopped racing through my mind. However, for some reason, later in life, I never felt satiated eating those Brazilian dishes I had dreamed about constantly, no matter how good they tasted nor how much I ate. There was always something missing. My stomach was full. But in my head, I wanted more. Looking back, my deprivation was intense. My need for food was never fulfilled; my hunger was never satisfied. Hunger remained in my brain, and hunger often carried me to the dining rooms where I smelled the Brazilian dishes that I could not eat. Their colors and aromas are indelible. There is the inexplicable, persistent feeling of a strange wanting as soon as I smell those dishes, even many years later.

In the afternoons, after lending a hand in the kitchen, I let the breeze fan my body and the sun redden my face as I planted eucalyptus by the dirt road leading to the farmhouse with Dona Clara. Other days, I followed her on visits to the farmworkers' homes. She planned weddings and baptisms for the farmworkers when the priests from the adjacent towns came to the farm. On one of my outings with her, I saw a young mother using coffee grounds on her infant's umbilical cord so it could heal and fall off faster. I had seen this practice cause infections and kill babies in Castro Alves, so I asked Dona Clara to run to the farmhouse for oxygenated water and cotton to remove the coffee grounds from the child and clean his umbilical cord. I was afraid that the baby would die. I visited the mother again to help her care for the infant.

While I lived on the family's plantation, I wondered about its size and hoped I could see how big it was. One afternoon, I found out. Seu Ariel, the head of the family, asked if I wanted to ride along with the two boys I tutored to visit his employees in the remote areas of the plantation. I spent the whole afternoon riding in the jeep and learned that we covered only half of the farm. During one of our stops, while Seu Ariel talked to the hired hands, I wandered around and saw a twig with pretty dried yellow berries. When Seu Ariel saw me holding the twig in my hand, he said the twig was pretty and that I had "artistic eyes." He told me that I could take the branch home and ask the maid to arrange it in the hallway of the farmhouse entrance. I felt proud to have "artistic eyes" and to see my twig displayed.

After Carnival in February, I returned to the *invasão* from the cocoa farm. Miriam had moved back from Angela's home to live with Mother. My sister had stopped attending the teacher preparatory school in the city and had found a job working at a home appliance store in *Baixa do Sapateiro*, where I bought my clothes and shoes. Miriam had a cheerful personality and made friends easily. She crossed the highway to meet with the two girls whom I tutored, Frieda and Anelise, as well as other youngsters in the nice neighborhood. In the evening, Miriam spent time with the group talking, listening to the Beatles on the radio, and dancing on the sidewalk. I stayed home. I never knew how to be comfortable with Miriam's friends or how to laugh so easily. I lived in my head and was a misfit.

During these gatherings across the highway, some young men who attended a nearby veterinary school joined the group. Miriam started dating one of these young men named Chico. Chico was very handsome, soft-spoken, and polite. He wore his long brown hair in a ponytail and walked to our house on Sunday afternoons to sit on the steps by the papaya tree and talk with Miriam. When Chico came to the house, he saw me sitting on the straw mat outside by the window with my books. On one occasion, he sat beside me and said that he thought that I was an intellectual.

"Me ... eu," I stammered, "an in-te-lec-tu-al?"

"Yes," he said. "Every time I see you, you're here with books in your hands," Chico repeated.

I did not have much to say to Chico and did not understand what he meant, but my family and I liked him. Besides having good looks,

Chico was very warm and relaxed. The stench and the lack of food and furniture in our house did not seem to bother him. It amazed me. He told us that he wanted to be a veterinarian and work on his father's animal farm in the interior.

For my new school year starting in March, I registered at the closest public high school, *Colegio Severino Vieira*, in the suburb of Nazaré. It was close to ninety minutes from our house; two bus rides and extra fares. Depending on how long I had to wait for the crowded buses, it could take even longer. With the money I had saved tutoring during the summer, I bought my new uniform, a different style of white blouse and navy-blue skirt, as well as supplies and thick biology, chemistry, and physics books translated from English into Portuguese. I set aside the money for my daily bus fare in a sock hidden under my straw mat because I knew that I could not get to school without it.

The new school year brought many new expenses. The bus fare consumed most of my savings. Sometimes I had to borrow money from my brothers. I transferred to night school after I found it too difficult to continue. I tutored more students during the day to cover the costs. My night classes began at 7 p.m. and ended at 11 p.m., Monday through Friday. Except on the days when the teachers did not show up for the classes, which happened often, I went home early. Many times, I arrived home well past midnight. At the end of my first year, I switched to morning classes.

My second year in high school, I befriended Cristina, an upper-class girl from an elite suburb called *Morro do Gato*—Cat's Hill. One day, she offered to pay for my midmorning snack when she noticed that I wasn't eating with the other students. I would sit on a bench at a distance because I could never afford to buy any of the food sold in the school cafeteria. My classmates looked forward to the *merenda*, checking the time as 10 a.m. approached, but I dreaded it. As soon as the bell rang, the students would rush out of the classroom to be the first in line to order the colorful tropical juices and snacks on display, the popular *sonho de valsa*, *pastel*, and *coxinha de galinha*. Sometimes I stayed in the classroom just to avoid looking at the food.

The day Cristina offered to buy my *merenda*, we chatted while we ate. She asked me where I lived. I said Ondina. She offered to give me a ride home in her chauffeur-driven family car. She lived in the same suburb. I accepted, thinking that I would save money for the bus fare that day. I didn't tell Cristina that I lived in the *invasão* in Ondina. I seldom revealed my address to anyone out of fear of rejection and put-downs. I only mentioned it when I absolutely had to. The *invasão* was the worst place one could call home. To a certain extent, people knew about the inhumane conditions we lived in. I was even more ashamed of our home in the shantytown after experiencing life outside of it.

After school that day, I quietly walked out with Cristina. We entered her car, parked by the curb in front of the school, and sat in the back seat. The chauffeur, Seu Ismael, drove off. Cristina and I talked about our sociology class, which we both liked. As we approached Ondina, I suddenly agonized over where to ask the chauffeur to drop me off. I was fearful about revealing my secret that I lived in the shantytown. When he asked for directions to my house, I told him to stop at the bus stop because I needed to wait for my sister Miriam to get off the bus so that we could walk home together. I explained that my house was not too far from there.

I mingled with other people at the bus stop and waited for Seu Ismael to turn the car around and drive away, disappearing in the distance until I could no longer see Cristina sitting in the back seat. I felt a huge sense of relief that the chauffeur had dropped me off without Cristina asking additional questions and insisting on driving me to my house. From that day on, I found many excuses to decline Cristina's offer to buy me the midmorning snack or drive me home.

On a Sunday afternoon in August, halfway toward the end of my second year of high school, a black car parked in the empty lot in front of our house. Dona Clara, the mother of the two boys I had tutored at the cocoa farm in the summer, walked down the stairs to the house. I met her outside when I heard her calling my name. She wanted to talk to Mother and me about an important issue, she said. I called Mother from where she was resting. We stood outside by the papaya tree. Dona Clara asked me if I wanted to live with her family for the remainder of the school year and again the following year. I was to tutor her sons in the afternoon five days a week. I would continue attending school and have some spending money in addition to room and board.

Mother was quiet. She did not have much to say. She seldom did. Eating three meals every day for the two months I had lived with the family left me yearning for the security of regular meals at our house in the shantytown. The food fantasies had returned. Also, the year-and-a-half I had spent attending a distant high school had made a large dent in my savings and therefore in my ability to keep afloat. I did not, however, consider the difficulties I might have living with the family for a lengthy period of time. All I had in mind was the food I would eat every day and the proximity to school. I told Mother that I would live with Dona Clara's family and that she didn't need to worry about me. I went inside, packed my books, school uniform and the few belongings that I had into a white plastic bag, kissed Mother goodbye and followed Dona Clara to her car.

The family lived in a large house on a steep hill paved with stones in a neighborhood called *Graça*—Grace. The home had eight youngsters of various ages, five servants, and many dogs. Besides the two boys I tutored, there were two young men and four girls. One of the girls was close to my age. The other girls were younger: ten, eleven, and twelve years old. The household had lots of commotion, from early morning to late at night.

The family chauffeur, Seu Duval, walked into the kitchen for coffee in the morning and stood outside waiting for the family to get ready. Dona Clara sat at the table with her younger children and insisted that they finish the oatmeal that the maid had prepared. Once the issue of breakfast had been set aside, as the oatmeal was usually left cold and uneaten, the issues of tangled hair, lost socks, and scattered books occupied center stage. The two maids rushed up and down the stairs looking for the needed items. Once the quarrels were settled, the children followed their mother to the car and the ever-patient Seu Duval drove off.

Wearing my school uniform, I silently approached the breakfast table and ate with gusto whatever Ambrosia had prepared that morning before leaving the house with my book bag, crossing the quiet cobblestone street, and climbing a very steep stairway to the bus stop. Although the ride was shorter, I still had to take two buses to get to school, which lasted forty-five minutes on a good day.

The family reassembled for the large midday meal, arriving before I did most days. And there was the same hubbub around the dining table. Some of the children complained that the food did not taste good, that they had no appetite, or that their favorite dish had not been served that day. After a while, the chauffeur would take off again with the mother and the three younger girls to be tutored at the private school they attended in the morning. I was left home with the servants and the two boys. The mother and the girls would return in the evening.

I helped the boys with their homework, leading them upstairs to a small den where I slept in a bed in the corner. We gathered at a small table at 2 p.m. and concluded our sessions at 5 p.m. We reviewed the school day and I re-taught lessons if needed. Most days, the frequent and long bathroom breaks the boys took, and the fighting with one another and the servants made the afternoons long and tiring for me. I spent a lot of time just getting the boys to the upstairs den and breaking up fights. By 6 p.m., I managed to get my books and flee to an abandoned garage in the back of the house where I did my homework and prepared for my classes the following morning. The maids knew about my hideout, and one of them would call me for dinner, after which I would return to my studying.

The oldest girl in the family busied herself with club affairs, dress fittings, friends, and phone calls. She was a pretty blonde and a popular girl. The second oldest boy attended college and kept to himself. The eldest, a tall, light-skinned, handsome young man with honey blond hair, was named Augusto. Later in life, when I saw a picture of Michelangelo's David for the first time, I thought of him. He had returned to Brazil from studying in Europe. Augusto did not work or study and often slept until noon.

I was home sick one morning when I heard an uproar downstairs, loud, angry voices. I hurried to the kitchen and found Augusto standing by the hot stove wearing a blue robe and holding a long, thick wooden spoon high in his hand. In front of him stood the cook, Ambrosia, a short, stocky, yet strong, black woman. She held a large kitchen knife. Young master Augusto had awakened before noon and gone to the kitchen to help himself to lunch. Ambrosia refused to let the young man meddle with her cooking or eat. She stood by the stove to protect her pots and pans.

"Lunch isn't ready yet," she said. "When it's ready, I'll set the table for the family to eat. I'm not letting you or anyone else mess up my cooking," she added.

Ambrosia raised a sharp knife in the air while cursing at Augusto.

He held the wooden spoon and insisted on his right to eat in his own kitchen whenever he wanted. The scene shocked me. I stood between the master and the servant, hoping to break up the fight. I was afraid that they would hurt each other by the hot stove with steaming pots and pans.

I pleaded with Augusto. "It's close to noon already," I said. "You won't have to wait long before Ambrosia sets the table and everyone will eat. Meanwhile, you can go upstairs, shower, and get ready."

"Leda," he said, "tell Ambrosia that I'm hungry. All I want is a plate of food so that I can get dressed before everyone comes home. I have things that need my attention this afternoon."

"Don't involve her in this," shouted Ambrosia. "There's no way you're going to get the food I'm cooking before it gets to the table," she warned.

"This is my house, this is my kitchen, and this is the food my parents bought. I'll do whatever I want," he said.

"It's your house, but you'll never touch the food I cook before it is set on the table," she insisted.

Augusto turned around, threw the wooden spoon in the sink, and walked away. Ambrosia shouted some more and returned to her work. I lingered, surprised and delighted at her victory. I had just seen a slave fight the master.

Another afternoon, while I sat in the upstairs den with the youngest boys and their books, I heard the bathroom door hit the wall hard. Augusto walked out wearing only a white shirt, naked from the waist down. He walked slowly with his legs apart, holding his bleeding penis with both hands and leaving a trail of blood behind him. I got up from my chair and followed him, but he quickly entered his room and slammed the door shut. I stood by his door asking him if he was all right; should I call a doctor?

"No. Leave me alone," I heard him say.

Later in the day the servants were talking and laughing. Augusto, they said, had learned overseas that, unlike he and his countrymen, men in other parts of the world were circumcised. So he decided to lock himself in the bathroom and do the job himself using a sharp razor blade. I thought he must have done a good job because no doctor came to the house to repair any serious damage from his circumcision. After a few days walking around with a limp, his spread legs apart, Augusto seemed fine again.

The father of the family, Seu Ariel, spent weeks and sometimes months away, traveling on business and meeting with other cocoa producers and exporters. When he was home, the commotion in the house grew. The maids busied themselves preparing his favorite dishes; the children sought his attention; the chauffeur had extra errands to run, and his wife stayed in the house more than usual, commanding the servants and chasing her husband, who liked chasing other women whenever he had the chance.

It became increasingly difficult for me to remain with the family and teach the two boys. I had to intervene in every fight they carried on in the kitchen with the maids, in the yard with the gardener, and in the house with their siblings. It was extremely hard to keep them focused on studying and doing homework when they showed no interest in learning in school with their teachers and peers. In addition, I started helping the four girls in the family prepare for their quizzes and tests.

After I moved in with the family in Graça, I spent most of my weekends at their home with the servants, catching up on my schoolwork. The family members were usually out visiting friends and family or at social clubs. Some Sundays, I rode the bus to visit Mother in the shantytown and brought her some money. I never talked about my life in Graça. No one ever asked. I did not have a fixed salary, and Dona Clara was not consistent with the payments. I had to ask for some cash for the bus fare, for books, and for Mother. There was never enough to buy anything extra. Dona Clara was nice to me but tight with money. The servants also had to constantly remind her of their payday at the end of the month.

Early in 1969, I returned to my family for a weekend visit and learned that the mayor of Salvador had sent a worker to the *invasão* to warn people that their homes would soon be torn down. I also learned that Miriam was pregnant with her boyfriend Chico's child. Her once curvaceous figure was now round, and her beaming eyes and broad smile faded away. Miriam stayed in bed with morning sickness during my entire visit. I did not talk to her that day or any day thereafter. I did not know what to say, and I couldn't tell her what I felt. Deep inside, I was enraged and sorry for Mother because I knew that she would end up raising Miriam's child.

Early one evening in November, Eduardo came to the house in Graça to tell me that Miriam had taken a bus to a public hospital in the city to deliver the baby. A few days later, I asked Dona Clara for some money for a taxi to bring Miriam and her infant son home from the hospital. My family had rented a small house in a poor wooded area away from the coastline until they could move into their new home in *Boca do Rio*—Mouth of the River. Chico, Miriam's boyfriend, who had promised to assume responsibility for his child after the baby's birth, disappeared from sight. No one heard from him or saw him again. Eduardo went to the veterinary school Chico attended to ask him for money to buy milk for the child. None of Chico's classmates would tell Eduardo where he was. Mother raised the boy, and Miriam found a job promoting a new Coca-Cola product that had come to Brazil.

I lived in Graça until December 1970, my last year in high school, when I left the family so I could find time to study for the college entrance exam. Shortly afterward, there was a tragedy with the boy whom I had tutored, Paulo. One afternoon, Paulo had a fight with his youngest sister. He threw a sharp metal rod at her that hit her in one eye and blinded her. I later heard that, Ambrosia had said at the time, "If Leda had been here, this never would have happened."

19. Removal of the Invaders

I n 1969, a crew appeared in the Ondina shantytown to advise the approximately 1,000 people living there that the city would be evicting them. The mayor offered cash for their shacks and a new site to build their new homes. The residents were told to claim their payments downtown at city hall. Slum dwellers were being moved to a savanna-like area called Boca do Rio, about one hour by bus from Ondina, ninety minutes or so from the center of Salvador.

At first, no one in the *invasão* wanted to believe the mayor's plan. The residents had no reason to trust the public officials who had nearly always ignored their plight. They had been invisible to society for years, so why the attention now? The dwellers had finally found a place to call home and had nurtured a sense of community in the *invasão*. They looked after each other in bad times and relished the few good times they had together. The daily struggle for survival was a common badge everyone wore. Sharing a bucket of water, a cup of coffee, or an aspirin with those who had none was as much a part of their lives as breathing the impure air that engulfed them. Caring for the sick and the needy was an unspoken and unwritten collective duty. The women would not hesitate to care for the sick, help with the chores, or house anyone whose shack the high waves had flooded. The men would walk from door to door collecting donations to bury the indigent or take the time to fix a shack destroyed by the waves and the wind. Drug dealing and crimes were unheard of in the shantytown. In our shantytown, the reckless highway drivers were the ones who committed the most horrendous crimes. They killed us like flies and fled the scene, showing absolutely no remorse or respect for our lives.

The strong bond that connected the people in the shantytown led them to believe that the mayor's plan to destroy what they had built was pure talk. However, a few weeks later, on a rainy and damp winter morning in mid-July, the crew returned to the shantytown— this time, armed with briefcases, pens, and papers. They demonstrated the city's intent to remove the shanties by documenting the dwellers' possessions and affirming the mayor's seriousness to raze the *invasão*. The workers quickly appraised the homes and told the people that they could claim the compensation that the mayor was offering at city hall and leave Ondina on their own, if they wished. For those who remained, the crew would return with dump trucks to move them to the new location in Boca do Rio.

The *invasão* had grown over the years. The collection of unfinished and dilapidated shanties packed together on the shoreline had become bothersome, a sore thumb, to the politicians and the elite neighbors across the highway. The daily deaths on the road and the many drowning deaths on Sundays and holidays when people bathed in the ocean had been brought to the public's attention. Also, the number of *invasões* in Salvador had increased along with the many homeless in the city. But most importantly, the tourist industry had been eyeing the prime oceanfront location and planned to build hotels as soon as the "invaders" were out. The shanties were in their way and had become an eyesore to the local and national authorities when their caravans and military convoys drove by them. In addition, the mayor of Salvador was campaigning for the governorship of the state. The tinted windows of the fancy cars that I saw speeding by our house were frequently closed. However, no matter how fast the chauffeur-driven cars raced by our shanties, the officials must have glanced at our faces waiting for a chance to cross the road with our naked children watching the parades go by. Unfortunately for the officials, it was the only route to the city's airport.

Depending on the size and condition of *invasão* properties, the Mayor of Salvador offered homeowners between 50 and 145 *cruzeiros*, the Brazilian currency at the time. Mother took a bus to city hall with Fernando to claim the fifty *cruzeiros* offered for our house. But the amounts were hardly enough for people to buy a new house or even a one-bedroom apartment in the poorest outskirts of the city. People couldn't rent a small apartment for more than one or two months, not to mention paying for living expenses. The *cruzeiros* that the mayor offered couldn't even buy the essential materials needed to build a small shack in the resettlement area. Indeed, it could not buy much of anything. But people had no choice but to accept the mayor's inadequate amount of money.

After a brief visit to Boca do Rio, some dwellers packed their few belongings and moved elsewhere. The area scared them. They preferred to build a shack in a shantytown closer to the center of the city and the elite suburbs where many of them worked or made their living as beggars and servants. The majority of the people, though, were forced to move to Boca do Rio, whether they wanted to or not. A few residents, like my family, rented a small ramshackle house on the outskirts for a few months while building a new place in Boca do Rio. My older siblings helped pay the rent.

The city crew moved in, loaded the people and their belongings into dump trucks and drove them to Boca do Rio, where they unloaded their cargo in an empty area across the main highway on the ocean side. The dwellers claimed their few possessions, which some lugged on their backs and heads for a mile to their new piece of land. Others had already started building their shacks, putting them together in a day or two, leaving out details deemed unnecessary, such as windows or indoor plumbing. With the paltry offer from the mayor and the building materials salvaged from their homes in Ondina, some people dug a foundation for their new homes and built a room on top of it. Yet others moved in with friends who could temporarily house them until their shacks were built.

The city trucks deposited more salvaged materials from Ondina and new sheets of Eternit roofing and building materials that the city donated at the site. People would gather around waiting for the trucks. They fought for whatever leftover materials they could collect and carried them on squeaking wheelbarrows. Under the hot sun, they pushed their carts with their possessions up and down the sand dunes and slowly added to the construction of their new homes like a colony of industrious ants. Thus, the slum of Boca do Rio was given life.

Once the dwellers had moved out of the *invasão*, the bulldozers moved in and razed it to the ground. Two high-end hotels, the Ondina Praia and the Othon Palace, were built on one end of the former shantytown. Today, the Meridien Hotel stands tall in front of the rocky beach on the other side. A few basketball courts and colorful metal exercise bars occupy the center.

On the scrubland and white sand dunes of Boca do Rio, a new village of feeble wooden shacks with Eternit roofs was born. Boca do Rio was built the same way that Ondina had been built: building codes were not adhered to and inspections were not performed. The location was a distance from the bus line and again near a dangerous highway. Now people had to cross a busy road to reach the ocean. Boca do Rio was a large, open and uneven brushwood area under a blue sky. The lots allocated to the residents were far apart from former neighbors. Consequently, the strong community bond prevalent in Ondina was blown apart along with the homes. The new shanties were unstable and had no protection. It took one heavy tropical rainstorm and strong ocean wind to shake loose the scraps of wood from the shacks and send their shimmering tin roofs and contents flying into the air or into the sand dunes. A female acquaintance from the shantytown, Dona Vanda, watched her new shack destroyed by the wind in just a few minutes after days of hard labor. She sought shelter in her neighbor's hut until her own was put back together again, scrap by scrap.

The new slum had no electricity, sewage, or running water. The crickets chirped in the dark; the fireflies flickered; the stars shone brightly, and the rattlesnakes roamed freely. During the day, men armed with shiny machetes and heavy wooden sticks chased away the snakes. At night, the women wrapped old rags around wooden sticks, soaked them in kerosene and set them on fire. They stuck the sticks in the sand near their shacks to deter snakes from entering. People in Boca do Rio were especially afraid that the poisonous snakes would bite the pregnant women. They tied a knot on the women's skirts, believing that the knot would prevent snakebites. It seemed to work. Many people in Boca do Rio suffered from snakebites; some died, but never the pregnant women.

Boca do Rio smelled bad. People left their shovels in their backyard to dig holes in the sand and bury their waste. The rain would unearth the sewage and carry it down the streets until it landed on a high sand dune where it stayed until the sun dried it out. The garbage piled up on the distant dunes. When the wind blew, you could smell the stench. Water was stored in a faraway tower, which the women climbed with empty kerosene cans under their arms. They carried full cans back on their heads, snaking down the dunes, in good weather and bad.

The sand dunes in Boca do Rio were infested with a dangerous parasite called *bicho de porco*—pig bug. It was a nasty pest that dug into a person's skin and found its way into the flesh anywhere on the body. It especially attacked children who played in the hot sand and ran barefoot. *Bicho de porco* ate flesh, causing deep wounds and high fevers. Mothers would carry their children to the bus stop by the highway and travel to the public clinics in the city to have the insect removed. I remember that a *bicho de porco* found its way into Rita's vagina. Mother carried Rita, Gaia's first daughter, to the bus stop, then to a clinic in an elite suburb called Canela to have the parasite surgically removed.

Electricity and running water came to Boca do Rio a year later, in 1971. The residents resorted to using a kerosene lamp, *fifó,* which left their nostrils and the walls of their shacks black from the smoke. An elementary school and a water spigot—*chafariz* were built in the Center Square. A few years later, more schools and a medical clinic were built, and bus service began. But as was the case in all of the slums, planning and infrastructure were lacking. This is still reflected in Boca do Rio today. There is some better construction in the midst of the many unsafe, dilapidated, and half-finished shacks. The commercial center, with a population of approximately 10,000, operates on its own. There are several resident-owned stores, many street vendors.

With the fifty *cruzeiros* from the mayor, Miriam and my brothers helped build a small house in Boca do Rio, and the family moved there. When I finished high school in December and left the family that I had been living with in Graça, I went to live with my family in the new slum in January of 1970 to prepare for the college entrance exam, the famous and feared *Vestibular.* The English exam worried me because I had only taken elementary English in middle school and was not prepared for the comprehensive and very competitive exam that required a higher level of reading and comprehension of literary and technical texts.

I rode the bus downtown one afternoon to a private, elite preparatory school called Nobel, famous for its success in preparing students for the exam. There, I asked the teachers who taught Portuguese if I could correct their students' papers in exchange for attending the English classes at the school. They gave me one student's composition to correct while they watched. After examining the paper that I corrected, the teachers handed me a stack of compositions, which I took to the public library. I spent the rest of the month riding the bus downtown to attend English classes in the morning. Afternoons, I corrected papers and prepared for the exam. The preparatory school was far from Boca do Rio, and the public library did not have most of the books on the exam's reading list. The ones that they had were old and many pages were missing.

Fernando lost his job with Petrobrás that year and started riding the bus to the city cemeteries, where he spent evenings gathering wax from candles left at gravesites. He came home on the late bus, and in the morning, in a corner by a coconut tree in the backyard, he built a fire, sat down and melted the cemetery candle wax in a large cauldron. He poured melted wax into tin candle molds of all sizes and let the wax cool. Then he removed the candles, dyed them with brightly colored paint, wrapped and stacked them in plastic bags to sell to vendors in the city.

Fernando wanted to expand his candle business with some of the money he earned. He bought tin molds of the much-feared African god Exu, one familiar to him. My brother would spend a long time filling the Exu molds with hot wax from the cemetery candles and painting the figures black. Exu's lips were tomato red. Fernando placed some of the small figures in his plastic bag and carried the larger ones in his hand. He walked to the bus stop with his figures to wait for the bus to sell Exu to the voodoo priests and priestesses to be used in *candomblé* ceremonies. When other passengers on the crowded buses recognized Exu in Fernando's hands, they quickly made the sign of the cross and hurriedly left their seats if they were near him, giving Fernando more space to enjoy the ride. Some passengers wanted to get away from Fernando and Exu as soon as possible and would get off the bus at the first stop, terrified of the bad luck Exu would bring them.

One evening, Fernando came home laughing. He invited Eduardo to ride the bus with him the next time he took Exu to the market so that Eduardo could witness the effect it had on the passengers. Eduardo told us that Exu worked well on the very crowded buses. When I left the house in the morning to take the bus to school, Fernando recommended that I take his figure with me. He was sure Exu would guarantee me a seat. I didn't take the god, but sometimes when I had to spend long hours waiting for buses under the hot sun, or in the rain, or when I had to stand the entire ride into the city I wished I had taken Fernando's advice.

Gaia and her three children also moved to Boca do Rio. She had to stay with Seu Amado's family, the neighbors who gave us drinking water in Ondina. Gaia's shack had collapsed during a storm. People usually sought shelter with neighbors whose shacks were constructed more sturdily. Those neighbors would stay put and pray that the wind and the rain would spare their shacks. During heavy rains, though, few people dared venture out until the soft sand had soaked up the rainwater and the sun dried it up, making it possible to walk again without getting stuck in the wet sand. If caught in a storm, one had to stay put until the rainwater drained away.

Early one evening, a neighbor woman named Dona Juju was caught in a storm. Back in the shantytown in Ondina, I had seen Dona Juju walking in front of the house in the morning as I climbed the stairs on my way to school.

"Good morning, Dona Juju," I said.

"Good morning, my daughter," she replied.

Calling me "my daughter" was Dona Juju's endearing way of addressing me. As I stood by the highway waiting for an opportunity to cross, I watched Dona Juju walk to the bus stop with her young granddaughters. Their father had abandoned them, and she was raising the two girls, Didi and Dilma. One was seven years old, the other nine, both pretty and lively. Dona Juju was older, perhaps in her 60s, but she looked to be in her 90s, as she was very slow and frail. I knew that the two young girls and the older woman spent their days downtown begging. Dona Juju took the girls with her because they made a compelling trio: an old frail woman with gray hair and two young lively girls with coal dark hair. People in the shantytown had seen them on city corners, holding their tin cans for passersby to drop in some coins. I always wished that I could have sent Dona Juju back home and sent Didi and Dilma to school in the morning.

At sundown, I would see the trio walk past our house, down the small slope, each carrying a plastic bag of groceries in one hand and a tin container with the change that they had collected in the other. The fatigued Dona Juju walked slowly. Didi and Dilma, bouncy and playful, were impatient and walked ahead of their grandmother. They would turn their heads and ask Granny to hasten her pace, "*Anda mais rápido, Vô*"—Walk faster, Granny. Dona Juju would take a few long strides but then slow down again, forcing the girls to slow down with her. But the girls soon would forget and walk ahead of Dona Juju, taking one long step at a time as if playing a game. Dona Juju would stop to rest and walk down the dirt slope all the way to their hut near the end of our row. I looked up from my books and watched them until they disappeared from sight.

Dona Juju later moved to Boca do Rio with Didi and Dilma. The neighbors built their shack. They walked the sandy road to the bus stop by the shoreline and returned at day's end. Didi and Dilma stayed close to their grandmother, understanding that the dunes were high, the sand hot and soft, and Dona Juju was frail. The three held hands as they walked to their shack.

Early one evening when Dona Juju arrived home from begging, she took some of the money from her tin can and walked to a store close to her shack in Boca do Rio to buy some groceries. The sky became dark. The rain came down hard, and Dona Juju left the store thinking that she could make it home if she hurried. As she ran, she stepped in the soft sand made mushy by the torrential rain. Her foot got stuck in a hole in the sand and she could not get it out.

No one heard Dona Juju's cries. The loud rainfall muffled her voice. The heavy raindrops washed down her tears. After the rain stopped, Didi and Dilma went looking for Dona Juju. They found her stuck in the sand, soaked and silent. They cried for help. Female neighbors came running but could not pull her out. Her right foot was shattered. They called for the men, who brought shovels and a chair to carry Dona Juju to the bus stop where they waited for a bus to take her to a public hospital in the city. The doctors operated on Dona Juju's leg. She received medical care for a few months but never walked again. When she came home, I went to see her.

"How are you doing, Dona Juju?" I asked. Lying on an old bed, covered with rags, she opened her eyes when she heard my voice.

"I'm carrying on as God wills it, my daughter," she answered and closed her eyes again.

I left Dona Juju's shack when the female neighbors came by to feed and care for her. Outside, it was calm and the sun was setting, causing patches of bright colors to appear over the horizon. I thought of God and asked Him to please help Dona Juju recover and not let her die. I liked her patient way of carrying on with life and felt sorry for her. Shortly after my visit, Dona Juju died. The women's care and my prayers were in vain. Maybe God knew what He was doing and that was the "way He willed it," as Dona Juju used to say. Since then, every time I think of Dona Juju, I ask God to listen to my prayers, hold her high in His hands, and give her the peace and comfort in heaven that she never experienced on earth.

20. College

S
tudents who plan to enter the public universities in Brazil start preparing for the mandatory national entrance exam called *Vestibular* during the last two years of high school. The examination consists of a long reading list of canonic literary works, a foreign language proficiency, and a challenging test in the subjects associated with the students' career choice. For instance, if a candidate wished to pursue a career in medicine, then biological sciences would weigh more on the average score, whereas math and physics would be the core requirements for engineering candidates. It takes several hours to complete the exam, which is given over an entire week.

Vacancies at public universities are very limited. Students fortunate enough to have attended private schools and students whose parents are able to pay for Vestibular preparatory courses have a better chance of passing the exam than students without such advantages. Roughly 100 university openings are available for 800 or more applicants in major areas like the sciences and engineering.

Most of my classmates enrolled in the afterschool and weekend preparatory courses, which were expensive. I had neither the money nor the time for them because I tutored the siblings of my former students and had added still others to pay for my transportation and expenses. Because I liked French and Portuguese literature, I registered for the *Vestibular* at the Universidade Federal da Bahia, UFBA, in the area of language. I knew that it would be impossible for me to pass the exam in any other area without more books, more time to study, and reinforcement from preparatory courses. My high school years had been far from challenging academically due to frequent teacher strikes, poor teaching, and my lack of books and time to study.

For most students, the *Vestibular* was their main worry, an exam they had prepared for since they began school. My main problems were food, transportation, and housing. Passing the exam, scheduled for January, was of secondary concern.

I was assigned to a testing center located farthest away from me in a section of the lower city at the tip of the Salvador peninsula in a colonial-era suburb called *Bomfim*—Good End. More than two hours away by bus, Bomfim is located on the opposite end of Boca do Rio. Buses that stopped in Boca do Rio came from an even more distant suburb called Itapoã. Buses were often late and overloaded with riders. Sometimes they did not stop, not even when passengers hoping to board desperately stepped away from the waiting crowd, waved their hands high in the air, called to the driver and begged him to stop.

The distance from Boca do Rio to the test center, the bus fares, and the early hour I needed to report to the site worried me, so I contacted Aunt Didi, one of my father's sisters. She had moved to Salvador to live with her children. One of her sons, Antonio, lived near the testing area with his wife Solange. I asked Aunt Didi if I could stay with Antonio and Solange during the week of the exam. They agreed to let me stay at their apartment on *Rua do Céu*— Heaven Street while I took the *Vestibular*.

In February, the newspaper *A Tarde* posted the list of students who had passed the *Vestibular*. I was one of them. I remember not feeling especially happy at the announcement. Deep inside, however, I knew that I would overcome the next barrier and graduate from college no matter what. I had learned to take things as they came and not to expect too much, but my dream to escape poverty was alive. I knew I would do whatever I needed to do. College would just be another phase of my life that I needed to embrace in order to stay afloat. Students who pass the *Vestibular* in Brazil have good reason to celebrate, so they generally combine Carnival week, which also takes place in February, with news of their success on the exam. For me, it was yet another test of my endurance, another samba of survival.

I was not only the first, I was the only person in my family to have taken and passed the *Vestibular*. In most cases, passing the difficult exam provided a path to a better life worth celebrating, but in my family, there was no fuss over my success. I do not remember receiving congratulations. No one mentioned the exam even though everyone knew I had been approved to go to college. My siblings were too absorbed in their own daily struggles. They had neither time nor energy for praise, and they did not understand what the *Vestibular* meant; they did not have any awareness of the difficulties I had overcome. Encouragement to do better in life was not embraced by my family. Everyone was left on their own to meet challenges and attempt to overcome, if able to, their own obstacles.

Because I started school late, at eight-and-a-half years old, I entered college in March 1971 when I was twenty-two, the age when most students are graduating. Most of my classes were in the suburb of Nazaré, in the same general area where I had attended high school. Boca do Rio was a long distance from campus. I would leave home early in the morning and return late at night. I had hoped to receive university housing for poor students, but I soon learned that few vacancies were available for undergraduates from the interior who had no family in the capital. From Boca do Rio, I rode two buses to Nazaré. One took me halfway to Campo Grande, where I transferred to another bus, paid another fare, and rode the rest of the way to an old building in Nazaré. I sometimes rode yet another bus for about half an hour to forty-five minutes from the main campus to another site in Canela, where I had some classes.

My classes were spread out throughout the day, one or two in the morning, for instance, and a few others in the afternoon. In between, I tutored some of the Graça students I had kept in and Barra. The money I earned tutoring was spent mostly on bus fares and for books. If there was any left, I bought food. There was no money to help Mother or to pay for anything else.

On more than one occasion, while waiting for the buses, I got totally drenched and had no other choice but to go on with my day. I would have missed all of my classes if I had gone home to change and had to walk back again to wait for another crowded bus. I loved the rain, and it never prevented me from leaving home or doing what I had to do. Traveling to the suburbs to tutor became a problem, though. At times, I was late for some of my college classes and had very little or no time left for my schoolwork. If I spent more time studying, I would have had no means to keep afloat. And worst of all, I couldn't afford some of the books and dictionaries that I needed.

Some days, instead of taking two buses to school, I would take the longer bus ride and walk to and from campus for an hour the rest of the way. One weekend, to alleviate my money shortage, I decided to take a bus from Boca do Rio to visit some of the mothers whose children I had tutored in Ondina. I walked to Dona Zélia's apartment and then to Dona Terezinha's house and asked if any of their children needed tutoring. They were happy to see me and to learn that I was in college. Not only did they arrange for me to help some of their children on weekends, but they also contacted their friends and neighbors to attract more students. In this way, I earned a little more money to pay my expenses.

I enrolled in six courses in my first semester in college. English, French, Latin and linguistics were mandatory for my double language major in Portuguese and French. The English texts that the professor brought to class were long and difficult. They were nothing like the simple greetings, daily vocabulary, and dialogues that I had memorized in middle school or the readings I had studied for the college entrance exam. The texts came from *Time* magazine and similar sources and had many words, expressions, and issues that I had never heard of and did not understand. I remember one text that discussed the habitat of the puma. Another described the many types of berries grown in the North. I found it difficult to visualize these berries because the ones I was used to in the South were wild. Each subject made the readings even more difficult to understand. In addition, I had neither the resources nor the time to prepare for class.

The public university that I attended did not have a library on campus where I could study, consult, or borrow books. The building was only a structure where students and professors met for classes. There were no gathering areas, lounges, or cafeterias. The professors were not available to help the students either. They taught their classes and left. There were no office hours nor any demonstrable willingness to help students who were falling behind. The students were on their own, the captains of their ships. One either sank or swam. Only the fittest swam, and those were mostly the students from the upper social class. They were the ones who lived at home and were supported by their parents; the ones who owned expensive cars or were driven by chauffeurs; the ones who wore designer clothes; the ones who could afford books; the ones who didn't have to work.

There were only a few poor students in my class, but none were as poor as I was. Most of my classmates came from the lower middle class or the elite class. Some had been taking private lessons in English. One girl, who was a stellar student, was a member of the Magalhães dynasty, the family that had enjoyed decades of

204

economic and political control and dominance in the state. The family had streets, roads, and public buildings named after them, including the city's international airport, whose name was changed from Dois de Julho—July second, the state Independence Day, to Deputado Luís Eduardo Magalhães. The girl was from the same family as the mayor of Salvador who had removed the dwellers from Ondina and relocated them in Boca do Rio. She knew the answers to the most challenging test questions. I overheard her one day explaining to some other girls that she had been studying English at the best private schools in the area "since she could remember."

She earned the highest grades in class. The professor looked to her for the answers that no one else knew. She would come to class well-groomed, wearing high heels and nice clothes. She and some of the other girls discussed the latest fashions from Paris. Her uniformed chauffeur always sat in the car by the curb waiting to open the door for her after class. Sometimes her mother drove her. On my walk to my second bus stop to save money, I watched her family car speed by me. In class, I felt intimidated by this girl, not because of her clothes, car, or chauffeur, but because she had the books and dictionaries that I needed and knew the answers that I didn't. I always sat in the back row. My worn-out shoes, my faded *Baixa do Sapateiro* clothes, and my frizzy, bushy hair often made me shy away from the elite group.

That first semester, I failed English and had to repeat the course twice. I also failed linguistics, which was in the afternoon when I had to tutor in the distant suburbs and spent a long time waiting for the buses or walking to save the bus fare. Since I had taken French throughout middle and high school, I was more familiar with the language and able to pass that course. French is closer to my native Portuguese. I had also kept the scholarship that I had earned in middle school to attend the *Maison Française* to study French.

During the school year on my way home late in the evening, if I had extra cash I would stop at a small butcher shop and buy whatever I could afford, usually a piece of liver or cow brain. I carried the meat home wrapped in newspaper ready to cook on our propane stove. Often, it was the only meal I would eat all day.

My busy schedule and the bus problem prevented me from arriving at my students' homes during their family's lunch hour, as

I had in the past. On the days that I had no money for lunch, I would visit either Eduardo, who worked at a parking lot near Praça da Sé, or Tatai, who briefly worked at a glass factory near the university. I would ask Eduardo for some cash or find Tatai among the workers getting ready for lunch and ask him if he could get a ticket for me to eat with him. Tatai would ask his boss for permission to buy me a lunch ticket for the same low price as the workers, and I was happy to walk into the cafeteria with Tatai.

A few other times when money was scarce for food, I visited another of Aunt Didi's children, a young English teacher named Maria Luiza who lived near the university. When she heard that I had passed the *Vestibular,* she gave Mother her address and said I could come to her apartment for lunch when I wanted. When Tatai lost his job at the glass factory and I could no longer eat with him, I walked down a steep cobblestone hill under the hot noon sun to my cousin's apartment. The maid answered when I rang her doorbell.

"I'm one of Maria Luiza's cousins," I explained. "Is she home?"

"No. She isn't yet but soon will be here for lunch," she said. "You may come in and wait for her."

I was overtaken by feelings of extreme awkwardness and embarrassment when I waited in the living room while my students and their families ate lunch. I hardly knew this cousin, or any other cousin who lived in the city. My family had only occasional contact with them, and most of them had kept their distance from us. I did not feel at all comfortable being at Maria Luiza's place to eat lunch. Besides, my cousin's apartment was stylish and clean. I believe the awkwardness I felt was a consequence of my deprivation and living on the margins of society. It is as if you get used to the inhumane conditions you have endured for so long and, once you are confronted with a different environment, you feel small and intimidated. And so it was with me.

Maria Luiza's hardwood floor smelled of fresh wax and shone so brightly it almost reflected my figure, like a shiny mirror. The scent of fresh flowers in every corner of the apartment mingled with the smell of tropical fruits and other food coming from the kitchen. The linen accented the orderly placement of the colorful dishes on the dining table. The maid rushed around in her blue uniform and matching cap and apron, attentive to details. My uneasy feeling grew deeper as I sat in the living room waiting for my cousin to arrive. I thought of what I would say and prepared an explanation for why I was in her living room at noon. I chose my words carefully and rehearsed them in my head. But when the doorbell rang and the maid hurried to open the door, I wanted to rush out so that I didn't have to recite the explanation that I had been practicing. Nevertheless, I stood up to greet my cousin when I overheard the maid mention my name and saw Maria Luiza walking toward me.

"Oh, your mother must have given you my address," she said as she approached.

"Yes, Mother said you mentioned I could come to your place for lunch," I said. "I don't have enough time to tutor as much as I used to and sometimes I run out of money," I added.

"I understand. You come here whenever you want to," she said. "We'll eat in a little while after I shower and my husband arrives."

Maria Luiza was friendly, but I wished that I could eat the food that I smelled and leave without having to wait any longer. After her husband arrived, the maid served lunch. I sat opposite my cousin and answered the few questions she asked me about school. After lunch I thanked Maria Luiza and left in a hurry, wishing she had asked the maid to feed me as soon as I entered her place. I wished that I was able to eat alone and leave. My discomfort was greater than my hunger. I never returned to Maria Luiza's apartment.

Late one Tuesday afternoon during my third semester, I was sitting on the warm cement steps outside the *Maison Française* in Canela, preparing for my French class, when I noticed a young man leaning against a nearby wall and looking at me.

"Do you study French?" he asked when I looked up.

"Yes, I study here at the *Maison Française*," I answered.

"I'm also studying French because I want to go to France after I finish college," he said.

"What's your major?" I asked.

"Architecture. I'm Fred," he answered.

As I got up and started walking toward the building, Fred turned toward me.

"And what's your name?" he asked.

"Leda," I answered.

"What days do you come here, Leda?"

"Tuesdays and Thursdays," I answered.

"Most of my classes are here in Canela. I may see you again," Fred said, then went on his way.

To my great surprise and delight, Fred was waiting for me by the entrance of the building the following Thursday when I arrived at class. We talked about French, school, and studying abroad. After that Thursday, I thought a lot about Fred but did not expect to see him again. He was good-looking, blond, blue-eyed, calm and soft-spoken, and just a bit serious. Before I said goodbye, Fred asked me where I lived.

"Boca do Rio," I answered.

"Boca do Rio is far away. Incidentally, I have a friend whose girlfriend lives there. How long does it take you to get to school?" he asked.

"It takes a long time, up to a couple of hours or even longer some days, depending on the buses. But I leave home early in the morning when the buses are a bit less crowded, and I don't return until evening," I answered.

Fred left for his classes. The following Tuesday, he waited for me by the entrance of the building. Our short conversation was again about French and school, but this time he asked if he could come to Boca do Rio on the weekend to see me.

I felt like a frog turned into a princess. The disorderly conditions of our house and Boca do Rio immediately flashed through my mind, though. My family lived in an unfinished, unpainted four-room adobe house with an Eternit roof made from a compound of cement and asbestos fibers that dispersed suffocating heat throughout the day. The house had a small entryway, two bedrooms, a living room, and a kitchen. There was no bathroom. We buried the waste in the sand in the backyard like everyone in Boca do Rio. Little by little, Miriam and Eduardo were helping to enlarge the house in which eleven of us now lived. The slum of Boca do Rio, on the other hand, still painted a grim picture: it was enveloped in a choking stench; had only a few roads with no signs; and displayed a great deal of disorganization and chaos during the day. At night, it was a dark sandy wasteland with insects and reptiles.

However, I was too excited about Fred and thought that I would scare him away if I mentioned the deplorable state of Boca do Rio. Instead, I said it would be fine for him to come visit me. That day and the following days, I didn't think about anything but seeing Fred again. It was the first time that a boy I liked showed interest in me.

I had never discussed much about my life with anyone in my family. I told Mother, however, that I had met Fred and that he was coming to see me. Despite all the goodness Mother displayed, she just wasn't engaged in her children's lives. I don't think she knew how to offer guidance to any of us. She was always very quiet and showed indifference to the life each of us led. I don't think that she knew what to say or do about most happenings around her. She just let them happen, and in one way or another, we later paid the consequences. We all dispersed in our own way. Mother never complained about having to raise two of my sister's children after raising her own, for instance. Was it because Mother married at fourteen, was robbed of her own childhood, and forced to raise so many children alone without having been prepared for the many difficulties that she would confront in life? I often wondered.

On the Saturday that Fred came to Boca do Rio, I woke up early and was excited. I decided that I needed a good suntan, so I walked to the beach and lay under the sun. I thought about Fred and what to say when he came. The nights had been bright, but the moon was appearing in the sky later in the evening, so I asked Fernando for some of his candles to light the entryway where I planned to visit with Fred. In the past, Fernando had given me candles when I needed to stay up at night to study for an exam.

I set some of Fernando's colorful candles on the cement wall of our entryway, where they were ready to light later in the evening. I drenched my head in coconut oil during the day and kept my hair tied up in a bun to tame it before washing it with the shampoo I had bought—a luxury that I could seldom afford. I normally washed my hair with bar soap, which made it even drier and wilder in the dense humidity. In the evening, I wore my best outfit, a white dress with small yellow flowers, and lit the candles in the entryway.

I waited for Fred, nervous as night fell. I wondered if Fred would get lost in Boca do Rio. I thought it might have been a good idea if I had offered to meet him at the bus stop to show him the way to our house. I feared he might never find it. Then, what to say when he came? An idea occurred to me. I was taking French poetry that semester and had completely fallen in love with it. Aware of Fred's interest in French, I thought that I would look over a copy of one poem that we had read in class. I appreciated the poem because it spoke to my secret dream of making life better for me and my family. I reread it and planned on sharing it with Fred. As I worked on my reading, leaning against the wall in the entryway, the moon peeked out from under a blanket of passing dark clouds. It appeared and disappeared before giving way to full brightness. I felt relieved, knowing that the moon would brighten Fred's way and the entryway to my house.

I blew out the candles and waited with the French poem in hand. When he arrived at last, Fred was wearing jeans, tennis shoes, and a blue shirt, almost as blue as his eyes. I was happy to see him but tried to disguise my excitement.

"Did you have problem finding the way?" I asked.

"I rode the bus with my friend Roberto. He came to Boca do Rio to see his girlfriend and they helped me find your house. Otherwise, it would have been very difficult," he said.

"I'm glad they helped you," I said. "How was the ride?"

"Long. It took hours for the bus to come and a long time to get here. I don't know how you do it every day," he said.

"It's a daily hassle," I said.

We held hands and talked. Fred asked about my family and my classes. I told him about feeling alienated and distant from my siblings and about the difficulties of living in Boca do Rio and attending classes in Nazaré. Fred said he was the only child of German immigrants and that he lived with his parents in the city. He wanted to have a place of his own but could not find a job to fit his schedule since his classes were spread throughout the day. I mentioned the classes I had failed and my fear of failing more subjects due to my lack of study time and my tutoring schedule. But French was going well. The professor had brought some poems to class that were melodious. I liked one poem in particular, I said, because it spoke about my feelings and my desire to free myself and those close to me from the conditions that we lived in. I asked if he wanted me to read it. Fred laughed and nodded in agreement.

I picked up a thick packet of poems I had been reading, opened it to Rimbaud's *Sensation*, which *I* read by Fernando's flickering candlelight.

Par les soirs bleus d'été, j'irais dans les sentiers,	*In blue summer evenings, I will travel the paths,*
Picoté par les blés, fouler l'herbe menue:	*Tickled by the wheat, trampling the short grass:*
Rêveur, j'en sentirai la fraîcheur à mes pieds,	*Dreaming, feeling its coolness upon my feet,*
Je laisserai le vent baigner ma tête nue.	*I will let the wind bathe my bare head.*
Je ne parlerai pas, je ne penserai rien:	*I will not speak, I will think of nothing:*
Mais l'amour infini me montera dans l'âme,	*But infinite love will fill my soul,*
Et j'irai loin, bien loin, comme un bohémien,	*And I will go far, far away, as a bohemian,*
Par la Nature - heureux comme avec une femme.	*Through Nature—happy as with a woman.*

Fred liked the poem and asked me to read it again. I reread it and commented that the voice in the text expressed a communion with nature and the surrender of the innermost self. Fred and I agreed that the poem conveyed connections to the present while projecting that connectedness into the future by wishing to flee to a distant place, free from worries and full of love. I told Fred about Castro Alves and how I felt free in the open space of our backyard, always in touch with nature and the wild. I remembered the raindrops pounding on the roof tiles, the ponds with the singing frogs, and the early morning trips to drink milk at the corral. I was trapped in the filthy conditions I had been living in Salvador, and I dreamed of searching for a better life. The poem expressed my silent longing to leave Boca do Rio and Brazil behind.

Fred liked the idea of wandering, of going "far, far away, as a bohemian." He wanted to finish college and travel to his European ancestral land, to let go of weights and worries, and to live lovingly and happily. I told Fred how good it felt to read Rimbaud by Fernando's cemetery wax candlelight. I told the story of the candle under the shining moon. I asked if we could read more French poems the next time that I saw him. We laughed, and Fred shook his head in agreement. It felt wonderful to have Fred and the French poets.

I saw Fred in Canela before French class the following week and then again in Boca do Rio on weekends. I kept the ritual of crossing the busy highway to sunbathe at the beach. I spent all of Saturday getting ready for Fred to visit for a few hours in the evening. After a few more weeks of holding hands and kissing, one evening Fred mentioned that his friend Roberto, who rode the bus with him to see his girlfriend, had shared with him the enjoyable sex he had with Bianca in the dark corners of Boca do Rio. Roberto had a good laugh when Fred told him that all we did was hold hands, kiss, and read poetry in a candlelit entryway.

Fred's visits became intense. His French kissing became longer and harder, and his hands started travelling over my whole body as if searching for hidden treasure. He found places that I did not know existed and awoke my dormant senses. I liked Fred's warmth, closeness, and comfort. Above all, I loved his friendship. I had finally found someone to talk to and share my thoughts and feelings with. But as Fred's breathing accelerated, my body quivered, my heart raced, and my inner voice began speaking loudly. A line from my middle school principal suddenly came back to me: "Your body is the Temple of God," and Fred was violating this temple. Guilt and fear took hold of me and muffled my pleasures. The thought of getting pregnant unnerved me. I drew away from Fred when his body and mine became entangled in a dark corner of the entryway after he blew out the cemetery candles. Because of what had happened to my sisters and to some girls in the neighborhood, I associated sex with pregnancy. They had sex, got pregnant, and their lives, for all intents and purposes, were over. I feared that it would happen to me and my now clear dreams of graduating from college and getting out of poverty would die.

One Saturday evening when Fred came to see me in Boca do Rio, I told him of my fears, explaining how Gaia and Miriam's boyfriends had left them pregnant and how difficult it had been for Mother to raise their children. Fred said he understood but that he would be very careful not to let it happen to me. He added that the ride to Boca do Rio was getting too long, and French poetry was a bit dull, especially in comparison to Roberto's stories of wild sex with Bianca. He could no longer take the long ride merely to hold hands and then ride back and listen to Roberto's stories. Fred wanted sex, too, and since I had not conquered the guilt and fear that the nuns had planted in my head long ago, he would no longer be my boyfriend and come to Boca do Rio. That was the end of my relationship with Fred.

I was heartbroken. I could not concentrate on tutoring or studying. I thought of Fred while studying French poetry and looked around for him when I went to class. I no longer sat on the warm cement steps. Instead, I waited for class to begin inside the building. I saw Fred in every slender young man with blond hair and blue eyes. I looked for him on buses, on campus, and everywhere else I went. Weekends were the worst. Instead of sunbathing on Saturdays, I took long walks on the beach and thought of nothing but Fred. Even the ocean reminded me of his blue eyes. It took me a long time to get over him. I still think of Fred's blue eyes and Fernando's candles in the entryway when I read French poetry. I wonder if Fred had anything to do with my marrying a man with deep blue eyes.

21. A New Beginning

Toward the end of my fourth semester, living in Boca do Rio became increasingly difficult for me. Balancing tutoring in the distant suburbs with the demands of my classes, then transportation, the busses often late and crowded, was exhausting. When I was unprepared because I did not have the books my professors assigned, I became anxious. I constantly feared that I would be asked questions that I couldn't answer and that I would fail all my classes. I began dreaming that I had taken the wrong bus to school and rode aimlessly through the city's unpaved, potholed, and muddy roads. In my dreams, I would be glued to the ground, tongue-tied, and unable to utter a word when my professors asked me a question even though I had the correct answer. In my dreams, I failed all my classes and never graduated, or I graduated but when the officials were handing me my diploma it would fly off into the sky so fast and so high it would disappear into the dark clouds. To me, my dreams were real. I would lie awake sweaty and worried during the night and would wait for daybreak. My worries and nightmares went on for a while.

In my linguistics class, I became friends with Norma, a kind girl from *Vitoria da Conquista,* located in the interior of the state where Father and Mother were married. Norma came to study in the capital. Her father had bought her an apartment in Graça. She noticed that I didn't carry books to class and that I looked very tense and distant. I was taking seven classes, had very little time to study and was consumed by my long bus rides and frequent nightmares. One day, Norma invited me to her apartment to eat cold beans and study for a linguistics exam. I was very appreciative and felt a tremendous sense of relief since I had failed the course in my first semester and feared failing it again. Norma let me borrow some of her books on weekends and let me copy her notes when I was late or missed class. She also started serving me food in her apartment when I slept over. I realized how much easier it was not riding the bus back and forth to Boca do Rio. It saved me significant time and money. I wanted to ask Norma if I could be her roommate but changed my mind when she mentioned that her parents and younger sister often came to visit.

Otherwise, my relationship with most of my classmates was

confined to the classroom. I was very self-conscious and felt the girls' eyes were fixed on me all the time. I sometimes would overhear them chatting and laughing about the movies they had seen, the nightclubs and parties they had attended, and their boyfriends. They sometimes giggled while discussing the many concoctions they had mixed in their kitchen blenders—the apples, carrots, and orange juice, or the extra palm oil they used in their foods for aphrodisiac effects. I was never a part of any of their conversations and stayed away from the groups of girls.

My world was different. I never had money to see a movie, never visited the famous nightclubs or the distant beaches, and was never invited to any of my classmates' parties or celebrations. My exclusion was easy to understand since the Brazilian culture puts a great deal of emphasis on physical appearance and material possessions. Social class status is important. My physique and clothes clearly revealed my low social and economic standing. My hair never shone or bounced in the air, my clothes were worn out, and my figure was frail. I did not walk with the swagger and charm of a typical girl.

Once, a classmate named Laura invited me to her bridal shower at a friend's house. In retrospect, I think she must have felt badly and asked me to attend after inviting everyone else in class. I wanted to go, so I bought a broom as a gift. It was the only thing that I could afford. When I showed up at the nicely decorated house holding the broom, I elicited lots of laughter and jokes. I felt like I had fallen out of an airplane and was out of breath and words. I could not even eat the many sweets the uniformed maids passed around on elegant silver trays. I found an excuse to leave soon after arriving. It was the first and last time I was ever invited to, or cared to be part of, any party.

In the middle of my fifth semester, Miriam traveled to Castro Alves to move Ua and her family to Salvador. Her husband Louri found little work after the Suerdick tobacco factories closed in town. Ua and her family of seven by then moved in with Mother and my siblings. I was again taking seven classes, including Portuguese literature. I had neither the time nor the money to read or buy the books. Consequently, I failed the class. The following semester I moved into the city with two girls, Bernadete and Alice, whom I had met at the school chapel while living in Ondina. I reconnected with the girls on the bus one day and learned they were looking for a third roommate to help pay for the small apartment they rented on Avenida Sete in the center of the city. I tutored more students to help pay the rent and was relieved that I no longer had to ride the buses. I slept on their worn-out cot and shared a room with Alice. On weekends, we shopped for food and cooked together. It felt great to have companionship and food to eat on a daily basis. The proximity to the university and to my students also saved me time and money in addition to easing my anxieties and nightmares.

Through Bernadete and Alice I met Ivan, a friend of theirs. Ivan stopped at the apartment on weekends and took us for a ride on the coastline in his car. As the four of us walked on the beach, he showed a special interest in me. I did not think much about Ivan. When he came to visit and I wasn't around, he asked the girls about me. One Saturday he came to the apartment and asked me on a date. After Fred, I wasn't interested in dating. My classes and tutoring occupied me and were all I could handle. The girls said that they had known Ivan since high school and that he was a good man, so I said yes to his request for a date.

One moonless and chilly Friday night, Ivan took me for a ride along the coastline. Without any explanation, he parked the car at a distant beach near many other cars already parked there. I had heard of these distant beaches in the *Orla Marítima,* the famous seaside, where lovers would park their cars and spend the evenings engaged in intimate behavior in the back seat. As soon as Ivan turned the engine off, I heard the loud symphony of "oohs" and "ahs.' It did not take me long to realize that Ivan wanted sex. When his hands reached for my body, the many voices in my head repeated the chant: "Your body is the Temple of God." And again, the idea of getting pregnant petrified me. This time though, I didn't bother explaining anything to Ivan and asked him to drive me to the apartment, where I locked myself in the bedroom and cried. Bernadete, a psychology student, was home studying when she heard my sobbing. From the kitchen table, she laughingly yelled out, *"Alguém deu o cabaço hoje"*—Someone gave away the gourd today, a popular saying that meant a girl had given away her virginity. I didn't bother explaining anything to Bernadete. Ivan stopped coming to our place, and I never saw him again.

In 1973, during my seventh semester in college, Eduardo rented a three-bedroom apartment in Parque São Paulo, a lower middle-class apartment complex in Avenida Centenário, near the elite suburbs of Barra and Graça. It was much closer to the city and the best area anyone in my family had ever lived in. Eduardo and Raimundo still worked maneuvering cars in a small parking lot. At that time, the city had torn down an old building with a larger vacant area nearby. Eduardo saw an opportunity to expand his parking business and rented the space. His business prospered, and he soon was able to buy the apartment that he rented. Everyone in the family moved into Eduardo's place, except Ua and Gaia who stayed in Boca do Rio with their families. I also needed to move in with the family a short time after my roommate Bernadete graduated and Alice moved home since we hadn't found a tenant to replace her and couldn't afford the place by ourselves.

For my family, the move to Eduardo's apartment was incredible. For me, it was an opportunity to reunite with my mother and siblings. I helped with the utilities and food and came home for lunch when my schedule allowed and when I tutored in the suburbs nearby. The money I earned at the time went a little further, and I could afford more books, a few more clothes, and a little money to give to Mother. I even bought a small LP of Puccini's *Madame Butterfly* that I had heard when I walked by a music store. I thought the music was dazzling. However, the LP stayed in its cover since I could never save enough money to buy a record player.

In 1973, Salvador experienced worker strikes, student demonstrations and protests against the military, especially at the universities. The military rule in Brazil that began in 1964 had become increasingly authoritarian and repressive. Students, peasants, and other citizens had lost their rights, and their voices were silenced during the years of dictatorship. Many protesters were jailed and persecuted. Classes were often cancelled without notice. Professors and the intellectual elite went on strike to challenge the lack of freedom of the press. Students often carried flags and banners in the streets, protesting the arrests, torture, and disappearance of many of their fellows. Groups of students from other campuses often gathered at our school to give the latest news of arrests and other oppression that they had heard about from underground groups. I tutored more when the students and professors were on strike and saved money to buy the books and clothes that I needed.

I graduated in December of 1974 with a bachelor's degree in French and Portuguese, after having completed eight semesters in college, with forty-four courses, 124 credits, and 2,610 credit hours. I was twenty-five and did not bother attending any kind of graduation ceremony. I do not even remember if there was one. In my last years of college, I nurtured a promise of change and a dream to live life as a normal young woman, doing the activities a young person normally does, such as dating, going to the movies and parties, and listening to music. I dreamed of traveling to France to visit the museums and cultural places that I had studied in class and to speak the language I had spent many years learning. I wanted to live in the land of the poets that I loved.

After graduation, I found a full-time job from 7 a.m. to noon, teaching French at a secondary school in a suburb called Rio Vermelho, a little past Ondina. In the afternoons, I taught Portuguese from 1 to 5 p.m. at my old school in Ondina. Both were full-time jobs though the salary was just enough to meet my basic needs. But life was easier for me. I was no longer going hungry and neither was my family. I still lived in Eduardo's apartment and depended on the crowded buses to get to work. A car was too expensive.

One weekend, while visiting the family that I had lived with in Graça, the mother invited me for coffee and dessert. She told me that one of her sisters-in-law had married an American and lived in the United States, in Arlington, Virginia. The couple was looking for a live-in nanny to watch their two children, a toddler and a newborn. Dona Clara had thought of me and wanted to know if I would be interested. I was breathless for only a second and said that I would be very happy to take the job. Dona Clara would soon talk to her in-laws and recommend me. She gave me the number and address of the woman who was making the arrangements for her sister. I couldn't thank Dona Clara enough.

I walked home feeling blessed and knowing that the change I dreamed about was palpable. I wanted to pinch myself and hoped that the job would come through. I radiated happiness when I told my family the news of my possible travels. My siblings were indifferent, as they had been in the past. Mother, however, wanted to know where the United States was in the world. I walked to a newsstand, bought a map and showed it to Mother. The size of the U.S. amazed us. I located Virginia on the map and began to imagine what it would be like to live there taking care of an infant and a toddler for a family I had never met. These thoughts later became secondary to the world of possibilities that would open up for me.

The next day, I walked to Graça to see Helena, the sister in charge of the travel arrangements, anxious to learn if the family in the U.S. was agreeable to the arrangement. I also would need to be instructed as to how to prepare for the trip. I soon found myself at the Federal Police station in line for photos and a passport. My excitement was boundless. I visited Helena every day after my teaching, wanting to learn if the plans were going well and if the family had sent my plane ticket. Helena must have been tired of my eagerness and frequent presence at her apartment, but she was always gracious and patient with me. To this day, I remain grateful to her. Though I could not see it at the time, the daily travails of living on the margins of society had burned me out. Leaving Brazil in search of a better life was the only thing I could concentrate on.

The day Helena handed me the ticket, I took the money that I had been saving for the trip and went to Baixa do Sapateiro to buy myself a new dress, a pair of shoes, and a small bag for traveling. I did not have much to carry and was glad when Helena told me not to worry about what to take because her sister would buy me what I needed when I arrived in the U.S. I continued to teach every day before I left. I was full of hope, even though I knew very little about my new family and country. I had heard of the prosperity of the U.S.; had seen the news of an American walking on the moon in 1969; and had heard of the American ambassador kidnapped in Rio by a group of leftist students and exchanged for the release of fifteen jailed political prisoners. Eventually freed, the prisoners were sent from Brazil to Mexico after the Brazilian military tortured them in jail.

On the day of my trip, I was up before sunrise and found Mother in the kitchen making coffee. I told her that I would send her some money every month. She was quiet but did not appear overly sad that I was leaving. We didn't talk. I had a lot to tell Mother but could not bring myself to say anything. I wanted to tell her that I loved her and that I wished that I had done more for her. However, deep inside, I resented her and could not disregard the feeling. I felt that I should have received more from Mother—more food, guidance, encouragement and stability. I wish now that I had had a better understanding of my mother and the reality we had dealt with. I only understood a fraction of that reality, only the part of the world that impoverished my family and forced us to frantically dance the samba of survival each and every day. I hadn't seen the bigger picture of the nation we lived in, a nation with a high level of tolerance for inequality. I wish now that I had respected and accepted Mother for who she was. She had given her children all she had. She had struggled desperately and fought mightily for the survival of her children in a nation in which the poor are children of a lesser God.

I quietly drank coffee sitting in the kitchen while Mother picked through the beans she was preparing to cook. She asked if I had any money to buy the ingredients to make *caruru*, a dish of fresh diced okra cooked in thick palm tree oil called *dendê*, with dried shrimp, farina, peanuts, and caju nuts. She knew I liked the dish. I said that I had some money, which I was planning to give her when I left. I took the money and walked across the street to a small neighborhood store where I bought the ingredients and came back to help Mother cook.

Early in the afternoon, Helena came to the apartment with her husband to drive me to the airport. Mother rode in the car with me. Eduardo, who had bought a Volkswagen beetle, packed the car with as many people as he could to follow me to the airport. We left the apartment for the 6 p.m. flight to Rio de Janeiro, where I was to take the 10 p.m. flight to Miami, then another flight to Dulles Airport in Washington where the family was to meet me. I had never been on a plane or traveled outside Salvador, except when I visited Ana Maria's farm. I was not afraid of flying, even though I had never been on a plane. I was struck with nostalgia as the car passed Ondina, the school I had attended, and the shoreline lined with coconut trees. The car entered a narrow road where tall bamboo trees bent over high in the air. The branches tangled with the other bamboo trees growing on the opposite side of the road to form an archway, shaded from the sun, like a tunnel. The cars drove through this archway to the departure terminal at the airport. I was passing through my last dark tunnel in Brazil. I would soon fly to meet with bamboo trees up high in the sky, soaring toward the sun that would light up my new life.

After the good-byes and some crying, Helena handed me a piece of paper with the new family's phone number, some coins and directions on how to use public phone in case I needed to call, and a twenty-dollar bill. I put these things in my purse, entered the departure gate, and walked a short distance to the airplane. I looked back a few times to wave to my mother and siblings, who were standing on a tall balcony. I took my seat by the window, knowing that when I woke up I would be in the United States.

The aircraft soared into the twilight. The setting sun spread dazzling rays through the sky, and the plane slowly assumed its flight path. I saw the enchanted Abaeté Lagoon that I had heard about, with its white sand dunes and crystal-clear water. The distant, shining shacks in Boca do Rio were hidden by the sand dunes. The tall buildings that housed the students I had tutored appeared in Pituba. The infinite ocean of my backyard stretched out before me, beauty streaming through it. It was clear blue at first, but as the plane flew higher in the air, the water seemed darker. The ocean became darker and farther away until it looked like nothing but a black hole. I was leaving behind a land of incongruities and contradictions, a land of abundance and splendor for the few, of deprivation, injustice, and indignity for the many—a native land that I could no longer imagine or dream of to call my own.

The plane ascended and billowy white clouds filled the blue sky. We cut through the clouds. My neck became stiff and my head grew heavy from looking down. I rested on the chair, closed the window shade and shut my eyes. In my mind, the white clouds had turned into the tall, frothy ocean waves in the backyard of the shantytown in Ondina. I saw them approaching, filling the caves in the rocks with clear water, finding me in a corner and gently sweeping me away. I rode the waves, my body floating slowly, caressed by the current and the wind. I surrendered my innermost self. I closed my eyes tightly, let go of my body and traveled farther and farther away from the dark hole into a new light, away from the captivity of poverty and deprivation to a faraway land of infinite possibilities. It was a wonderful feeling.

Epilogue

While attending Northern Virginia Community College, I stayed with a host family, Nieta and Sandy. I learned English, earned a Bachelor of Arts degree, and met people from different countries. The family gave me room and board and a weekly allowance for personal expenses. In exchange, I took care of a baby boy and a toddler girl. I saved any money I had left after expenses and took on an additional job delivering the morning Washington *Post* in the neighborhood to earn some extra cash to send to Mother. My host family treated me well and included me in all of their social activities, exposing me to social etiquette and a variety of foods. They were very socially active and well connected. Although I was very busy taking care of the children and going to school, I gained some insight into American culture and history during my stay by visiting many wonderful sites, museums, and monuments of the nation's capital.

In the summer of 1979, after I'd lived in the U.S. for almost two years, the head of my host family was transferred to work overseas. The family had to move, and I was not permitted to come along. I returned to Brazil, where I took back my teaching job at my old middle school during the day, rented an apartment nearby, and brought Mother to live with me.

In the evening, I taught Portuguese to speakers of other languages, professionals and their spouses working for multinational companies in Brazil. In addition to teaching Portuguese, I planned cultural activities and guided my students through a day-to-day living in an unfamiliar culture.

One of my students, an American named Paul Hogan, approached me after class one evening to ask if I could give him private lessons on Sundays because he wanted to become proficient in Portuguese but did not have enough time to study during the week.

Mr. Hogan and I began meeting for lessons late on Sunday afternoons. After a few weeks of meeting for a couple of hours, Mr. Hogan asked if I would come to church with him to hear Mass together Sunday mornings. We ended up spending a whole day together, and after a few weeks, Paul asked me on a date. We enjoyed going to the beach, theater, and grocery shopping together.

Paul was an Irish Catholic, extremely religious, conservative, and hard working. One day he asked me if I wanted to return to the United States to attend graduate school after I had mentioned to him my desire to attend an American university. He helped me secure my student visa and paid for room and board and my graduate work at Saint Cloud State University in Minnesota, where I graduated with a master's degree in English.

After I left Brazil, Eduardo lost his parking business. The city would not renew his contract and reclaimed the space it had rented to my brother. Eduardo could not pay for the apartment and the car he had bought. Both were repossessed.

Some of my siblings moved back to Boca do Rio. Mother moved in with my brother Tatai, who was married then. After years of bouncing in and out of small businesses and misfortunes with a wife and four children, Eduardo developed lung cancer and lost his last battle in 2003. He died in a public hospital in Salvador with little relief from the severe pains he suffered for one month—in a similar way that my father had died in Castro Alves forty-seven years earlier.

Ua heads a multigenerational household of four adult daughters, two sons, two daughters-in-law, eight grandchildren, and two great-grandchildren, all living in a kind of housing complex with units attached to each other on top of Ua's house in Boca do Rio. Her husband Louri died from liver cancer after years of heavy drinking. He had abused his children and Ua and left her a small pension that she uses to maintain the house and help her children and the poor people around her.

Gaia's husband, Zeca, died in a public hospital, afflicted by lung cancer from drinking. He also suffered from tuberculosis and many venereal diseases. Zeca left Gaia with nine children, seven girls and two boys, and no money or pension of any kind. He also left ten mistresses and ten children with nothing. Zeca died so destitute that my brothers took up a collection to buy clothes and a casket to bury him. Gaia lives in Boca do Rio with three of her children in a structure that is a great improvement from her previous tin roof shack.

Miriam left Salvador to live in the interior with a man whom she met while working at a furniture store in Baixa do Sapateiro. After twenty-five years together and three children, Miriam separated from her abusive partner and had to go to court to be granted the upstairs of the house which they shared. Miriam's first-born son has a degree in chemical engineering. He and his two sisters lived with me in the United States and are doing well for themselves.

Célio died from a stroke in 1982 after years of alcohol abuse. I do not know how he was able to keep his job for so long. He never married, retired with a small pension at thirty-eight years old, and lived with Mother until his death.

In 2001, Mother died of heart failure at the age of eighty-five. She lived with one of my younger brothers, Raimundo, who had married and was separated. He worked at many different jobs but never held a steady one for long. He has four children and now works for himself, fixing rental houses.

My fun-loving brother Tatai, who never had children, died in 2019. He had worked as a chauffeur for a retired general and lived in Boca do Rio, near my other siblings. My youngest brother, Wilson, is married with two children, both college educated. Wilson had endured many episodes of fainting from hunger at school and graduated from technical school with a degree in soil inspection and evaluation. He works for the city of Salvador and lives a decent life with his family in Boca do Rio.

Fernando, who I imagine was getting tired of scraping wax in the city cemeteries for his candle business, gathered the cash that he had made during one week in 1978 and headed to the bus station without telling anyone. He saw a bus pull in with the word *Belém* written in the destination slot and later told the family that he had difficulty reading the word at first—*Be-be ... Be-lém*. Fernando finally put it together. The word sounded pleasing to his ears so he bought a ticket and boarded the bus. Fernando traveled for two and a half days before arriving in Belém, the capital of the state of Pará, very far north, near the Amazon basin. He continued moving around the area and the surrounding states for seventeen years, confronting all kinds of hardships, from going hungry for days to getting sick with malaria, beriberi, snakebites, and yellow fever. Fernando slept in cemeteries and in a hammock in the woods, tied up high in trees so he wouldn't be devoured by the wild animals of the jungle.

In 2003, a woman neighbor went to city hall to ask for

information about my family in Salvador. She then called Ua with the news that Fernando was destitute. He had fallen very ill in São Luis, the capital of the northern state of Maranhão, where he lived at the time. Fernando's neighbor said that he wanted to be with the family but that he had no money for a ticket or to buy food and medication. I sent him a bus ticket to Salvador and some money and later bought a small house for Fernando in Boca do Rio near Ua and Gaia. Soon after he arrived, he developed kidney problems and spent six months in and out of the public hospital. Social services provided my brother with medical assistance and some of the medication he needed. He required dialysis treatment three times a week, but there was no ambulance service available to take him for the procedure. Either the drivers were on strike or the ambulances were too busy with other patients. I sent him a small monthly allowance for food, medication, transportation, and for a woman to stay with him until he died in August 2008.

As for me, I graduated from Saint Cloud State University in 1982. Paul returned to the U.S. and we married in June 1982 before settling in Eden Prairie, Minnesota, where I taught seventh grade English at a public school. Paul worked installing elevators for Westinghouse. Our beautiful son was born in 1985.

Paul was killed in an accident at work in 1987. I suffered a great loss and went to Brazil with the baby for a while before moving to Rochester, New York, to be close to Paul's family and to raise my son, Paul Hogan II.

When Paul II left Rochester to attend college in Boston, I also left to enroll in a graduate program at the University of Massachusetts Amherst, where I received a Ph.D. in Hispanic Literatures and Linguistics in 2014.

Pulling my family out of poverty, especially the women, has remained a strong passion. I have bought and rebuilt a number of homes; given capital to my brothers, nephews, and nieces to start various small businesses; sent some of my nieces and nephews to school and have brought others to live with me in the United States. Some members of my family have become quite successful while many of them are still not doing so well. Times continue to be rough in Brazil with an unstable economy and an environment very hostile to the underprivileged.

In the United States, I feel privileged to have worked as a

translator and interpreter for various companies; privileged as well to have taught Portuguese, French, and Spanish at all levels for schools, colleges, and businesses. I now live in West Hartford, Connecticut, with Bruce Grower, a wonderful companion. My son, Paul, lives about a five minutes' drive from me.

Acknowledgments

I am indebted to my friend Deborah Brown for her patience and valuable readings, crucial in the initial stages of this work. Without Deborah's feedback, it would have been difficult for me to continue. Michele Jacklin, a free-lance editor, helped make this book better by ensuring a clear structure. I am grateful to my colleagues at Litchfield High School: Lynn Rice Scozzafava, Lisa Ferrari, Andrew and Andrea Schacht, and Sandy Carlson for their important comments and suggestions; to my partner Bruce Grower; and to my son Paul Hogan II for their valuable support. My sisters in Brazil spent many hours in person and over the phone sharing their stories, helping me remember, and adding to the accounts related in this work. To all of them, I am grateful.

About the Author

Maria Leda Souza Hogan was the eleventh of fourteen children born to a mother who gave birth to her first child at age fifteen. Maria and her family endured dire poverty throughout her childhood and adolescence. She spent her early childhood in a small Brazilian town, Castro Alves, before moving to the slums of Salvador, a capital city in northeastern Brazil. Her family never had running water or basic sanitation. She excelled in school and was the only member of her family to attend college. In 1978, after graduating from a Brazilian university with a bachelor's degrees in French and Portuguese, she left to study in the United States.

The author recalls her mother begging the townspeople for help to feed her children. She remembers that her siblings resorted to stealing the neighbors' chickens; taking money and merchandise from vendors; venturing to the crossroads at midnight to steal the gifts left for the African gods; her sister sleeping with the town priest for money to buy food.

Maria earned a Ph.D. in Hispanic Literatures and Linguistics from the University of Massachusetts, Amherst. She lives in West Hartford, Connecticut, and teaches Spanish at Litchfield High School.

"Although at times I ponder over my past, for the most part, I have risen above it. The life I lived heightened my humanity. Like a sunflower, I now dance the samba around the sun, celebrating it, trying to keep pace with its light, and hoping to brighten up the life of those left behind and those I can reach. There are seeds of light I want to plant. I want to let them grow and trail the sun around the world, spreading light where darkness reigns."

—Maria Leda Souza Hogan